ANTONY

Viscount Knebworth in 1931

ANTONY

(*Viscount Knebworth*)

A RECORD OF YOUTH

BY HIS FATHER
THE EARL OF LYTTON

WITH A FOREWORD
BY
J. M. BARRIE

αἰὲν ἀριστεύειν καὶ ὑπείροχον ἔμμεναι ἄλλων
μηδὲ γένος πατέρων αἰσχύνεμεν.
HOMER

LONDON
PETER DAVIES

Published in December, 1935
Second Impression December, 1935
Third Impression December, 1935
Fourth Impression December, 1935
Fifth Impression February, 1936
Sixth Impression June, 1936
Cheap Edition, October, 1937

PRINTED IN GREAT BRITAIN FOR PETER DAVIES LTD. BY ROBERT MACLEHOSE AND CO. LTD.
THE UNIVERSITY PRESS, GLASGOW

'It is not growing like a tree
In bulk, doth make man better be;
Or standing long an oak, three hundred year,
To fall a log at last, dry, bald, and sere:
A lily of a day
Is fairer far in May,
Although it fall and die that night;
It was the plant and flower of light.
In small proportions we just beauties see;
And in short measures life may perfect be.'

BEN JONSON

AUTHOR'S NOTE

This book was first put together for private circulation, but as a few friends to whom it was shown pressed me to give it a wider circulation, I have yielded to their suggestion and allowed it to be published.

FOREWORD

THERE must be few that knew him who would not be proud to write a 'foreword' to the book of Antony. Nevertheless I first heard of the project with some misgivings, fearing that he could not have left behind him a sufficiency of himself to show him to others as the glamorous creature we, his friends, knew him to be. I was not then acquainted with the letters, the galleon of treasure, into which he had poured himself to his nearest and dearest; but reading them now with admiration and wonder, I feel—and believe other readers will feel with me—that to have let this self-portrait remain in some sacred hiding for the eyes of love alone would have been unfair to Antony as well as to many others like him in the first flush of manhood. I say others like him because it would be a poor thing to say, in the familiar phrase, that never shall we look upon his like again; let us rather add to our confidence in the youth of our land by hoping that there will be many such. One of his crowded ambitions was to write a worthy book, as we find in these spontaneous letters, and lo, though unaware, he was in these letters doing it; little thinking that the one book of Antony was to be a gay autobiography, gay certainly for even when he was, as he trusted, in the doldrums, his high spirits scattered them. Some one said there was always something 'high' about Antony, and nothing truer has ever been said of him. Here in these prodigal letters you shall find him in his bewildering many-sidedness, but always the brave heart, sometimes surveying himself with a rush of delight in the picture, and before the pen has dried it becomes to him an ecstasy of scorn. One of the reasons he loved

ix

boxing was obviously that with his staggering right or unexpected left he could knock himself out and triumphantly count ten over the fallen. Few on the whole have had such a happy life, and it could not have been as happy without his jolly miseries, which were as entrancing as all the rest of him. Perhaps his laugh was his richest part. However grim the mood, it was sure to be caught out by his laugh. I have never heard a more glorious laugh in man or boy; it overfilled him: I think he laughed last in his last moment, or one prefers to believe that his laugh accompanies him still.

There are other letters in the book, not so young as his, but wiser, and even more loving. He had one to guide him who was both lover and counsellor, of whom a discreet word should be said, the one to whom we owe this book. Those other letters are his, and surely they are as good letters to a son as have ever been penned.

J. M. BARRIE

CONTENTS

INTRODUCTION

A MEMOIR is often a sad document, but there can be no sadness in the record of Antony's life. It is a tale of sustained health, of progressive achievement, of vitality unimpaired, of courage undaunted and high spirits that never flagged. Life was for him 'speed, colour and bright bliss.' A child of the morning, he 'outsoared the shadow of our night', and has joined the great company of those who will never grow old. To those who knew him he will ever remain the embodiment of all that is young, strong, healthy, chivalrous and gay. Like Faithful, he could say, 'I had sunshine all the rest of the way.'

In the main this is a story of family life—necessarily so, because Antony was only on the threshold of public life when he was called to another sphere. But what makes the story almost unique is the fact that his parents, with whom his relations were those of complete intimacy, confidence and affection, were separated from him for a long period at the moment when he was emerging from boyhood. The letters which passed between father, mother and son give a contemporaneous picture of the development of a fine mind and character to which it would be difficult to find a parallel.

Though typical of his generation, he possessed unusual gifts and capacities. He was a supremely good letter writer, and his letters gave expression to all the changing moods through which he passed. His self-understanding and self-criticism were exceptional, as was also his power of lucid and vivid statement. Both in speech and writing he showed two tendencies, which time would have cured; one was an inclination to over-emphasis or exaggeration, the other was a love of paradox; and allowance must be made for these youthful imperfections in the letters which are contained in this book.

His strongest characteristic was his gaiety. His smile, his laugh, the light of happiness in his eyes—these are the things which those who knew him will recall when they think of him. He allowed nothing to be sombre. Having expressed himself with vigour, even with passion, when anything touched the depths of his feelings, he was quick to banish the serious look, to laugh away the serious situation, to smother the bitter disappointment.

He had a genius for friendship. From his Mother he inherited a love of people and of animals, and from his father a love of ideas; but the first was the stronger of the two, and he did not live long enough to develop the second as fully as he might have done in later years. As Browning said of Luitolfo in the *Soul's Tragedy*, he was a 'friend-making, everywhere friend-finding soul. Fit for the sunshine, so it followed him. A happy-tempered bringer of the best out of the worst.'

In games and sports his tastes led him to prefer those that had the most movement. For this reason he preferred football to cricket, ski-ing to skating, pig-sticking and hunting to shooting or fishing. Though fond of an active open-air life, he was also fond of books—both reading and writing them, and preferred the companionship of people to either. Above all things he was conscientious and thorough in everything which he undertook. He disliked drudgery, but he never shirked it either as a boy or as a man.

The story of a life may have an intrinsic value apart from its achievements. This story is of that kind. Others have delivered greater speeches, written better books, moved in

more stirring times, made more history by their actions; but
no man was ever a better son or brother, few have faced the
world more gallantly, or expressed more vividly the emotions of a very vital nature. This is a record of youth, and its
title might well be *Juventus Juventuti*.

Chapter I

CHILDHOOD AND WEST DOWNS

1903-1916

'The Childhood shows the man
As morning shows the day.'
MILTON: *Paradise Regained.*

ANTONY KNEBWORTH was born at 32 Queen Anne's Gate, on May 13th, 1903. He was christened at the Chapel Royal, St. James's, in the presence of his Royal Godfather, King Edward VII, from whom he received the name of Edward. His third name, James, he received from his second Godfather, Viscount Cranborne, the present Marquess of Salisbury, and his second name, Antony, by which he was always known, was given to him by his parents after no one in particular. The red-robed choir sang, 'In token that thou shalt not fear', and looking back now through the twenty-nine years of his active young life these words seem to have provided the motif which characterized them throughout. He was from first to last absolutely courageous.

He developed quickly, was splendidly strong, active and nimble, quick both in body and mind. Even as a baby he was extraordinarily articulate, and this quality he retained throughout life. Whether in speech or in writing, he never found difficulty in expressing himself. He loved the sound of words, and committed easily to memory the passages in prose or verse that pleased him. But his own choice of words was original and expressive.

At eighteen months his mother wrote of him: 'He likes

A   I

enterprise and doing things. He is never still, and expects everyone to be interested in what he is doing.' He would make use of anything that was at hand, and improvise games and entertainment for himself throughout the day. Whenever I visited his nursery I was always greeted with a joyous shout of 'Daddy, come and see what I'm doing', or 'what I've made'!

His relations with the unseen world were as joyous as those with the world of men—the joy of companionship and friendship was the mark of both. His first prayer at night was 'Angels come', to which he soon added 'and soldier boys too'! When he was three years old he said to his mother one day, 'I never talk about Angels now, Mums, 'cos Jesus always comes when I sing.'

'Does he, darling, what does he say?'

'He doesn't say anything, he only laughs and laughs while I sing to him!'

About this time he had his first love romance, with Joan of Arc, in Boutet de Monvel's illustrated book. Every evening he would kiss her picture tenderly and say 'Dood night, dear Joan of Arc, till to-morrow night.' The battle pictures were his favourites, and also the one he called 'the dark picture'. Then he fell ill with a feverish cold, and even Joan of Arc failed to comfort him one gloomy day. When his mother offered him the book, he said, 'I simply tant, Mummy, I'm so tired of her.'

One day, when only about two years old, he went upstairs to fetch a small red fez which he used to wear on his head at that time. As he was rather a long time absent his mother called out to him from the bottom of the stairs to hurry up. His shrill voice replied excitedly from the upper floor, 'I'm coming, Mummy, I'm coming, I sees it everywhere but I haven't caught it yet.' Has lost property ever been more vividly described?

The first four years of his life were spent in London at 32 Queen Anne's Gate, the house where he was born, with occasional visits to the seaside and to the houses of friends in the country. His sister Hermione was born in the same house in August 1905. In 1906 we moved to the Manor House at Knebworth, and to Knebworth House in 1908. Our third child Davina was born there in 1909.

Antony was always gay and active. When he was four he announced one day, 'Mummy, Mummy, I'm as happy as twenty fairies in a row, all saying Good morning and Goodbye.'

At this time his heroes were Robin Hood and Richard Coeur-de-Lion. He asked what Coeur-de-Lion meant. His mother told him 'lion-hearted, brave, strong, splendid, what every man wanted to be.'

'I shall be, then, Mummy.'

'I hope so, darling.'

Then, after a pause, 'I almost am.'

In 1908 he became acquainted with the *Jungle Book*, and this remained a favourite for many years. He was Mowgli, and everyone else in the house was an animal. The garden became the jungle, with Shere Khan lurking in the bushes. His baby sister was a willing wolf cub. One day he came bounding up to his mother in great excitement, saying, 'Mummy, Hermione has sent word that she doesn't want me to play in the garden with her. Oh! I am longing to meet it, to meet it!'

'To meet what?'

'Her anger, Hermione's anger.'

'What will you do with it?'

'Drive it forth!'

Once, when expecting my return from abroad, and trying to keep awake for my arrival, he said, 'Do you think Daddy will arrive before I disappear?'

He would help his mother in the garden to pick off the heads of the roses that 'had gone to death'.

One day he said to his mother, 'Mummy, Mummy, I'll give up everything for you, but not my wildness. Do you mind? I must keep my wildness.'

Of the various accomplishments at which he became proficient, riding was the first to be acquired. He began to ride at five years old, a small Shetland pony called 'David'. In January 1909 his mother wrote:

I told Antony one afternoon, when I was out in the Park with him, that he might make a beginning of riding without a leader, and away he went across the grass towards the house. I thought he was going rather too fast. I am short-sighted and could not see clearly after a bit, so I made Frank, his groom, describe to me what was happening—

'He is going a bit fast.

'He seems going amongst the deer.

'It's all right, his lordship has got the best of him and is coming back.'

Sure enough the speck became bigger again and was soon with us.

'Well, Antony,' I said, 'did you like it, or was David going faster than you liked?'

'Oh, I loved it', he answered, 'and he quite ran away, David did. But when I found that out, I just made him go faster and faster and pretended to chase the deer.'

'Weren't you afraid of tumbling off?'

'Oh, no, Mummy, I simply couldn't, 'cos you see I jammed my knees in, just like a bradawl into leather!'

'I don't know what a bradawl is', I had to say.

'Don't you?' answered little Antony, 'then call it a spear into its sheath.'

This same winter there was ice on the lake, and Antony first learnt to skate on a pair of tiny blades. He learnt quickly; his balance was perfect, and he darted about at a tremendous pace, erect and eager, like a swift over the water.

In the summer he learnt to swim with equal ease, starting with inflated wings, which he was able to discard after two or three days.

The chief event of the next twelve months was his introduction to the Odyssey in Church's *Stories from Homer*. He loved it, and could never bear to be away from a new chapter for longer than two hours. He would run about the house shouting 'I am Ulysses, King of Ithaca', humbly followed by his adoring but silent little sister, Hermione, who he explained was his 'bravest and strongest man.'

'You see, Mummy', he said one day, 'it's his strength that is so wonderful to me. You can't think how Ulysses strengthens me.'

The Odyssey was followed by the Iliad, which he found even more enchanting, and instead of Ulysses he became Achilles, ever brandishing his 'Pelean spear'. He wished to have a correct Grecian dress of the time of Achilles, and would not be satisfied with anything that was not exact. I took him one day to the British Museum to look for a model. Sir Sidney Colvin, the Keeper of the Print Room, was very kind and patient with us, producing many illustrations for our inspection. Antony was grave and critical. Flaxman drawings he rejected as mere modern imitations. He was better pleased with some designs on old pottery, and finally found what he wanted on a coin. The dress was carefully made from the model. He had a huge gold helmet with red plume, tunic, skirt and greaves, and a large round shield. Then we designed for him a small chariot, standing upright in which he drove his little Shetland pony at a gallop about the park. We heard that in the village it was called 'His Lordship's milk-cart!'

One day Antony reported to his mother that his governess had disputed his statement that Pallas Athene was the goddess of war as well as of wisdom. His mother replied that she

was so beyond any doubt. 'I knew it, Mummy,' he cried
delightedly, 'I knew it, 'cos I said it must be wise to fight for
anything you really wanted and that was worth while.'

During this year he sat for his portrait to Sargent. It so
happened that the stories from Homer, which his mother
read aloud, were also favourites of the great painter. Everything was therefore congenial, and the charcoal drawing
which Sargent made of him was one of his masterpieces.

Early in 1910 we went to London, and John—the last of the
family—was born at 11 North Audley Street on March 10th.

In the spring of this year King Edward died, and we took
Antony to see the Lying-in-State in Westminster Hall,
which impressed him greatly.

He was now seven years old, and from this time onwards
his letters begin to be worth recording. There are not many
of them, as we were mostly living together, but during the
occasional absences of either his mother or his father he
wrote delicious little letters that contained expressive
phrases and were nearly always accompanied by drawings
that showed much imagination.

At the Coronation of King George, in the summer of
1911, Antony was Page to Prince Arthur of Connaught. He
himself had first announced the news in a letter as follows:
'Isn't it jolly? I am going to be a page and to Prince Arthur.
My first Historical Event June the 22nd 1911. Do tell me
what I have to do and what I shall have to wear?' It was a
great event, and he bore himself with becoming dignity.
Someone said that he and Lord Curzon were the two that
walked best in the procession in Westminster Abbey! We
had a house in Buckingham Gate that year, and we got
home early from the ceremony. We waited a long time for
Antony to arrive. He had gone to Clarence House to be
photographed. The street was thick with people, and when
the Royal carriage arrived they all rushed to our porch to see

who was in it. A Royal footman opened the door and little Antony stepped out, very calm and erect, with a beaming rosy face—beautifully dressed in smartest scarlet livery, with sword and plumed hat. He looked so dignified, the crowd cheered him as he walked into the house.

While I was in Switzerland during the winter, Antony had written to me, 'I do like your postcards, they make me want to be out in Switzerland very much.' In the following year he got his wish, as in January 1912 we took him and Hermione with us to Wengen and Mürren. He was then eight and Hermione six. Antony and I and his governess, Miss Glasspool, started first, his mother and Hermione following a fortnight later. The first journey abroad was a great excitement, and Antony enjoyed it thoroughly. On the steamer crossing the Channel he became very nautical, examined every part of the ship, and talked about his 'sea legs' and 'the focsle'. At Calais the Douane was very crowded, and at times I thought he would get squashed by the jostling porters with their luggage. Antony was disappointed when the Customs officer chalked our luggage at once, without even asking us if we had anything to declare. He had hoped for an exciting search through his attaché-case for contraband!

Later, as we were going round the *Ceinture* from the Nord to the Lyon station in Paris, Antony was looking out of the window and asked me if there was any exhibition in Paris. I said 'No, not at present.'

'No Crystal Palace?'

'No, not exactly.'

'Oh, haven't they got any enjoyments at Paris?'

The weather was very unsettled for the first few days after we arrived, with little snow and poor ice, but Antony had never known anything better and he was enraptured. The day of our arrival I got him a pair of skis and we went on the nursery slopes.

The next day he wrote to his mother: 'Yesterday I went out for my first days ski-ing, it was the best fun I know. The Rink opens at 12 o'clock this morning. I hope I shall go luging with a very nice girl that I have made friends with before we go to skate. I love luging. The girl has a most heavenly little brother called John, no bigger than Davina, and he has a ball and plays with me a lot.'

The next day, January 7th, I wrote, 'It has been an awful day! In the afternoon we all three sallied forth to face the weather. There was a wet sleet falling, and a wind blowing, and the whole landscape was blotted out. The prospect before us was a dismal one, but Antony found everything enchanting, and could not have been better pleased if it had all been carefully arranged for him. We walked up the hill above the hotel and got into some very jolly woods where we were sheltered, and every boulder made a mountain or a cave, which evoked fresh shrieks of delight from Antony. "See the mountains up-towering high above us", he shouted. "We shall be the first to reach the top of the Jungfrau without the loss of a limb", and again, "Here is a fortress made by nature for herself against the envy of less happy lands!" It was all pure rapture, and we returned to the hotel with glowing cheeks and happy hearts.'

A few days later we had a rather exciting adventure. As it was thawing at Wengen and there was no skating, I took Antony with me up to the Scheidegg. If the weather had been clear, and if the railway had been open all the way, it would have been a possible though strenuous expedition for a small boy. But neither of these conditions was realized, and what is a very simple ski-run for the experienced proved for us a real adventure. Owing to the recent heavy snowfall the railway was not open beyond the Wasser Station, and from there we had to climb on our skis to the top. The snow was deep, and Antony found the climb very tiring. For the last half-hour I had to carry him on my shoulders. It was a quarter to two by the time we got to the top, and all the other people who had gone up in the train had finished their luncheons and were starting down again. We spent an hour resting and eating, and then found when we came out of the restaurant that we were enveloped in cloud and could not see more than a yard in front of us. We had neither of us ever been there before and I had no idea of the way down. There was nothing for it but to point our skis downhill and follow the tracks into the mist. I put my arm round Antony and held him up as best I could. As long as the ground was fairly even we kept our feet, but bumps, dips or unexpected changes of gradient generally brought us down. We picked ourselves up laughing and started on again.

After one of our spills, when I had fallen on the top of Antony and asked anxiously if he was hurt, he replied cheerfully, 'Not a bit', and then added, 'You know, Daddy, in funny pictures when people fall down they draw stars over their heads. I never knew what it meant—now I do!'

'Did you see stars that time?' I asked.

'Yes', he replied, 'a few, it was so funny.'

In this gallant spirit he kept going and faced the unknown without the slightest anxiety. It was very mysterious speeding downwards in a thick cloud, our eyes glued to the narrow thread at our feet, and in our ears the distant thunder of avalanches on the Jungfrau.

At the Wasser Station we struck the railway and were able to follow this for a time. Presently, however, the railway turned in to a wood and our tracks led us away from it over a shoulder to the right. By the time we rejoined the railway line it was already getting dark. The tracks here became very confused and I did not know which to follow. I chose the wrong ones, crossed the line and struck down the hill till suddenly I saw the lights of Lauterbrunnen below me and realized we had come too low. So we had to turn and climb back along the railway till we came to Wengen Station. It was 6.30 when we arrived at our Hotel, and we found everyone in a great state of anxiety, about to set out with guides to search for us. Antony remained gallant and cheerful to the end. He had come down on his own skis (with the help of my arm, it is true, but still on his own feet) 2,600 feet from the Scheidegg Hotel, and had been out for $7\frac{1}{2}$ hours—yet he was but eight years old and had only put on skis for the first time four days previously!

Two days later Antony came into my room at 9.15 in the morning, and I asked him if he had slept late. 'No', he answered, 'I woke ever so early, but I couldn't help indulging in the luxury of telling myself a story'. I asked him to let me write it down. 'Oh, no', he said, 'it will go on for months, perhaps for a year. My chief delight is in describing clothes. My present story is about a cavalry regiment and the uniforms we wear are wonderful'.

We spent the summer at Knebworth, and on May 13th— Antony's ninth birthday—he played in his first cricket match. It was between his own team of boys from the village and the household. Antony's team won easily. He himself made 30 not out.

That autumn we took a place in Scotland for the holidays and paid a visit to the fleet at Cromarty. This was a wonderful experience for Antony, and he lived every moment of it with intense keenness. He had a passion for ships at this time, and was determined to become a sailor. He would draw pictures of ships all day long, and knew the names and tonnage of all the ships in the navy, distinguished their silhouettes, and even knew the calibre of the guns they carried.

In November 1912 he got the measles. When he was first told what was the matter with him, he asked anxiously if it was 'something you cut', and was relieved to hear that it only meant staying in bed! He wrote to his mother, who was in the south of France:

My darling Mumsie,

I'm covered in spots just like a leopard. When I look-ed at myself in the glass I was *horrified*, I hardly recognised myself. My cheeks are rather hot but my spots don't tiggle *nearly* as much as they did. I feel quite well otherwise when I'm lying down; when I sit up my head feels giddy. Measles aren't at all bad things, are they? Do you remember when *you* had measles how I earned my sword by having grease put on without minding? This morning when the Dr. came I had made up a rhyme which I told him. It was really a very funny one, but I don't think he *saw* the joke; and he said *quite* seriously he didn't want to treat brain fever as *well* as measles. . . . Hermione is in the best of spirits, and has got *anything* but the measles. . . .

Goodbye, with a whole trainful of kisses and little aero-planes of love.

Your loving

ANTONY.

I also wrote reassuringly, 'Antony has had a very good day and is quite peaceful. He asked for buttered eggs, sardines & blood!'

We had a very happy Christmas all together at Kneb-worth, and with the year 1912 ended the period of his childhood. It was a period of great happiness, and every year disclosed new depths and richness in the development of a nature which was all that a parent could desire.

The year 1913 was an eventful one in Antony's life. It began with the first big change from home to school, and it ended with an operation for appendicitis which seriously affected his health for nearly a year.

In January Mr. Helbert, the Headmaster of West Downs, the school we had chosen, wrote to say that he had an unex-pected vacancy and wished Antony to come at once, as he would not be able to take him later. Antony himself was much excited during the days of buying and trying-on his new clothes. He was so astonished at his changed appearance that he used to stand staring at himself in his mother's long glass.

One day Mr. Helbert came to our house in North Audley Street to see Antony and prepare him for his new life. He spoke kindly and wisely, stressed the importance of modesty, and warned Antony that boastfulness on the part of a new boy would be resented by the other boys. Antony listened gravely, and then asked naively, 'Does that mean that if someone asks me if I can ski I am to say I can't?' Helbert laughed, and explained that he might say he had been lucky in having opportunities of learning how to ski, ride, swim, etc.

When the last day came—January 28th—he had to make an effort to keep up his spirits and was very gallant. In the morning, while he was lacing up his new boots, he kept repeating, 'Life is hard', but when parting from his sister at the station his one thought was to keep her cheerful, and he made her polka with him on the platform till the train started.

He made a good schoolboy, as he was naturally sociable and played all games well. Joyous and keen, he made the best of everything, and from now onwards his letters were a never failing delight whenever we were separated from him.

On the second day we got a postcard from him saying 'I am just going out to play footer. I am getting on very well. I have not made many enimes, much love.' A few days later he wrote: 'My nickname is LITTLE TIGER, rather nice, don't you think? Dent gave me it. He is exactly like a rabit, so his nickname is RABIT. I love sosages now. Will you bring me down THE STORY OF ROME when you come. I am getting on very well. A boy said this to me, "If you go on as you are now you will be liked by the school. You are liked now." '

He wrote frequently, not only the regulation Sunday letter but several times during the week, telling of his friendships and his activities. Here is an example of his descriptive power:

What do you think happened on Thursday? Just at the beginning of the first brake we saw an aeroplane flying very close, and it went round and round in a circle getting nearer the ground every time. At last it descended out of sight down the bank, and the whole school ran after it, over the fence, over the road, down to the valleys of the golf course, till we came in sight of it, a big yellow thing looking like a boat upside down. When we came up with it we found it smashed up. It was an army one, and the man had come down to look at his map and was running along on the ground when he saw a bunker and pulled the leaver to send it into the air, it did not act and he was wrecked. His wheels were smashed and the screw broke in two, he had a narrow escape with his life, but I touched it for the first time.'

In the summer term he was very successful in the school sports. I was unable to be present at the finals, but his mother was there, and he wrote to her the next day: 'I was so sorry that you had to go before the prizes were given, I got three medals—the high jump, hundred yards and school handicap. The school handicap one has gone to have my name put on, so have the others. The school handicap one is gold and the others are bronze.'

On July 13th he wrote: 'On Friday the school race was run. West Downs won (Browning Ma). Perhaps two years hence I shall be running for West Downs, and may I pray that I shall have as good luck as Browning 1 did.' *

The autumn term was an eventful one. On October 5th he

*See page 25.

'wrote to me: 'I am in the senior game, that is to say I have a chance of being in the 2nd 11', but the next week he wrote: 'I am not going to be in the 2nd XI I am quite certain, because the games master Mr. Kirby who arranges the games and 11's does not like me, and so he puts me in the place where I cant play, so that his excuse may be that I am too bad, which I call very unfare. Do not tell anyone except Mummy, not even Hermione, until I tell you further, which I will do on Thursday.'

To this we replied that Mr. Kirby had probably merely been trying to test him, and he answered at once:

I was not in the 2nd XI, I knew I should not be. Of course Mr. K. did not put me outside right to test me—it was simply because what I told you on Sunday, but I hate him 1000000000 times more than he hates me. But I have again another chance of being in the 11. I will prove to you that he did it out of hatred, because the day of the match, after it was finished, there I was back in my old place.

In his Sunday letter, however, he qualified this opinion by saying, 'I have just come to the conclusion that it was not out of hatred that Mr. K. did not put me into the 2nd XI, but I was never good enough. But in the 3rd I may take a place. I have bought a new game, the same as Attack with ships, only quite different. Will you please send me a kite that will fly up a very great height.'

A fortnight later he was laid up with chicken-pox, but no invalid ever wrote more cheerfully. This is how he announced the news:

THE SANATORIUM, *Nov.* 8, 1913.
Dies bonus tibi Pater et Mater meus.

Here I am happier than a Saint (pom-pom!) in bed (Hurrah)! with (chickens and pox) otherwise chicken-pox (pom-pom!) If you will (*I* should be delighted) come down with 9,999 books to read to me. Please come. Very comfortable lodgings. Have I thanked you for the kite? If not 'Thank you'. Love by the ton from me.

On the following Sunday he wrote:

Thank you again and again for the toys you sent, they comfort so (what little comforting I want) I have not got a headache ς Do you know why I put that funny sign? because it is the answer to a question. This is the sign you put after a question—?—and this is the sign you put after the answer to a question—ς Please come and see me, I shall be in bed for a fortnight because I have been told so.

He had only just recovered from this minor ailment when a much more serious trouble occurred. We were at a shooting party in the North of England in November when I was called to the telephone and told by Mr. Helbert that Antony, who had been playing football in the afternoon, had developed an acute abdominal pain in the evening. The doctor diagnosed appendicitis and recommended an operation. We had no alternative but to accept the surgeon's advice. We travelled through the night by special train from Chester to Winchester. When we arrived at the nursing home about 5 a.m. we learned that the operation had been successfully performed at 2, and we found Antony propped up in bed with a face rather white, but beaming as usual. It is impossible ever to forget his smile of recognition on seeing us. He threw out his arms when we came into the room, and then winced at the pain which the gesture caused him. He was amazingly cheerful and only begged us not to make him laugh. During the next fortnight he played happily with the Meccano toys which we brought him, and made a most astonishingly rapid recovery. His mother stayed at Winchester and was with him daily until he could be moved to London. He used often to say in later years that these days in hospital were the happiest he could remember !

By December we were able to bring him home in an improvised ambulance to Sloane House, which we had taken
for the winter. The wound was completely healed and he
seemed to be as well as ever. As Knebworth had been let for
a year to the Grand Duke Michael, brother of the Czar of
Russia, we had planned to go to Mürren for Christmas, and
Antony was passionately looking forward to this. I consulted
the surgeon, who said it might be very good for him, provided we did not let him do too much. This warning was not
sufficiently emphatic, and as it turned out the holiday in
Switzerland was a serious mistake.

We went to Mürren. Sir James Barrie was there with
four Llewelyn Davies boys, and we all spent a very happy
Christmas together. Nicholas, the youngest of these boys,
became Antony's devoted friend in later years at Eton and
Oxford. We took every care of Antony during these holidays. We only allowed him to skate or ski once a day,
and I don't think he ever got tired. It was impossible
not to be deceived by his high spirits and apparently
perfect health. The operation was completely forgotten
and seemed to have left no bad effects. Antony was
entirely his normal radiant self, and it was very difficult
to restrain him. But the excitement of Christmas and the
company, and the sport which he loved, were in fact too
much for him and brought on a nervous breakdown before
the holidays were quite over. I was out ski-ing with him one
afternoon on a bad day; the snow was deep and difficult, and
he fell down more than usual. Then he began to cry, which
was so completely surprising that it ought to have warned
me that he was not well. We put him to bed when we got in,
and next morning he seemed to be completely normal and
happy. But for many weeks after that day he would suddenly collapse in the afternoon and have attacks of acute depression that he could not account for. After he got back to school

he wrote most pathetic little letters describing his unhappiness and adding: 'I am trying to be brave, but it is very hard.' I visited him and found him quite unlike himself.

Mr. Helbert agreed that he was suffering from some kind of nervous breakdown, and that I had better take him away. He came to live with me in a hired flat in London for a short time, and then I took him out to join his mother and the rest of the family in the south of France, where we had taken a villa, and where he was soon made happy and tenderly cared for by his mother and the children's Nannie, Mrs. Butler.

He gradually recovered and went back to school for the summer term. But this experience had a permanent effect on his nerves. Hitherto he had literally not known what fear was—he was never afraid of the dark as a child. Standing on the high diving-platform, or at the top of a steep slope, he would say to me, 'Can I do this, Daddy?'—never 'Dare I do it?' If I said 'Yes, you are all right', he would plunge into the water or down the slope without another thought. I often used to wonder whether the knowledge of fear would ever come to him, and if so in what form. In fact it came to him during this period of nervous breakdown and never again left him. Hereafter he knew what it was to be afraid, but to the end of his life he remained completely master of his own fears.

He returned to West Downs at the beginning of May, and from now onwards until he left the school he kept a diary of each day in the week, which he used to post to us on Sunday, and sometimes when we were in different places he would take the trouble to make a second copy, so that we could each have one. He was very keen on scouting at this time, and his letters make constant reference to this interest.

At the end of a July letter he wrote:

Mr. Helbert never looks nice now but always looks cold and dull and stern.

B

I don't know the reason for this last remark. Was it
Antony's imagination, or had Mr. Helbert already a pre-
monition of the dark days that were coming? At the moment
the newspapers were full of stories of impending civil war in
Ireland, and a fortnight later came the news of the Serajevo
murders and the Austrian ultimatum to Serbia. That week-
end we spent with some friends at Overstrand. Returning
to London on Monday morning, we met Winston Churchill
on the platform at Cromer. He looked unusually grave and
troubled, and I asked him the cause. He told me the news
and added, 'This will mean a European war, and the world
will never be the same again.' Those words have always
stuck in my memory, as they have since been so completely
realized. The world has indeed never been the same again,
and never will be. Between the pre-war and the post-war
worlds is a deep gulf of four years which darkened every
household and left scars that will never be obliterated. The
summer term at West Downs ended happily enough, but
with it ended a whole epoch in the history of England.

As Knebworth was still let, we had taken a lease of the
Kirk House at Innerleithen in Scotland for the summer
holidays. We travelled north by road at the end of July, and
broke the journey with the Archbishop of York at Bishop-
thorpe. The horizon was dark and stormy. The whole world
was crumbling to pieces around us, and the machinery of
civilization seemed to have broken down during the days of
the moratorium. Everyone hoped for peace, yet feared a war.
The Archbishop talked of peace the whole time. He had a
special service in the Minster to pray for peace, and we
prayed with him night and morning in his Chapel. But
things had gone too far, and in those days there was no alternative. We left York on August 3rd, and war between England and Germany was declared the next day as we arrived
at our Scottish home. The holidays were completely over-

shadowed by the terrible anxiety of those early days and I left for London to raise a relief fund for the aid of Belgium from the exhibitors who had supported me in Brussels in 1910.

The children, however, were scarcely affected by the tragic happenings in the outside world, and had a very happy holiday among the hills and burns.

We were very glad when the Grand Duke gave up Knebworth a month before his time, to return to Russia and take part in the war, and we all rushed back there the first week in September. The children cheered loudly as we drove up to the house.

Antony returned to West Downs on the 17th. The war had made great changes in the school. The boys were organized into Scout patrols, the senior boys acting as patrol leaders; and route marches and scouting exercises largely took the place of games. They were allowed to have their bicycles, which somewhat relieved the monotony of the marches. Antony wrote, 'The School is divided into 6 patrols (Lions, Bears, Buffaloes, Swifts, etc). I am in the Swift Patrol, a very nice and good one.'

His mother organised a hospital for wounded soldiers, rank and file, in London, which she kept going with one or two changes of address from September 1914 till six months after the end of the war. Antony wrote on October 13th: 'How is the Hospital? Can I be of any use as messenger or anything connected with the hospital as scout in the holidays? I can only write very short diaries now, as we are all so busy. We do nearly the same thing every day and I will tell you the exceptions.'

The year 1914 closed in gloom and anxiety, and the Christmas holidays were the first of many to follow, in which the usual gaiety of the season and its association with peace were completely at variance with the tragic realities of a world at war.

During his last two terms at West Downs Antony gave up keeping diaries each week, and instead wrote little letters almost every day. He also kept our own letters to him this year, so the correspondence is more complete than in any previous year.

He was now at the top of the school and had more responsibilities, and his reports tell of harder and more concentrated work than before.

I wrote to him describing a fight between his fox terrier (Binks) and his sister's Sealyham (Roger), in which the former had been bitten in the leg, and he replied, 3rd Feb.:

'We be all of one blood ye and I'. I have found new hunting grounds O my Lair-Father and from this day forward I shall hunt alone. 'Good hunting to you.'

Many thanks for your lovely long letter. I feel proud of Binks and I long to congratulate him on having had a fight with his equal and having lost the power of a limb in fair fight.

I have got the calendar and I do tear the leaves off, and I will send you any good ones. I am going to make a jungle calendar and I have done some of the animals, cut them all out and painted Shere Kahn, Bagheera, Hathi and his 3 sons.

Love from
ANTONY the black panther.

'Good Hunting O old pack'.

On February 24th, 1916, he wrote:

It has been snowing most of to-day and we have only been able to get out once to have a little game of chivy. Captain Roland Philipps has been here today giving us some lovely tips. He is a Commissioner for all school troops. He is telling us some lovely yarns about the front now. It is awfully exciting, He has been telling us some glorious indoor games. He is talking all about bombing, glorious! We have got a God in the Room, it is great fun. He is talking so well that he makes you think you are in the trenches. Good-bye.

His Yarn.

They are just going out to bomb at 9.30 p.m. He is over the parapet now. The next one is over, they are all over, they are through their own barbed wire. He walks forward, he has found his landmark. He thinks he knows where the Huns are. He is coming to the Hun trip wire.* He has cut the German trip wire, he cuts a bit off to bring home as a souvenir of the war. He has come to the Hun barbed wire. He is lying in front of the German trench. They have thrown their bombs. They throw them sideways so as not to get hit by Germans shooting straight in front of them. First he hears a shouting, then he hears a yell and laughs, then he crawls away to the left, so as to get out of his original position. He sees a German loosing off into the dark and he fires 3 successive bombs in his direction, that is the end of him! then they retire. He has just got home past his own sentry when he hears a voice saying 'English Pigs'.

Captain Philipps was killed before the end of the summer, and his death was Antony's first taste of sorrow. He had written from the front in June, 'Dont forget that if I live through the war, you and other West Downs boys are coming down in a few years time to help me with my Scouts in East London.' Antony did not forget his East-End boys, and the last years of his own life were devoted to their service.

The following is a typical letter of this time:

WEST DOWNS SCHOOL,
Near the town of WINNCCHHEESTHEER.
7/3/16.

Hallo! Mudisse,

I am so sorry that I did not write yesterday, I quite forgot to. I had a horrid thing happen to me today. I was copying someone running on the run and I ran into a thorn bush and tore my face to atoms. I went on with the run and you could have traced me by my blood in the snow. When I got home Sister put some iodine on it. Ow! I can feel the

---

*Wire for tripping people up.

pain still, but she gave me a piece of cream toffee for it. This story is rather exagerated but the iodine did hurt and Sister did give me some toffee. . . . It has been snowing quite a lot here today. What else have I to tell you? Nothing! Ah! but wait, oh! my Lord you have overlooked a bully trifle, now list thou whilst I speak.

My stomach is empty within me and (paratus sum ad cacem recipiendum) I am ready for a *cake*, if you please.

Good-bye,

Love, love, love xx love, love, love, love. Stop!

From James.

On the 18th of March he came to London for the day, and his letter describing his return journey was characteristically vivid:

. . . Directly the train started I tried to do that puzzle and did not even look up to say good-bye because I did not want to feel miserabler than I could help. Then I just opened the parcels, so as I could see what was inside them—there was jam-sandwiches, cake, 2 plums, a bottle of milk, 4 caramels and lots of toffee. Then I started off and fairly well gorged, looking at the Illustrated War News in between the bites....

I walked up to West Downs and gave various people some toffee, then I went to Shakespeare and saw some slides of old boys which L. H. was showing. When I went to bed I read 3 of Stevenson's prayers, which made me think of you. 'For Absent Friends', 'For Family', 'For Renewal of Joy'. Then I ate half a caramel and fell half asleep. I pictured 4 things, 1st a back spare room at Grannie's with the lamps turned down low and 3 children romping and laughing, and Nannie telling them to shut up. 2nd a Room at the Admiralty with green shades on the lamps and lots of papers on the tables and the scratch of a lot of pens and a man writing with a brown stylo-pen. 3rd a big double bed in our house in London and Mummy in it reading, and last myself. . . .'

His mother replied:

I think your Sunday last letter was the best I have ever had. I often picture you like that, just as I am going to sleep

—A large dim room, with rows of little beds—and one far down on the left, by the balcony door, that I make for, with you in it—*so* rosy and fast asleep—very wrapped up with odds and ends as well as blankets on your bed—and a delicious feeling comes over me of your safety lying there—so warm and sleeping off the happy day's work and play—and I kiss you hard and tease you a little, like I always have ever since you were born, *without waking you*! . . .

I long to hear the result of your exam—don't forget to tell me—I am very glad you liked your tea basket. Goodnight, darling little friend and son.

The scouting was vigorously pursued during the term, but as usual when anything became too serious Antony got nervous and failed to do himself justice. It was the same with his games and his boxing. When he was playing for pleasure, he was always at his best, but when he had to be extra careful for a match or a competition he generally failed.

On his return to West Downs on May 4th for his last term, Antony found himself a Patrol Leader, which meant responsibility as one of the leaders of the school, but he missed his two best friends who had gone to Eton. His mother went down to the school for his birthday, and I wrote to him when she left:

This is to take the place of Mummy when she goes. I did not write to you yesterday as I knew Mummy would be with you, but tomorrow you may be feeling sad after she leaves, so I must send you a little line to tell you how much you were in my thoughts on your 13th birthday. It will be an important year for you, in which you will complete one stage of your life and begin a new one. May you be as happy and successful at Eton as you have been at West Downs. Everything will depend on what place you take, so I hope you will make a *very* special effort this term. It is awfully hard to work in the summer, but do try.

Next Sunday we are all to put our clocks and watches on one hour, so that we may get more daytime. It will be

rather confusing at first, but I think it is a very good plan.
I wonder how you will like it at school? . . .

Antony's account of the first daylight-saving experiment
was amusing:

I lead a very strenuous life in our days—especially as the
daylight savings bill is in force. I get up at 5.45, go down and
change into my running clothes, then I go out and practise
running for the school race, then I go and have a swim, then
I change and do work, then I have breakfast, then I do work
till quarter to 12, then I go out for half an hour, then I have
lunch, then work to 3.15, then cricket to 4.45, then work,
chapel, work and bed at 7.30. That is all the ordinary time,
not daylight savings—daylight savings it is an hour later.

To this his mother replied: 'Your full day gives me a
great feeling of strength. Running like the deer, and working like the Philosophers—what a *splendid* combination. I
do love it and envy it. This weather is gorgeous, and the
flowers come up in shoals from Knebs, and make the house
smell like a garden. . . .'

The great event of the term was the school race, in which
Antony represented West Downs with Knollys, a boy much
bigger than himself:

. . . Next Tuesday is the school race and I am going to run.
It is the most awful feeling, so please wish us luck. Last
Wednesday we played water polo against the Owls four a
side. I have never done anything so strenuous in my life, it
nearly killed me, in fact 2 of the people who are not such
strong swimmers as I am did kill themselves—for the time
being. So I had to do nearly all the work. . . .

May 30th.

Today has been one of the most exciting at school. I loved
your telegram. The school race is run between Twyford,
Winton House, and us. We each send two runners, Knollys
was our fastest and me the second. Knollys is miles faster

than me. Well, we have been training all last week, and you can imagine how awful I have felt this last two days. The day came and we ran. Knollys won by miles, and wonder of wonders I was second. That is the first time that any two have been first and second from the same school. I got for my prize 3 parcels of sort of Fortnum & Mason things to send to people at the front. Can you suggest anyone? I thought of Gale.* It is my Lesson next Sunday. We had a lovely gorge after the race, fruit salad, sponge cake and lemonade. Try and pop down and see me on Sunday. I am so happy at having achieved a record.

Antony fell ill at the end of the term and was unable to do himself justice in the entrance examination for Eton. But he took Upper Fourth, which everyone felt was creditable in the circumstances.

Mr. Helbert wrote in his final report, 'He will be ready for any form of mischief and will get into innumerable scrapes and scraps; but his wickednesses are all of the healthy order, and he is straight and clean.'†

In reading through Antony's letters from school I was amused to note the variety of his signatures. He rarely signed two letters the same way and had great fun in ringing the changes on his names and nicknames. During the first term 'K.10' was his commonest signature, 10 being the number assigned to him in the school, but this does not appear after 1913. Other variations were A., A.K., E.A.J.K., 'Antony', 'Antony Knebworth', 'Knebworth' (which at the end of one letter he spelt in 9 different ways!) 'Your baby', 'Your little boy', 'Someone', 'Me'. Other variations included 'Someone some day to be famous', 'Viscount Knebworth the

---

*Our chauffeur, who was at the front.

†Mr. Brymer, a member of the staff, who took over the school after Mr. Helbert's death in 1919, wrote to us in 1933 and said of Antony 'I don't know of any old boy whose life has brought more honour to the school.'

somebody', 'Me and my sham', 'Me and mine', 'Me or somebody else', 'Antony and Marmaduke', 'Ya-pa', 'Antony
P.L.' and once only 'Tony'. On one occasion he finished a
letter, 'I have forgotten who this is from' and on another,
'from your all loving, most beloved, most meet to be loved,
most happy, most miserable, most excited, most longing and
hoping great things of Mudisse, Aannttoonnyy.' His signatures were nearly always accompanied by pictures repre-
senting his mood at the moment.

His 3½ years at West Downs had been both happy and
successful. He developed along the lines of which his childhood had already given promise. He lost something of his
originality, as all boys do at school, but the pattern to which
he conformed was the schoolboy type at its best. He excelled
in all games and sports, and brought back eleven medals for
running, jumping, swimming, throwing the cricket-ball,
etc., but he retained his fondness for reading and his love of
good words. He never acquired the reticence so common in
schoolboys, and expressed with the utmost ease everything
which he felt. His capacity for making friends was strongly
developed and remained with him always.

Chapter II

ETON: WAR YEARS
1916-1918

'How I love this place, at least I do at present.'

IN SEPTEMBER 1916 began a new and very important
phase in Antony's life. Eton, while it lasted, had a tremendous hold upon him and also upon his parents. Now
that it has faded into a mere memory it is difficult to believe
that the school continues to have the same intensity for each
generation which passes through it. Antony loved every
minute of his Eton days. He was popular and successful in
all its activities, and made friendships which lasted throughout his life. For the next six years there was no Eton event
which we did not share with him, either in person or
through his vivid descriptive letters. For the first two years
the school was in the grip of the war at its worst, and the
shadow of that terrible time had not wholly passed away by
the time he left. The normal rigours of school life were
accentuated by the exigencies of this period of scarcity.
Fires were few and far between in the cold months. Food
was greatly restricted. Every home was saddened by losses
among the flower of the young generation, and the great
anniversaries, like the 4th of June or the Eton and Harrow
match, which took place at the school and not at Lord's, were
almost unbearably sad for those to whom they were but re-
minders of happiness that could never return. But Antony
had not known the days before the shadow of war fell upon
them, and his Eton time was a crescendo of enjoyment.

We took him down to the school in September 1916, and left him in Mr. Ramsay's house. There was no doubt about his happiness, for in his first letter to his mother he said:

I am radiantly happy here. I am fag to the Captain of the house with David Dawnay. I passed the swimming yesterday. It wasn't half cold. The food here is fine. We dont begin fagging till Oct. 4th. We have only got 10 lower boys and only one of them knows the game (the Eton game of football) so I dont expect we shall have a very good eleven! My Tutor (please pronounce m e r) is awfully nice and quite killing in some of his ways. We have learnt one saying lesson which we weren't heard. What Ho! My room is looking nicer. I had a hot bath last night.

On September 25th he wrote:

I adore this place, it is glorious. We haven't done any work yet except a little history. We had sardines for tea and boiled eggs and cake. The next school is at 10.50. My bath has come. One only gets one can full of water and that fills it to about the depth of $\frac{1}{2}$ an inch. There was early school this morning. It is bitterly cold and my hands and feet are icy. How I love this place. At least I do at present.

We have the most wonderful teas ever known. We had two poached eggs each today which may amuse you. We have finished the Gentlemen's Relish and the potted meat (which we can get for 8d a pot here) and the sardines which are very welcome. There are still loads of Fortnum & Mason caramels left. I didn't know there were so many in the world. I have 52 every day, so does David, and Furze 42, and there are as many left as there were at the beginning! I am writing this in David's room between prayers and supper. . . . I play short (sudden change of subject but I must write it before I forget). I have just finished an extra work. We have lots of spare time here—Prayer bell—there it goes.

Goodnight,

ANTONY.

As soon as regular work and fagging and football began the days passed quickly, and Antony's letters had little to record, except the weather, which seems to have been abnormally cold for the time of year, and his lower-boy football matches. He read Callender's *Nelson* this half for the Lower Boy Rosebery History prize. He wrote on November 22nd: 'We have most certainly begun fires. I should be dead without one. I am trying hard at the Nelson now and have read it once. I am now making notes on it. I am sitting bang in front of a blazing fire, rejoicing, and trying to get warm so that I'll be very warm when I get into bed. I had quite an adventure today. There is a fallen tree across Jordan, and I was out along it trying to get a football when I lost my balance and went in. It was about 3 feet from the water, so I went clean under in all my clothes. I swallowed most of the Thames and my clothes sucked up the rest, so you will not be surprised if you find it high and dry tomorrow.'

St. Andrew's Day, which fell on a Thursday this year, was kept on the following Saturday. Antony wrote to his mother:

You must come down next Saturday, and Daddy. It is St. Andrew's Day, when any amount of things happen. The Rosebery History Prize exam is on next Wednesday, very soon, so I must work like blazes. I have got a topping fire. Come as early as you like on Saturday with a crowd.

In another letter he wrote, 'I have finished the *Nelson*, thanks to the fires. You dont feel you want to rag with a fire, you want to sit down and read. . . .'

On 1st December he wrote: 'The old exam is over. It was not a bad paper. I enclose it. I feel that I have some chance. I wrote 14 pages on it all told.'

His next letter told of the result:

I am so sorry that I have not written to you before to tell you of my triumph. I was 3rd in the Rosebery and got a prize, it

makes me so happy. But as if to cancel my happiness I have
had 4/- stolen. It must have been stolen I am certain of that,
at any rate it is missing. My Tutor knows. He was awfully
nice and said that he expected it had been taken but that he
couldn't do anything. Since then 1/- has turned up.

At the end of 1916 Dr. Lyttelton had resigned the Headmastership, and Dr. Alington had been appointed in his
stead. With traditional loyalty to the old and mistrust of the
new, the boys were reluctant to open their hearts at once to
the new Head. Antony wrote later in the Lent half: 'I dont
think Alington is going to be too popular. He certainly has-
n't started too well, and as far as I know is not popular at
present. He is not so nice as Lyttelton I dont think. But as I
know neither I cannot judge!' At any rate, Dr. Alington at
once established the reputation, which he maintained for
the sixteen years of his Headmastership, of preaching ser-
mons which the boys loved, for before the end of the term
Antony wrote: 'We had a splendid sermon from Alington on
Sunday night. One of the best.'

He was now in Remove and found the work much harder
than in Fourth Form. Most of his letters this half speak of
the pressure of work and complain of having no free time in
the evening. There was a hard frost at the end of January
and beginning of February, and several letters tell of the
joys of skating.

To his mother:

Feb. 2nd, 1917.

. . . What a glorious day we had, didn't we, and how lonely I feel without you. But whenever I feel homesick your
wonderful saying 'Nothing lasts' rings through my head. . . .
I have just finished an extra work and a torn over ditto for
tomorrow. That is the supper bell. How beautifully this is
written. The maid has just let down the bed and displayed
the ever growing splendour of my eiderdown. Nothing can
compare with it. I am warm, you will be surprised to hear.

But there is a baking fire in my room now. Think of me tomorrow at 7.25 sallying forth into the cool scented dawn. And envy me!? There has just been a 'boy'. The trolls* are getting quite energetic. I am sick about leave, I simply long to come home, but 'Nothing lasts', not even the frost. It is about time to cease fire. . . . I hope the hospital went all right. . . .

The hospital referred to above was at 37 Charles Street, Berkeley Square. This was the third house in which his mother had maintained a hospital since the beginning of the war.

After the sports at the beginning of March, he wrote to his mother an amusing account of them:

Thanks so much for your letter; how I loved our day together. We have had our sports. The day chosen for them was the coldest day that there has ever been with howling N.E.NE.EN, etc. wind. We started with the hurdles in which I won my heat and then the finals, but in so doing I put my leg out most painfully. Then came the long jump in which I might have been second, only I did a bad jump at the end and that finished my leg for the rest of the afternoon. The high jump was next. I couldn't jump that high— after that came the 100 yds in which I won my heat, but the chap behind me dug the point of his running shoe through my ditto and my stocking and deep into my foot, so that the red blood poured forth. I then ran in the final in this state and before I had got my breath from the heat. Net result:—'Not even 2nd'. I nearly fell out I was so exhausted.

Then last of all came the house $\frac{1}{4}$ handicap, in which I got next to no start. I fell out. So on the whole I did poorly. I had a poor walk home in the cold with both legs hurting. But I am now before a warm fire with my foot swathed in bandages. It was not very much fun owing to the intense cold and the pain in my leg. But still I mustn't complain, seeing that I won the hurdles.

*His name for the Upper boys.

Will you send me—

    (1) Money.
    (2) Chilblain lotion.
    (3) Eggs.
    (4) Biscuits.

Please, thank you. That'll be twopence. I am tired but happy.
        Love to all

                from all = I.
    Yr
      Very very loving
        Me
           Antony.

In a letter a few days later he said: 'I am very happy and
seem to be raking in friends and getting to know new
people.'

His mother replied: 'Thank you for dear letter with a
merry peal of words about "raking in friends". Perhaps we
shall go to Windsor on Monday for the Duchess of Connaught's funeral. If we do I will telegraph to you and come
on and see you. I am very sad that she has died. The last
time that she went out was to open my new hospital on Feb.
12th. The Russian news is intensely interesting. I wonder
which will be the next monarchy to go! Do you realize the
intended Regent is the Grand Duke who took Knebworth in
1914? Where is the Czar? The Czarina is a prisoner in her
own Palace. It is like the story of Louis XVI and Marie
Antoinette. But I pray there will be no reign of terror in
Russia. When the Czarina was accosted in her room by a
revolutionary officer, she said "I am only a Sister of Mercy
now, looking after my children." '

Of the holidays his mother wrote in her diary:

We spent Easter in London. . . . On the 15th of April we
came to Knebworth and watched the winter die. The icy
cold winds subsided and the world burst into a summer

spring by May 1st. The chestnut leaves are still only in sticky buds—nearly all the trees are quite bare, but the daffodils are rushing into flower, and the sun is very hot to-day. . . . Last night Antony and I walked in the moonlight, and we saw the flashlight working from Norton Green. . . .

Antony's first summer half was not a happy one. It often happens that the longer days and greater leisure in the summer create restlessness and discontent, rather than happiness. Work is less congenial in the sunshine, and for most boys the recreation is less organized in this than in any other half. For those who play cricket in a regular game, or take to the river seriously, the summer half is full of delights, but those who neither row nor play cricket regularly find themselves too often unoccupied, and grow dissatisfied. The majority of the boys, unfortunately, belong to this class, as it is only for the good cricketers that games are well organized.

Antony started full of expectations, for he wrote on May 5th: 'I have arrived safely and am quite well and happy. I have been on the river all today. I am up to Butterwick, who is top hole. I am really quite awfully happy.' But already two days later he was writing about plans for the next holidays and said, 'I wish this half was over'; and by the end of the month he said: 'I feel as if I had been here three years instead of 3 weeks. I shall almost have forgotten the beginning of the half at the end of 13 years!'

All through June his letters were still depressed. We tried to cheer him: 'I had many unhappy days when I was at Eton', I wrote, 'and I shall be able to understand and sympathize with all you are feeling. . . . Keep up heart, old man, and don't get discouraged. Remember the old saying, "Lose money, lose nothing; lose honour, lose much; lose heart, lose all." '

As, however, the causes of his discontent were mostly intangible, they were not easily remedied. It was not till the beginning of July that his letters became happier, and as

c

always it was from friends that his happiness came. He wrote on July 2nd : 'Have we found a house yet for the holidays? and will it be all right if I ask someone to come and stay? A friend of mine called Allen* has got his Sixpenny, I'm awfully pleased. I am very happy with a great band of friends. Though all the same old gang, we have only just got to really know each other, and call each other by our Christian names.'

I wrote on 8th July: 'I will come down to you next Saturday for the Harrow match. I hope we shall have a fine day. The air raid yesterday was very exciting. I was working in the Admiralty when the alarm bell rang about $\frac{1}{4}$ to 11. I went to the window and almost immediately afterwards I saw a flock of about 20 aeroplanes coming towards us over the tops of the houses. It was very bright and the aeroplanes were very big, so they seemed to be quite low down. The large ones which carried the bombs were accompanied by smaller fighting machines to protect them. They looked very beautiful flying in regular formation like a flock of wild geese, with 2 or 3 stragglers behind. It was difficult to believe that they were deadly enemies, but the little clouds of smoke from the shrapnel bursting in the middle of them reminded me that they were dangerous. Then it dawned on me that they were all flying straight at me! and that in a few minutes they would be right overhead raining down bombs. I watched them coming and wondered whether they would actually strike the Admiralty. They looked very close though actually they were a long way off, and it seemed as if such a crowd of them must cause the most terrible destruction. I have never seen so many together before. On they came, very slowly, and the noise of the explosions came nearer and nearer. Then they swerved and turned south, and I went to the windows on the other side of the building

*G. O. Allen, the well-known English Test cricketer.

to watch them. Although they seemed to have passed so close, they actually went over the city, and the bombs they dropped were all round St. Paul's Cathedral, in Newgate Street, etc. Considering the number of the machines, the number of the casualties has been very small. Some of the shrapnel fell in Piccadilly Circus and broke some windows in Swan and Edgar's shop and the shops opposite in Regent Street. Mummy was at home with the children and they had a great fright. . . . Cyril, the small footman, ordered the rest of the household from side to side of the little courtyard outside the kitchen, as he thought the aeroplanes were coming first over one side, and then over the other! It was not at all a pleasant experience.'

We were unable to leave London at the beginning of August, and as Knebworth was let we had to scatter somewhat for the first weeks of the holidays. Finally we all met at Cranborne Manor, where, through the kindness of Lord Salisbury, we were able to spend a perfect month in ideal surroundings. Antony returned to Eton on September 19th.

The winter school-times were always favourites because of the football, but this next half, though very happy, was a stormy one. His letters told of three quarrels, one with fate over the drawing of the football ties, one with his dame over his gloves, and one with his tutor over one of his friends. They were not serious rows, but they called forth very spirited protests in each case. He had a new room this half and took a lot of interest in the decorating of it.

During the month of September there were continuous air raids, and our letters were full of them. We used to go to Birchington for week-ends, for the children were safe there, though there was much firing every night as the enemy machines passed overhead on their way both to and from London.

On October 19th occurred the historic raid when a whole fleet of Zeppelins were scattered and most of them destroyed. In a letter of the 21st I wrote: 'What a magnificent end of the raid on Friday. 5 Zeppelins in one day! The bomb which dropped in London fell in Piccadilly near the Circus and smashed all the windows of Swan & Edgar's shop and the neighbouring houses. It made a great mess in the street, and it looked as if half a dozen bombs had fallen. The Zeppelins lost themselves completely in the night and five of them drifted over to France, where they were discovered yesterday morning and chased down by the French aeroplanes. I should think this would put a stop to Zeppelin raids for a long time.'

Antony's letters continued to describe victorious football matches. Then came the drawing of the lower-boy ties which called forth a very vehement protest. 'Damn! Damn! Damn!', he wrote, 'we've been considered a bad lower-boy by the person who drew the ties, and so we're playing Hare's, a side that beat us 7–0 when we last played them. It is rather rotten luck, dont you think? But we hadn't got Dawnay or Fullerton when we played them before, so I do hope we beat them this time. My God I am annoyed. I expect we shall play next Thursday. . . .'

To his mother:

You know I told you that I had bought myself a pair of lovely fur gloves for 12/6, which was very cheap. Well I have had them a week, and last night the dame came and bagged them and took them to M'tutor—who said that he didn't like them because he thought that it gave a show of luxury to the outside people or something. The dame has taken them away and says that she is going to try and change them for another sort. I think that it is the most awful rot and cheek and goodness knows what else. Will you write and say that it is rot, and although they can forbid me to wear them they cant take them away, because I want them for the holidays. I dont want the other pair because I dont like them and I shant have them. I hope New & Lingwood's wont change them. I am having a rest today which is quite nice for me but rotten luck for Dads just the day he came down.

To the same:

My darling,

I am so bored about the ties, it was a mad thing to go and do. We were beaten 2–0, it was a frightfully good game, but I cant describe it to you because I hate dwelling on a bitter subject. At any rate I feel bitterly wretched now. The thing that I should like most in the world at this moment is a telegram from you saying that Daddy had got Paris and that you had got leave for me to come home and go over and settle down with you. I am bored with this half. The cold is so intense that it is absolutely wicked and there isn't a fire in the house. Miss Ramsay has told the maid that she is putting them off as long as possible. . . . The dame bought me a beastly pair of gloves (a cross between green and yellow) hard and woolen and nasty, that I wouldn't be seen dead in. It is all very well to say that I am well again, but it is not true. No one could be well under these conditions—

(1) temperature 0°F.
(2) Not a fire or heating apparatus of any sort in the house (except the kitchen and M'Tutor's study).
(3) Just been beaten in the first round of the tie when you are one of the best sides.
(4) the middle of the half.
(5) The dame.
(6) Miss Ramsay.
(7) Mr.   do.
(8) No sign of the holidays.
(9) Extreme hunger.
(10) No supper to look forward to.
            But my bath night—
                 10 min. of supreme happiness!
                 Cheers!!!

I have suddenly remembered that you are coming down for the week-end. Do come early, for luncheon! Let me know.

> Hoorah,
>> must stop,
>>> Love from
>>>> Yr devoted son,
>>>>> K.

P.S. I am out of bed, but I wish I wasn't, it is at least warm.

P.P.S. My hatred for Wilson (the boy who drew the ties) is something which I shant get over this side of Xmas.

Antony's 'row' with his tutor is told in the following remarkable letter to me:

I have had the following conversation with M'Tutor, I think that this is the best way of telling you—(things in brackets what I thought but did not say).

Tutor. Are you great friends with X at Y.'s?

Me. Yes.

T. Well, do you know anything about his behaviour, etc?

M. Yes, he has been caught cribbing and beaten and was complained of for bad work and beaten again.

T. Yes, he was. He is a boy with a very bad past record and he is not the sort of boy I like my little children to be friends with. In fact so bad a record has he that I had to write to his tutor and say that I wanted him to leave at the end of this half, and it was only by an accident and at a special request that he is not leaving. He seems to me to be a boy with a great lack of honour. What sort of a boy do you think he is?

M. I think he is a very nice boy.

T. How can you think that a boy who cribs is a very nice boy?

M. I dont see that it makes any difference to a boy whether he has had the bad luck to be *caught* cribbing or not.

(I did not tell him that there wasn't a boy in his house, or for that matter a boy in the school who hadn't cribbed, and it was bad luck on anyone who happened to be caught.)

T. Well, that's just the trouble. I can understand a boy of your age not thinking any the worse of a boy who is idle, though you will learn to, but I think you ought to think the worse of a boy who cribs.

M. (I should have an impossible chance of finding friends in that case.)

T. What do you see in X that you think nice?

M. I dont quite know, Sir, only I'm very fond of him.

T. Well, you ought to know.

M. Well, I know that he's the right sort of chap in that there's nothing nasty about him. He came to stay with us last holidays.

T. (annoyed) Oh! he came to stay with you, did he? If I'd known that, I should have strongly opposed it, I think that it is always a good thing before a boy asks any other boy to stay, for him to ask his tutor.

M. Sigh——!!

T. I think that your father would be very sorry to think that you were friends with a boy who is thought so poorly of by the masters as X. I think your father ought to be told, will you write to him or shall I ?

M. You may if you like, I certainly shall.

T. Alright. Then perhaps in future I hope you will be less with X.

(no answer)

T. Will you?

M. No, Sir.

T. Well, that's a great pity. I think that you ought to see something wrong with a boy who cribs—but never mind. Will you write to your father?

M. Yes.

T. Good. Because I think he ought to know exactly how things are. Of course, if your father doesn't mind, well then that's alright.

I did not say but I thought:

(You have caught 4 or 5 boys at this house cribbing this half and you have said nothing about it. You also had one of the same boys complained of. You gave him a white ticket.

Thus a boy in your own house gets off with a white ticket while a boy at another house is swiped twice for the same offence. Is that fair?

If X had been at this house, he would not have been swiped at all, he would have had an unstained character in your eyes, and he would be standing here being spoken to by you in the same way as you are speaking to me now.)

I have never been so angry in my life as I was then, I've never heard such cheek as saying that I ought to ask him if I wanted to have anyone to stay. I call it rather rot trying to take away a boy's best friend . . . simply because he's been caught cribbing. Surely he must know that everyone cribs if necessary, and if anything can be gained by it.

He told me to write to you and I have. . . .

Although I greatly admired his courage in standing up for his friend, and the spirit in which he had acted, I thought it necessary to emphasize the real values involved in the matter. I wrote the next day as follows:

You have written me an awfully good letter and stated admirably your own feelings, as well as those of Mr. Ramsay—your own perhaps more strongly than his, but that is only natural, and I shall hear what Mr. Ramsay has to say some day when I talk the matter over with him. What I shall ask him to tell me is whether he has any other reason for regretting your friendship with X besides those he mentioned to you. If not, I think he would have done better to have appealed to you, as his friend, to get him to mend his ways. A boy may be in trouble with the school authorities without being a bad friend. I don't know X well enough to express an opinion of my own, but I think you have a pretty good judgment, and I should trust you to find out before long if a boy was really a bad lot, even if you were misled at first. I have great confidence in you, and I admire you for standing up for your friend. But don't make the mistake of thinking

that things don't matter, because they are done by someone
you like. It is one of the tests of a good friendship that it
calls forth and encourages the best qualities of the friends.

With the exception of G., I think most of your Eton
friends are poor workers, and I should regret it very much if
you allowed them to keep you back and destroy all your
enthusiasm in school work. Without being a prig or a sap I
should like to feel that you could like some of the work, and
could encourage your friends to like it too. Cribbing is a
more serious matter. I know it is very common, but I don't
like it, because it is rather mean. There are several forms of
it, and I don't know which form you refer to. Copying other
people's work and showing it up as one's own, or looking
over another boy's papers in trials, or having a book under
the desk when you are construing or repeating a saying
lesson—and all that class of dishonesty, is only mean, and I
should be awfully sorry if you ever thought that did not
matter. To be found out in that sort of thing is not merely
bad luck, it is a disgrace. If any of your friends think differently, don't agree with them. The standard of honour one
forms at school one generally keeps through life, and a man
who is not absolutely straight is no good to anyone. The rule
to lay down for oneself is simply this: Don't ever try and
obtain a success or avoid a punishment by a subterfuge.

Using an English translation to prepare a Latin or Greek
construe is rather different. I don't think that is a crime, and
I think they are a help to learning a language. If I were
teaching a language, I should encourage the use of a translation, provided it was a good one. But schoolmasters take a
different view, and as cribs are forbidden it is not playing the
game to use them. My advice to you is to obey the rules in
this matter. It is not worth while to go against them, and to
use a crib merely to save time and trouble in preparing a
lesson is to go against the principle which I have just laid
down.

I will come down and talk the matter over with Ramsay,
and I hope I may help to get things right. I am so glad you
wrote to me so fully—and I hope you will always confide in

me like this. I try to help you as much as I can. Life—
especially school life—is so full of rules and prohibitions that
it is difficult sometimes to keep one's sense of proportion and
to distinguish between what does matter and what doesn't....

The Christmas holidays of 1917-1918 were spent at Knebworth, and were made happy by a long frost which provided
plenty of home-made winter sport. Antony came home on
December 19th and his mother wrote in her diary:

The cold is great, but frost and sun and skating provide
the kind of cold we like. Davina says her 'nose sparkles'. The
pairs are very happy these days, Antony and Hermione, and
Davina and John. D. and J. are like twins, and the gayest
liveliest twins on earth. We skate all day. Some of the sunny
days on the lake were glorious, and the crowd of children in
bright coloured jerseys, flitting about on skates, was a
lovely sight. Davina and John had skates for the first time.
They soon got on quite easily and very fast alone. They did
not learn their edges. Antony's skating was first rate, and
Victor taught him heaps of very difficult things. When V.
was at home they skated the whole day long, like people
from another planet.

During these holidays I suggested to Antony that he
should henceforth have an allowance and pay for the things
he bought, instead of merely getting orders on the shops
from his dame. I said I thought it would teach him the
value of things and be a good education. I asked him if he
would like to begin it next half. He replied with a shrewd-
ness that almost took my breath away: 'Daddy, will that be
an extravagance or an economy for you?'

On returning to Eton he found himself in Fifth Form, and
his letters throughout this half were extremely happy. The
boys were troubled neither with the air raids, which were a
nightly experience in London whenever the moon shone,
nor with the terrible anxiety that followed the break-
through of the German Army in France in the spring of this

year. It was in fact the last despairing effort of a nation that
was on the verge of collapse, but we did not know it at the
time and the months of March, April and May, 1918, were
almost the worst in the war.

At Eton all was serene. Antony was surrounded by a devoted band of friends, his room was comfortable and bright-
ened by a new chintz, he enjoyed the runs and the fives, and
we kept him well supplied with food. His only trouble was a
persistent pain in the foot, which the doctor ascribed to flat-
footedness and which proved very difficult to cure.

His first experience of Upper Chapel was thus described:
'Today I had my first experience of Upper Chapel. I was
awfully frightened. It always makes one nervous doing something for the first time in front of people who are used to it.
But it was all right and very nice except that "the knife-
board" is not " the best seat in the house" by any means.'

This was followed by a very happy account of the advan-
tage of being an Upper:

I am so sorry that you have been having these air raids.
You must be so tired. How tiresome. I'm sure that my foot
is something more than flat-footedness, it is throbbing and
baking and kicking and aching now while I write. It is awfully nice being an upper, but you have much more work to
do, only of course there is no pupil room, which is a godsend.
I will try and enumerate the advantages, although I shant
be able to think of them all—

(1) No fagging, and hence (a) you do not have to be
changed by lock up (b) you do not have to have your
door open [to hear the calls].
(2) Lights out at 10 p.m. instead of 9.30.
(3) You may go to the school library.
(4) You may go into other houses.
(5) You may go to 'Tap' which is a very good sock shop.
(6) You get off all pupil room.
(7) You are in Upper Chapel.

.Buck de la Warr is starting a socialistic paper here, and the Headmaster said that it must not be too socialistic, so it is not going to be. George & David Cecil are both going to write for it; according to George (Malcolm) D. Cecil is laughing at it.

In other letters at this time he said, 'My God! what a place Eton is! There's nothing like it in the world. You were quite right in saying that it was worth being a boy for the sake of going to Eton. I am most radiantly happy.'

There is little to record of the summer half, 1918. Antony was now playing in Upper Sixpenny, therefore he was more regularly occupied and consequently much happier than in the previous year. We spent the 4th of June with him, but it was overshadowed by the great anxiety caused by the critical period of the war this summer. His letters were short and happy, and no special incident occurred.

In his first letter, on May 6th, he said, 'I am up to nice quiet Masters whom one can do what one likes with, which isn't bad for the summer half.'

This brought a rebuke from his mother, who reminded him that summer days were not meant only for pleasure. She was herself working day after day among the wounded soldiers in her hospital. Her body was tired and her heart heavy, and she looked for a little more purposefulness in her son. 'My darling', she wrote, 'God "endues us plentifully with heavenly gifts" that we may make use of these. But he cannot use them for us. What use were the wings of Perseus to him, until he found by the effort of using them that he could fly? I want you beyond anything to make powerful the powers you have been given, and this can only happen through effort and will, and the love of being.'

He started well at cricket, but then had a run of bad luck. First of all his bat was stolen—then he got a ball on the nose —and finally a blow on the hand, which broke a small bone in one of his fingers so that he could not play at all for some time. In one letter he tells of making 15 and taking 8 wickets, and in another he says, 'I have been up to my eyes in work just lately and I have still got more than I can cope with. I have been doing pretty well just lately. I did the "hat trick" this afternoon and took 5 wickets and made 26. I think I have some chance of getting my Sixpenny next year, but I scarcely dare say so. I enclose a piece of wood for you to touch.'

The Michaelmas school-time of this year was the most eventful half that Antony had yet spent at Eton. On his return he went into tails, and at the end of the half he was confirmed, which marked the definite passing from boyhood into manhood. He joined the Officers Training Corps, and Dr. James was installed as the new Provost in succession to Dr. Warre. But the greatest of all the events was the Armistice, which came in November, and the dispersion of the war cloud which had hitherto overshadowed the whole of his school life.

At the end of September I was asked by Lord Beaverbrook to go to Paris as Commissioner of Propaganda, and after consulting my political leaders and receiving their encouragement, I decided to accept the post. On the 24th Antony's mother wrote: 'Isn't the Palestine news huge? Capturing Nazareth reads so strangely!' Antony replied: 'Thanks for your letter, and the gammon which is delicious. We had a terrific show today for the installation of the Provost. We all got into the school yard and the Provost knocked at the door and was admitted, and all the ushers wore hoods and everyone made Latin speeches and we cheered and sung Latin hymns and psalms in Chapel. It was altogether very exciting and foolish. . . . The news is too marvellous. Does Bulgaria's surrender mean anything really good? How near to Cambrai!'

On October 13th he wrote to me to Paris: 'The news is too
frightfully good, so that I am afraid it will all be over by
Xmas and we shall never any of us get to Paris.'

We both went to visit him on October 22nd, and he wrote
to me the next day:

Oct. 23.

I hope that this will catch you before you start, if you do,
on Thursday. What a glorious visit it was. . . .

I said that I was alright for money, but as a matter of fact
I am not. I feel always so ashamed about asking for money
and sort of frightened, even though it is my own father. I
have had to buy a lot of boots and shoes this half and I have
got exactly enough to pay for them, not counting any odds
and ends such as tooth-paste and hair-wash, etc., and leaving
me nothing over for Xmas presents. Also I must have
another pair of shoes which I can wear in Paris because all
my present ones are old. They cost £2. 5. 0. Thats enough
begging for one letter.

I replied to this:

Paris is very interesting just now. All the Ministers and
all my friends from the Admiralty are over here discussing
the terms of armistice which are to be offered to the Germans, and almost every day brings some fresh development.
It really looks now as if the fighting would be over before
the end of November. But the talking stage will probably
last for many months.

I am so sorry that you are finding money matters a difficulty, and still more so that you should have any hesitation
in telling me so. If you ever get frightened of telling me
anything you will break my heart. I have always told you
that if you found your allowance insufficient I would give
you more, but you must help me by accounting for all you
spend so that I may know exactly what your needs are. I
enclose you a cheque for £5 which I hope will ease matters
for you. If it is not enough don't be afraid to tell me so and
let me know exactly what you want. Darling, you will never
be afraid of your Father, will you? It would be too terrible if

you came to look upon me as an ogre! and if ever you are ashamed of anything remember that it is better if it is shared, and I shall always understand everything and help you about it, even if you think it will be hard to explain.

It has been such a disappointment to me that I have not been able to share your confirmation preparation with you this half. I had so looked forward to seeing you every week-end and having some real good talks about everything. I do hope you will be able to take your confirmation seriously, and feel that it is a great and important time in life. It meant so much to me when I was confirmed, but I was very unhappy at that time, as it was just after my Father died, and I was so lonely. Many people think that religion is only of use to those who are unhappy, and that there is something sad about it, but that is quite wrong. The great thing is to under-stand what it means and to make it part of one's life at all times. Will you write and tell me if in your talks with Ram-say or the Head there are any things you do not quite under-stand? As we cannot meet and discuss things together, we shall have to write about them, but this is more difficult. There are several religious doctrines which have puzzled me at times, but I got to find an interpretation for all of them in the end which satisfied my reason and fitted with the facts of life and human nature as I have found them in the world, and I should like to help you to find these interpretations too. But your difficulties and puzzles may be different to mine, so you will have to tell me what they are when you come across them.

I want you to make a really big effort this half to put forth all your powers, so that you may know what your best can do. If school work seems dull and boring, don't let yourself be beaten by it. It will always bore you if you only give to it as little time and as little thought as you can. The more you give to it the more interesting it will become. You have so much happiness in your life—so many good things, that you owe it to yourself to do all you can to earn them.

Antony wrote to his mother on November 3rd: 'I had a sweet letter from Daddy, such a wonderful one! It inspired me with such a sense of duty and love and loyalty to both of you.' He replied to me:

Nov. 4th, 1918.

Nobody but you *could* write such a letter, it was *too* perfect and I cant tell you how I adored it. Of course I'm not really frightened of you, I am not such a fool. Thank you so much for the cheque, it is too splendid and makes everything perfectly alright. It is indeed a pity that you cant be down here to talk about confirmation. It was such a glorious plan. Ramsay is very good but he's not the same thing. He says that 'gravity' is the word that he thinks expresses the conduct which he wants to see in candidates for confirmation. Does that mean that I ought not to rag about in the evenings when I'm not working? It seems to me as if he expected me to be walking about thinking of nothing but confirmation and I cant do it. I dont expect that he means it like that, but I must ask him. . . . I am really going to try and do well this half especially in trials for several reasons, besides merely wanting to do well. I am awfully happy and have a glorious life and am looking forward passionately to next holidays. You will come down for the actual confirmation service, wont you? At any rate you will come down again this half and settle all about coming over. . . .

The news is too good for words. I do believe we shall have peace by Xmas, do you think so? When peace comes will your job be at an end? . . .

His mother joined me in Paris at the beginning of November, and our letters from there tell of the exciting days that immediately preceded the Armistice. I wrote on Nov. 10th :

Thank you for your letter. Yes, of course, Mummie and I will both come down to Eton for your confirmation. Ramsay is quite right in asking for 'gravity' from his confirmation candidates. Of course this does not mean that you are never to smile or rag, but it does mean that he wants you to think seriously about your preparation. It is a time for self-examination and stock-taking, and the more you can fill your time with work and reading good books, the less you will want to

spend the evenings in ragging. But you must ask him about
this yourself. Confirmation is a sort of coming of age—the
passing from childhood to manhood, and you will want a
good deal of time to think over all that this means, but you
must not let it overshadow your life or cast a gloom upon it.

We are all on tiptoe of excitement here, hourly awaiting
the announcement that the Armistice has been signed. The
situation in Germany is very desperate—a starving population in open revolution, and a beaten army in full flight.
Before you receive this letter it will be all over. I wonder
what form of rejoicing you will have at Eton. I think everyone will go mad with joy. Do you remember the lines in
'The Ballad of the White Horse', where King Alfred asks
the Madonna of his vision 'if that which is forever is, or if our
hearts will faint with bliss, seeing the stranger go'? For
France and Belgium that hour of supreme joy at 'seeing the
stranger go' has come at last. The punishment of the Germans will be terrible. The soldiers who for 4 years have
exercised their brutal tyranny over the unfortunate French
and Belgians are now being driven out with the execrations
of the entire world ringing in their ears, and for them there
will be no home and no peace to return to for years to come.
At first they will find hunger and revolution, and then they
will have to submit to the occupation of their country by
foreign troops until they have paid for all the wanton destruction they have caused. But it is always so in this world,
with nations and with individuals. The most pitiless judge
is the Nemesis of one's own acts.

Our first intimation of the great event on 11th November
was seeing from the windows of our hotel a *midinette* run
down the Rue de la Paix shouting '*Ça y est*'. The streets
were absolutely empty at the time, but immediately, as if by
magic, they became thronged with people, and when we
emerged from our hotel the crowd was so dense that it was
hardly possible to move. In the Rue de Rivoli we encoun-
tered Admiral Sir Rosslyn Wemyss, who had just returned
from the signing of the Armistice. He was very tired, and on

D

his way to his hotel to have a bath. We arranged to join him
later at luncheon at the Hôtel Meurice.

When we rejoined him at one o'clock we found him in
high spirits and very hearty. He gave us a most graphic and
dramatic account of the ceremony he had just come from.
The German train and that of General Foch had drawn up
side by side in the middle of the Compiègne Forest on Sunday, November 10th. There was no friendliness, no saluting,
no handshaking, only the most distant and freezing civility.

Foch said to the German delegate, 'What do you want?'

He answered, 'We want your armistice.'

Foch drew himself up and said, 'My armistice? I do not
know what you mean. Have you come to ask for an armistice?'

The German, with downcast eyes, answered, 'We have.
We want an armistice.'

'Then you shall have it', replied Marshal Foch, and produced the conditions, which he read to them in French, and
then handed the document to them.

The Germans were deeply moved—'they whined' was
Admiral Wemyss' expression. One of them read a prepared
document describing the terrible state of their country, and
almost begging for mercy. Sir Rosslyn Wemyss said that,
having just come from Soissons, he was not touched. They
took the terms away to consider.

That night Foch and Sir Rosslyn Wemyss sat up talking
till late, and the Admiral was just going up to bed when a noise
in the court of their Château made them aware that the
German delegates had returned. The conditions of the Armistice were discussed till 5 a.m., when they were signed.

All this was reported to Antony in the diary which his
mother kept of these days. This diary describes our stirring
experience at the Place de la Concorde in the afternoon,
when a British military band played, the Kaiser was burnt
in effigy, and everyone went mad; also our dinner at

'Henri's' in the evening with Sir James Barrie and Sir
David Henderson, when further scenes of abandoned joy
took place. In the spring of this year, when things were at
their worst and all the officials feared the Germans would
take Paris, I had asked Sir James Barrie, who was lunching
with us, whether he thought the Germans would get to
Paris. He had replied on that occasion, 'I think the Allies
will get to Berlin.' I reminded him of this now and we drank
to 'the Allies in Berlin', and then to 'the English in Paris'.

'The curious thing about it all', wrote his mother to
Antony, 'is that whatever one sees, or does, or says, or feels,
is so small compared to the huge gigantic truth. One does not
seem able to realize it, it is so great.'

We had thought ourselves lucky to be in Paris on this historic day, but Antony's letters describing the scenes at Eton
made us feel that it must have been even more wonderful
there. He wrote three graphic letters on the subject, of
which I reproduce the last:

Nov. 14.

Book I

I must write you an accurate account of everything that
has happened here lately, because it is very thrilling. I shall
start from the very beginning, even if you have heard it
before. Also I am going to give names for my own benefit
afterwards (assuming that you will keep the letter).

On Monday 11 *Nov.* Everyone seemed to know that if the
armistice *was* signed fighting would stop at 11.10. I dont
know how everyone knew but they did, or thought they did.
There were all sorts of rumours that the armistice had been
signed, and we all agreed before 11.0 school that if Blacker
led it we would all cheer at 11.10. Eleven fifteen came, and
then Blacker got up and said 'It is 10 min. past 11, hip-
hurrah', and no one backed him up. I dont think he got much
of a *poena*, but I dont know. When I came out of school I
found a huge crowd assembled outside the school, and the

headmaster stood on the steps and gave out, 'French official wireless. All fighting ceased at 11.0'. There was a pause, and then he went on 'There will be no parade or work this afternoon, and tomorrow will be a *non dies*'. Then Eton went mad and yelled themselves purple. First of all I went to tap and ate till my money ran out. Then I got hold of Frank Stacey, and we went down to Selly and Clifford and bought a flag about the size of a pocket handkerchief for 2/-. Led by Armitage and Shirley with a gong, we rushed all over Eton yelling. We stopped outside Chitty's, and sang 'God save the King', with someone rolling a drum. I got hold of the lid of a tin and broke a bit of box on my fender, and beat it furiously. Finally, Armitage got up on the steps outside Chapel and said, 'We've made enough row, now lets go home', and we all went. Monday night nothing much happened; there was a continuous blowing of a bugle, and yells from street cads, and a few fireworks, and Ramsay came round very annoyed and said that we must be dignified and not make a row. Tuesday was the ideal day. We had the Lower Boy tie, and won 19-2, which was splendid. There was a house match against Marten's, but owing to my knee I wasn't allowed to play. In the evening there was a concert, of which I enclose the programme. From now the fun began.

Book II

We all sang the songs, and the Coldstreams' drum and fife band came down and played too lusciously, and we all yelled ourselves purple. The headmaster got up before it began and said that he was very proud of the school and the way in which we had behaved, and that if we had held ourselves back, let rip now. And by God we did! When it was over we were all mad and yelling, and when I came out I found that they had hoisted the drum major, and there was a terrific mob going on. The Coldstreams rescued the drum major and struck up and marched off towards Windsor. Then the whole of Eton linked up arm in arm in thousands of ranks, and marched behind the band, yelling loudly; at Windsor

Bridge Billy Marsden stopped us, and people who were just
beginning to be nervous turned and came back. But that
wasn't the last. For a long time we all ran about the streets
and watched the fireworks which were being sent off to
right and left. There were coloured lanterns hung all across
Keate's Lane. Then we all rushed to the Burning Bush, and
Glyn climbed up it and tried to pull it down, and stuck a flag
on it. And we all stood round and crossed hands and sang
auld lang syne (I forgot to say that just before we went to
the Burning Bush some other fellows and myself led another
rush to Windsor; we broke through Billy Marsden and Butterwick at Barnes' pool, but there were too few of us and we
were too scattered, and so we had to come back). After the
Burning Bush there were more cries of 'Windsor, Windsor',
and so led by some Pops we went marching back to Windsor.
We charged Butterwick, Billy Marsden, and the constable
(Hindenberg) and knocked them over, and on we swept.
Davies, me and Rhys pulled a flag off Hills & Saunders and
carried it in front of us. Away we went, yelling like maniacs.
I was in the last line, and my knee was hurting like hell. They
started running furiously and it was all I could do to keep up.
Dick and Harry were in front. We stopped (very foolishly) outside the Castle Hotel, but the fellows behind yelled 'On and to
the barracks'. This time our line, who were too tired to
move, got left behind. When we came to the barracks we
found the gates shut and all the street cads yelling 'They're
in there'. We thought that the army had turned traitor and
shut them in, and so we went on, about 18 of us in two long
lines, arm in arm. We meandered round Windsor, and came
up Peascod Street, if you know where that is, and very fortunately came in with others just outside the White Hart.
All this was with a crowd of street cads yelling behind us,
and of course in the dark. When we got back we found Eton
empty. We got in at 8.50. I was sweating all through, and in
such pain from my knee that I could scarcely move. I had a
bath. There were seven from M'Tutor's. We heard that
Rayner Wood had looked out of the window and obtained
silence and made a fine speech, ending up by saying he was

retiring from being C.O. of the Corps, and that his last order to us was to go home quietly, and they all went home as quiet as lambs. The next day the Praepostor came round with the following notice: 'All boys who came into their houses after 8.40 must do Georgic I by Chapel Friday'. I have just finished it, and it took me all my time.

. . . There was going to be another show on Wednesday after school. But there were only fireworks. I didn't go, but I was ready to get out if anything happened. It was the best thing that has ever happened at Eton, or is ever likely to happen again, and it was worth 30 Georgics! I wouldn't have missed it for £1,000000000000000. I left out about the glorious service we had in chapel on Tuesday morning, with 'Mine eyes have seen the glory of the coming of the Lord', and the *Marseillaise* and *Rule Britannia*. Eton was a splendid sight with all the flags, and I wished you could have seen it. I tried to play football again today, but my knee was much too painful. The Georgic is just finished, and I feel awfully pleased with life. My tutor has given a few of us his other study as a sort of library while the cold weather is here, so that we can get warm, as there is a fire. Thank you so much for your letters. . . .

The last event of this stirring half was Antony's Confirmation, which took place on Saturday, December 7th. After this we returned to Paris to pack up, and found the City very gay welcoming President Wilson. The streets were stiff with shouting Americans, and the houses beautifully illuminated at night. Then we returned to Knebworth to prepare for the arrival of the children.

On January 22nd Antony returned to Eton. He passed through London with his mother, and they went to Fortnum & Mason together to buy provisions for his teas. She wrote: 'He left his Macbeth behind: we meant to finish it in the train. It was his holiday task. So I went to Hatchard's to buy him another copy. None to be had, "so many young gentlemen had been in and bought Macbeths that day", they said!'

Chapter III

ETON: AFTER THE WAR

1919-1921

*'I think it is just the most wonderful thing in the
world what Eton means to Etonians.'*

ALTHOUGH FIGHTING had ceased, war-time shortage, both in food and fuel, continued undiminished. Antony's letters in the winter months complained much of the cold, and stressed the necessity for romping and ragging to keep warm. He came to London to line the streets with the O.T.C. in March 1919, on the occasion of the return of the Guards from the front. He had his first experience of the 4th of June kept in the traditional way, and of the Eton and Harrow match at Lord's. Gradually the school resumed its normal life.

In the summer months Antony's letters exhibited his usual restlessness, and after receiving many complaints about trivial matters we wrote to remonstrate with him. He replied, 'You mustn't get alarmed or made unhappy by my letters, just remember that when anyone gets unhappy the natural thing to do is to think of people he loves, and then to write to them, but when one is happy the joy of living and doing whatever one is doing is so great that one forgets everything but one's immediate surroundings.'

His cricket as usual suffered from over-anxiety, and only improved when it was too late in the half to be of value, and he was very disappointed at not getting his Sixpenny. His mother wrote to him about this: 'J. M. B.* is here, and he

*Sir James Barrie.

says he knows it so well. If you had not Sixpenny in your
mind, you would be running all the time. He says when it is
to get into the Eleven it is even worse—not only no runs but
sore throats and things added!'

The great event of the end of this summer was the final
conclusion of Peace. All through the spring and summer
months the Peace terms had been discussed. No one asked
whether they were wise or likely to ensure a durable peace,
but only whether they were severe enough for an enemy
that had wantonly caused such untold suffering and only
been defeated at the price of such terrible sacrifices. And
when at last the conditions of punishment, rather than of
peace, were agreed upon by the victorious Powers, the only
question was, 'Would the defeated Powers accept them?'
Early in May Antony had written, 'Tell me all the news
about Peace terms and people. The terms seem terrific to me
in the *Daily Mirror*. I cant think they'll sign.' His mother
had answered by sending him a copy of the Allies' reply to
the German delegates' Note of protest against the Peace
terms. 'It is very well written', she said, 'quite clear and
easy to understand. It is a clever document, actually composed, I am told, by Lord Curzon.' By the middle of June
the end seemed almost in sight. On the 18th she wrote,
'Fancy, as I write, the Germans are actually reading the
peace terms!'—and the next day, 'Will they sign?'

Then came the news of the scuttling of the German Fleet
at Scapa Flow. On June 23rd his mother wrote: 'My mind is
full of the German fleet. It's the cleverest thing they have
done yet, for after all the ships were ours, no longer theirs!
What a disaster!' Antony replied, very shrewdly, 'I dont
agree with you about the German ships. I think that really
it is the best possible thing that could have happened. We
could hardly have claimed them, already having the largest
Navy in the world, and we dont *really* want them to go to

France or Italy. Though it may not be the right thing to say, surely it suits us down to the ground, since it leaves us with far and away the largest Navy, and there is no country except America which could ever afford to build as big a one. I do hate the way the Germans keep on saying "We'll sign to-morrow", or "We'll sign on conditions" or "We'll sign next month, if we dont have to keep any of the clauses". Aren't they beastly people?'

At last the great day arrived. Antony wrote: 'Isn't it too wonderful about Peace? I wonder what will happen here about it?' On the 16th he said: 'There's scarcely any news, only preparations for Peace. We are going to have a torch-light procession and songs, a concert, etc., great fun, also a parade.' The actual celebrations were described in his letter of the 20th:

Oh, I feel an absolute wreck this morning, dead tired and awfully sleepy. We didn't get to bed till after 12 last night. Our peace celebrations were great fun. We had the annual inspection in the morning, which I think was rather un-necessary, but once over we lined the streets for the Windsor procession of demobilised men. Then Ramsay got a scratch team against us in the afternoon, and gave us an awfully good tea, the only trouble being that it rained nearly all the time, but it was great fun and awfully good of Ramsay. We then had a sort of yelling sing-song in the school hall with 'Katie', 'Smiles', etc. and 'Auld Lang Syne', and we just screamed till we burst. Then a sock supper, awfully good, and cheers for A. B. R., Miss A. B. R., Dame, Cook and ser-vants. We all dressed up madly with moustaches and hats and pyjamas, then took our torches and marched out into the rain to line the streets again. Rayner Woods' clothes were absolutely marvellous, you could hardly recognize the boys, but they were all sent back by the Adjutant. It was a most glorious sight, all the flaming torches from Barnes pool to the Burning Bush. The Windsor procession came round the Burning Bush, firemen, soldiers, bands, and awful women dressed up as 'Rule Britannia', etc. After that we all went into the school yard, where the smoke of paraffin became intolerable, but must have been wonderful to look at, and sang songs like 'Mine eyes have seen the glory', 'God the all-terrible', etc.; then we mobbed about the streets for about quarter of an hour, trying to get together for a definite sort of mob somewhere and failing, finally bed, and very tired too. The torches were a great success and great fun.

I wish that I could paint, because it was the best scene to paint that I have ever known. Pitch blue sky, the faint outlines of the buttresses and pinnacles of the Chapel all streaked and dark, four torches burning solemnly on the Chapel steps, and a thousand in the yard; boys all at attention, and the Last Post dying away from the roof of College, only to be taken up and played again in the distance. The Chapel was the most beautiful looking thing that I have ever seen . . .

At the end of the summer half Antony went with the O.T.C. into camp at Tidworth, and described his life there as follows:

Brief outline of our days, which are always the same, and of which I have consequently long ago lost account—Get up rather cold and wash slightly in cold water—freshening. Then kit—and clear out—and roll up tents, etc. Then comes the grind, a long, rather tedious, sometimes *very* tiring, tho' lately not very, so far always hot parade, miles away over the downs. Then luncheon, generally *filthy* but once good (for here). Then period at canteen and digestion, then another parade, always less tedious, generally nearer, and pretty slack, practise 'sighting' or something like that, home and a wash. God, that wash! It is the most divine thing I know. The washing here is really awfully good. A long bench with a trench down the middle for the waste water. A sort of round tub and delicious cold water. What makes it so much nicer than civilized washing is the absence of all clothing but trousers, the extreme need of it and the feeling of splashing as much as one likes. The feet are greatly relieved thereby. I

have a free evening, delicious canteen, writing, slacking,
talking, etc. . . .

It is great fun on the whole, and the only feature to spoil
it is the alternative—being home. I dont think I have ever
been so well before. Of course one's feet get very tired and
sore from the marching, but that is inevitable. The weather
is divine and I expect I shall arrive back brown as a negro
and strong as a lion. There is one thing which is foul, i.e.
when one has to be tent orderly, which means that one must
draw rations for one's tent every meal, but worst of all wash
up! A beastly job as you all know, especially when the plates
are greasy! . . .

He came home after ten days of this life in the best of
health. As Knebworth was let, the holidays were spent in a
round of visits. First came ten days with a party of cousins
and friends at Thorpeness, a delicious Suffolk seaside place
with a large shallow lake. Antony wrote ecstatically from
here, 'We bathe before breakfast, bathe after breakfast,
bathe in the afternoon and again by moonlight—and thats
the best bathe of all! The lake is great fun, full of tiny children in boats all rowing like the oldest sailors.' Then came
three weeks at Boughton, near Maidstone, with tennis and
bathing in a neighbouring river, and lastly the great excitement of two visits in Scotland.

Antony and I went to stay with the Duke of Westminster
at Lochmore on September 2nd, and we were both in tremendous spirits. It was my first holiday for five years, and
Antony's first visit to Scotland since he was quite a little boy.
We had some lovely deer-stalking on the hills, and caught a
salmon our last day. We then went to the Colquhouns at
Rossdhu on Loch Lomond, and here Antony shot his first
grouse and a capercailzie. This visit was a milestone in his
life, for Sir Iain Colquhoun became his intimate friend, and
remained to the end his ideal of perfect manhood and the
inspiration of all that was best in his life.

Antony wrote from his grandmother's house at Knebworth, on September 18th:

I'm afraid that when I was made I was given rather too much love of people and places; I expect it was a mistake, but there it is. Whenever I leave any place I have been happy at, or anybody I like, I have the most heartrending days afterwards. So now, when most people would think themselves very happy I feel low, merely because after having been sublimely happy, mere happiness seems unhappiness. It is too silly but I can never bear leaving any place, and whenever I have left it is worse. I felt just the same after Thorpe, and I feel it now. I felt so sentimental when I arrived in London last night; it seemed so large and romantic and wretched—little Glasgow and Perth seemed so small, and yet I felt as if we were the only people in the whole city. I thought of Scotland absolutely crammed with people and all the London houses empty and dreary and lonely, and when we got here it seemed worse. Knebs looks so stately and large with its mown lawns and flower beds. It feels quite strange as I haven't seen it for so long. I think of the other day when we were all there, and people staying, and can scarcely believe it. It reminds me of the poem 'Our England is a garden that is full of stately views, etc.' which always meant great loveliness to me.

We had a marvellous journey down, everything went smoothly and well, and travelling by day isn't really half as bad as it looks. . . . Oh, how I loved Rossdhu and Sir Iain and everyone. . . .

Early in the Michaelmas school-time he wrote to his mother: 'Do you mind if I learn boxing this half? I think I must have been inspired by Sir Iain, but I have a longing to learn. This half is perfect. I adore Eton and am very happy.' A few days later he wrote:

Oh, I do love this place, and my friends, and life in general. There is a depressing sort of feeling on waking up in the morning—cold water, whole schoolday, dull all the afternoon. But when the evening comes, and one just lives, everything is too divine. I adore football, too, oh, yes, I love it. I want to get very strong and well and in tremendous training—boxing and football. Oh, I am going to get so strong. I have just finished *The Jacket*, it is such a good book and yet so terrible! But I love awful books—the sort which never end right, where the hero is shot, and the heroine dies just before they're happily married. I think the everlasting successful ending to all stories is too boring. That's why I adored *The Cloister and the Hearth* so.

To encourage the desire expressed in this letter to achieve fitness, I wrote:

I send you a few notes on training, to help you to keep fit. I don't suppose you will follow them—fools learn by their own experience, etc., you know—but at least you may as well know what has been proved by the experience of others.

Notes on Training

After hard exercise it is natural to be tired and you need not worry about that.

What you have to avoid is:

1. Feeling tired before your exercise.
2. Getting blown when exercising.

These symptoms come from bad condition, which training should cure.

What is not generally recognised is that the mind wants training as well as the body—and like the controversy over the hen and the egg, experts will argue for ever whether it is the mind that injures the body or the body the mind. It is sufficient to remember that if either is ailing the other will suffer, and if both are healthy the condition as a whole is good.

Feeling tired and slack without a cause is nearly always the result of mental rather than physical conditions. If the brain is not actively employed in creative work, the body will feel slack and disinclined for exertion. By that I mean if you let yourself be bored, or worried, or indolent, you will be in bad condition. Physical exercise will not cure it. Therefore keep your brain alert on something interesting. Fill your thoughts with healthy vigorous creative ideas, don't dawdle, potter, or dream. Keep something to do every minute of the day—reading, writing, school work or something—fill up your time. If you fritter away the morning, you won't be able to run in the afternoon. If you have been busy and well occupied, you will feel as fit as possible when you take off your coat for the game.

I expect you will say rot, but try, and tell me if you do not find it true. Boys don't think of this, trainers don't tell it to them, and by the time they find it out for themselves their running days are nearly over. In nine cases out of ten, when you are feeling slack, if you examine your mind you will find that it is vacant, bored, or worried with some moral conflict, and that is the cause.

For physical fitness a few rules will suffice:

Don't overdo the exercise, and rest well when you are really tired.

Don't eat between meals. This is a cardinal rule—you *can't* be fit if you break it. It matters much less what you eat *at* meals than that you eat nothing—*nothing at all* between meals. You can do what you please in the holidays, but if you want to be in *training* this condition must be strictly observed.

Don't forget your teeth morning and evening. The mouth is a fruitful source of poison if neglected.

Remember that it is impossible to fill the lungs completely when breathing through the mouth. Train yourself to keep your mouth shut as long as possible, and when you get blown at the end of a run, take two or three *deep* breaths through the *nose* and blow out through the mouth. It will give you back your wind at once.

Boxing is good because it will develop your arms and chest, which are not otherwise used in your games.

At the end of this half he got his house football colours.

In the last half of 1920 Antony's chief occupations were boxing and running with the beagles, and they both kept him very happy. He wrote to say that beagling was great fun, but that hares had 'a remarkably silly habit of always running across ploughed fields!' He added, 'I am getting so lazy now that I can fag that I never do anything for myself.' At the end of March he wrote to his mother:

I don't know what to say, I think of boxing almost entirely now, I am beginning to feel that I understand myself more than I used to, and to realise the things that I really care about. I seem to feel that rather than anything else I should like to be very strong and frightfully fit; also I find what an enormous amount of hate there is in me. It seems a silly thing to say and even sillier when written, but the slightest little thing will sometimes send me off into a fit of rage with someone, and then I set to work to pick to pieces everyone I know, and see only their faults, and what beastly people they are, and how I really hate them. This puts me into a real bad temper, which eventually gives way to intense misery, and then I go to bed very unhappy, and wake up again more or less at peace with everyone. Oh, but jealousy is much my sorest point; any little thing I can generally trace down to jealousy, and hence to self-conceit and pride. I don't know why I should sit down and write all this, I hope it doesn't bore you, darling, and I don't want you to think that I'm either unhappy or continually bad tempered, but it is a new sort of thing that has just come to me, which makes me look through and through myself and other people, which makes me continually thinking and hating, and then wondering why I am hating and if it isn't really my own fault. It is very nice to write about oneself at length, and I just happen to be in a mood to pour it all out. It isn't unpleasant, but it is new and strange. It isn't, either, that I am always like this, but there are moments when I feel that I loathe everyone, and that all I want is to be alone and to be supreme, and to be feared and respected by everyone, and not feel that they count—and then it all goes and I begin to think, and there at the bottom of it all probably lies jealousy. The mood is leaving me even as I write, and if I were to read this through I should think what awful rot I had written, but I won't tear it up because when I wrote it I meant it, and it is something rather extraordinary which I feel you will understand. . . . When I feel worst of all, and most full of myself, and most thinking about self, it occurs to me what a great thing it is to be entirely unselfish. We had a very good sermon this morning preached on unselfishness, and that has set me to think again, and now I'm going to start all over again. I realised how very far I was from seeing other people's point of view, or from wishing anyone else success if I haven't also got it, how the only thing that I ever longed for really was to be superior to other people and to beat them in everything that I care about and to win. And then comes the thought—Is it wrong to win? To try to win? To wish to win? Surely not, or what would nature be if no one ever tried to win, but was everlastingly helping other people to? And yet winning is surely selfish, and unselfishness the basis of all that's really good and all that really matters. Well, I don't know what I am talking about now, I've got well out of my depth, but I do wish I could be a little less selfish.

I replied to this on the 23rd:

. . . Your long letter to Mummy pleased and interested me very much and I am longing to talk to you about it. I am glad that you are keen to get very fit and strong. At your age that is the best possible aim to follow.

Boxing is a splendid exercise for this purpose, and I hope you will stick to that. It is quite a right and proper thing to want to succeed and excel, even though that means beating others in competition. Rivalry is quite a different thing from jealousy and hatred. If you find yourself *hating* someone who has beaten you, this really means that you are angry with yourself for not having done better, but you conceal the fact by transferring your anger to the person who by beating you is always reminding you of your own shortcomings. The remedy for this is not less competition but more. Compete as much as you can in all directions, in work, play, sports, exercise, etc., and always put forth your utmost. If you are quite satisfied that you have tried your utmost and yet are beaten, you will always be able to say without any anger, 'that man is better than me'. As he will not give you cause for self-reproach, you will not hate him. Also unselfishness is not inconsistent with healthy rivalry. It is not selfish to try and win, and in his turn your opponent will not hate you or resent your victory unless (as I have explained) he is dissatisfied with his own achievements. . . .

His mother expressed the same thought in somewhat different words, when she wrote: 'Thank you for your dear intricate letter. Perhaps your jealousy is a form of disappointment when you don't win. You are very competitive and not quite ambitious enough. This makes things difficult; it leaves you wanting to beat your opponent, yet not having tried diligently enough to do your best. Am I right? I think, if you were clearly sure of having done your best, losing the game would not make you feel "jealous". After all, one would not really choose to have everything and leave nothing for other people—one's own joys are not always the greatest, the joys of other friends and life companions are tremendous —and you know this.'

Either the unburdening of himself in this long letter, or the encouragement he received in reply, had the effect of making Antony completely successful in the boxing competitions at the end of this half. His triumphs are recorded characteristically in the following two letters:

Wednesday, March 24th, 1920.

You can never realise what my visit to Rossdhu last summer has meant. Sir Iain inspired me to box, and now I am crazy about it. I have just won the ante-final of the Lightweight boxing against D. Dawnay. I won the first bout last night, and to-morrow evening I have to fight the final against one Nettleton K. S., a very slow, very heavy bruiser, a terrific hitter who I'm rather afraid of, but if I keep my head and box well I *might* beat him. Oh, I can't tell you

E

what the joy of winning a fight is. I was really loving it to-night, and was boxing rather well with my left, hitting him again and again. . . . I do feel so happy to-night, it's the most glorious feeling in the world to have just won. To-morrow is a *non dies*, and I suppose I shall spend it by slowly getting the wind up the whole day.

Nothing more to say, think of me to-morrow night being chased round the ring about 7.15 or 7.30.

26/3/20.

I bet I'm one of the happiest people in this world at the moment. Not every little boy wins the Light-Weight boxing and brings home a huge cup for his Tutor's—not every little boys gets all the praise that I've got, and not every little boy has the luck to beat a bigger and heavier one, or to be lamented when he does not enter for the public schools boxing, which I should like to go in for, but I'd rather go to Malta.

Oh, what the joy of last night was no words can express, unless it's

'One crowded hour of glorious life
Is worth an age without a name'.

I look forward passionately to seeing you tomorrow, let me know your train. I hope you will get this in time before you start.

The words 'I'd rather go to Malta' in the last letter referred to a plan which I had made with him for the holidays. I was paying an official visit to the dockyards at Gibraltar and Malta, and offered to take Antony with me. He accepted gladly.

Antony came home on the 6th. He had four days in London, and we left on the 10th, travelling as far as Gibraltar in the P. & O. liner *Naldera*, which was making her maiden voyage, having been used for other purposes during the war.

This journey was a great experience for Antony; he enjoyed himself thoroughly the whole time.

We returned home via Rome, arriving there on May 1st, to find—in those pre-Fascist days—that it was a *dies non*.

There were demonstrations in the streets, and we were warned to remain in our hotel. This excited Antony intensely, and he asked me eagerly whether it was a 'real revolution'. He was disappointed to find that it was not, and consoled himself by an equally eager interest in the antiquities of the Roman Forum. We heard that there was a railway strike in France, and that no through trains were running. We were therefore obliged to stay in Rome a few days, which meant that Antony could not get back to Eton on the appointed day. When at last we got home on May 8th I sent him to Eton by the first available train on Sunday, with a letter to his Tutor full of apologies and excuses, lest he should get into trouble for being late. My anxiety, however, was unnecessary, for he wrote to his mother the next day—May 10th:

I went to Ramsay and said I had come back (most unnecessary remark as I was standing in front of him). Then I gave him Daddy's letter and said therein lay the reason of my conduct. So he said of course there was nothing to explain, and Daddy needn't have written anything so long and explicit, and how very good of him it was, but how he quite understood, and was pleased to get me back at all, etc.! Very nice. It is very hard being back here again after seeing such a lot of life, and everything being so wonderful. But there it is, and it's great fun seeing friends again. I have got a new boy for a fag, which is rather a bore, because he doesn't start fagging for a fortnight. . . . I went to Lower Club nets this evening, so I had my first taste of cricket, as you might say. I am gradually drifting away from things holiday. It happens very quickly. You come to Eton thinking how hard it is to leave the world with its fun and people, and then after you've been here a wee bit you think Eton is the world and ever one else is just out of it and come here when they want to see it. It's rather a helpful feeling. . . . I have spent most of the day getting my room straight. Everything's very nice, and happy, and enjoyable, and fun, and warm, and calm.

We did not go to him for his birthday on the 13th, and he wrote to us that day:

I made 32 in the game on Tuesday and was put down for Upper Club nets yesterday in consequence, but as it never occurred to me that I should be I never looked, didn't go, and never knew till afterwards. Rather a pity! My room is looking quite nice with all my photos of Rome up on the walls. . . .

On the 17th he wrote:

No more runs at cricket. I have been too interested, and trying too hard. I can only make runs when I'm bored with the game and don't care whether I get out or not. Then I make some, get interested, and hence nervous, and then fail to score. Funny thing nature!

Antony was happier than usual this summer, as lawn tennis and boxing gave him outlets for his energy. He wrote on May 23rd :

. . . I have been playing lots of tennis and you will get an awful shock next holidays when you see how good I am! I have terrific singles with the Baldwin boy, who is pretty good, and we are very even; it's such fun and I enjoy it much more than cricket, which I am only considering as secondary this half. It is all such fun and I am so happy. . . .

I am going to read the books of Ruth and Samuel in Luxmoore's garden now, by way of a quiet Sunday occupation. I don't know whether it's the weather or what, but I am crazily happy and in tearing spirits. . . .

The Eton and Winchester match this year was played at Winchester, and Antony made use of the occasion to visit his old school at West Downs. His description of the day is an amusing account of a series of muddles:

June 26th, 1920.

. . . I enjoyed Winchester yesterday enormously and my visit to W.D., but I have never in my life mismanaged anything so completely. To begin with my tailors sent up the wrong clothes, and so I had hardly any time for breakfast. Then I watched the matches after 2 hrs. in the train, and about quarter to 1 started off to lunch at W.D. at 1.30, as I had been told. Arrived, after wandering about town, at 1.15, to learn lunch was at 1.0. Hadn't the courage to go in late, so missed luncheon. When they came out I was delighted to see everyone. Went and helped Mr. Brymer inspect the boys who were going to watch the match, and see if they were tidy. Perfect relationship, and Mr. Brymer *so* good, and boys quite unself-conscious. Lots of other O.W.Ds. Bathed in swimming-bath and went back to match. Ate 4 dishes of strawberries and cream by way of luncheon, then got interested in match and missed car which was taking chaps to W.D. for tea. Walked up again just too late. However, bathed again and in the joy of bathing forgot dinner at 6.45 with chaps at God Begot; 7.0 said goodbye and dashed down to town, arrived 7.15, all finished. Went to station, buying acid drops en route. Found I'd lost my ticket, man wouldn't let me through. Hadn't enough money to pay for another. However, someone kindly lent me some, and eventually got home. Mr. L—— was too sweet, and Mr. Brymer *very* good headmaster. A new man is going to be head soon, as Brymer is coming into a place in Dorset. Mr. K. very ill but kind, swimming-bath very hot and great fun. It is a most perfect place, and I do so wish John was there. I shall always be really sorry he didn't go; there's no other place to touch it or anywhere near, and after all as we have seen, education is anything but the most important thing. But it's no good crying over spilt milk. . . .

This year Long Leave over the week-end following Lord's was instituted for the first time, and Antony wrote amusingly about this to his mother on July 4th :

Darling,

       This is just a line to ask you to write a letter to Ramsay on the subject of Lord's & Long Leave. Now it must be understood that there are two things:

(1) *Lord's Leave*, extending from Friday morning to Saturday night.

(2) *Long Leave* from Saturday night to Monday morning. They are entirely different, so if one wants leave for both one must not ask leave for one, and if one wants leave for one, one need not ask for both, but *must* ask for the one one wants and not the one one does not want.

This at first may seem a trifle complicated, and even a little unnecessary, but one must not be too hasty in one's criticism of school regulations. *Par exemple*, supposing some one's parents, wanting their boy to go to Lord's, asked for Long Leave for him, but didn't want him for the week-end, how awful if he were to have to return here Saturday night having had leave granted till Monday, or even having had leave till Monday to stay till Saturday night, or having stayed till Sunday to have leave for Wednesday, or even if he got Monday for leave to Sunday back here that night!

All these involve very grave complications, and it must therefore be stated *clearly* whether leave is wanted for Lord's, Long Leave, both, neither, one (if only one, state which one) or the other (if the other, state which one) (or other).

Well, well, well, I should like leave for both (i.e. Lord's & Long Leave) so could you write to the tute and ask same.

You really ought to have seen Nicholas (Llewelyn Davies) swimming across the stream just above Sheep's Bridge in all his clothes amidst the cheers of Lower Club, for the sum of 1/6 from each person—total about £1.10. Worth it, but needing courage!

I boxed rather effectively after 12 to-day, though I am not quite so fit as I used to be. You really ought to see the muscles round my shoulder and biceps, I think they'd fair make you whistle (an American expression, generally used with a view to cabs or dogs—quite effective). . . .

I'm quite mad, moonstruck, or thunderstruck more likely. Goodnight, my darling Muzzy.

Yours to a pin prick,

BUBBY.

On August 27th I took Antony to Scotland for a few visits. He wrote to his mother on arrival at Kildonan:

Saturday night, August 30th, 1920.

This isn't really a letter about our journey or this place, but about the future, because all the time up in the train I was dreaming about what I was going to do. I had got two ideas, of which at present I am in favour of the latter:

(1) I go into the Diplomatic Service. I become the greatest Englishman in Europe, sworn by in 5 capitals, deified by the Hindoos while Viceroy, and eventually Foreign Minister upholding every high-handed action of our agents all over the world, the idol of my friends, and the terror of foreign nations, insulting America with impunity, with the whole world cowering at my feet. Then perhaps P.M. and a grave in Westminster Abbey, the biggest diplomat of the 20th century on a level with Palmerston and Bismarck, and leaving England absolutely supreme in the world, with her hand in every pie, grasping, successful, feared and honourable.

(2) I feel that I might be all this and that I might be one of the biggest men that ever was, and yet I don't really want to be. The baby side of my character is so predominant, and so superior to the social and grown-up life of the world, that what I want to do is to go into a business, marry a divine wife, live in the country at a divine farm, keep animals, etc., and meanwhile pile up a pretty fair sum of money; then Knebs and a London house and society and life, leaving money to my son, who may do the diplomat stunt and who may be the big public man and keep up the family traditions. Even while I write this I feel that I have put the case so strongly for the first that I have convinced myself that it would be the best, but when I started this letter and when I started to think it out, I felt that I should really be happier as the business man, the country squire and farmer, than the world-famous diplomatist. There is the struggle going on in me between your love of society and your ambition, and Daddy's great ideas about politics and Statesmanship, and your country instincts and love of animals, and Daddy's of

solitude and sport. To-day I am ambitious—I am the master
—I am strong, hard and magnificent. Yesterday I was humble, a child caring for love and happiness, England and
animals; living with mankind, not playing with it, adoring
my home and having only one home, not with the world as
my home. To-day I leave a great name in the archives of the
Lytton family, and a greater name in the memory of Englishmen to come, but I leave my family poor. Yesterday I
left nothing to my family but money, but I paved the way
for my son to become what I might have been. Yesterday I
was a child and full of love—to-day I am a man and full of
sociability. This sounds all very silly, but, oh, how I puzzled
over it all yesterday in the train, how I dreamt and built
castles—I saw my home, my wife, my children, and now I
feel much more like the great man. . . .

On his return to Eton Antony was Captain of the Games
in his House, and had the interest and responsibility of making and training the House football team. He was also in
First Hundred and did special work.

On the 26th he wrote that he was playing in the Field
Game and was enjoying it. 'We have won all our House
matches this week', he said, 'but they haven't been difficult
ones. The side hasn't been playing as well as it has got to if
we are going to do any good, but it is great fun managing it
and choosing the people and trying to produce the best
result. . . . Did I tell you that Luxmoore had enlisted me in
the Shakespeare Society? We are reading " King John ". I
have been reading some of our old friend "The White Horse"
this evening. How wonderful it is !

> The man of the cave made answer,
> And his eyes were stars of scorn,
> "And better Kings were conquered
> Or ever your sires were born".

I think "His eyes were stars of scorn" is perfectly wonderful!
I have just finished *Jane Eyre* and I loved it. It is awfully

exciting, but I still think *Catriona* is the only love-story I have read where you really feel the people are in love with each other.'

The week-end of December 4th-6th Antony spent at the Eton Mission at Hackney Wick, and he wrote about this on December 8th:

We had great fun at the Mission and it was well worth going. Two things struck me most

(1) The extraordinary absence of real poverty, the sort of awful thing one imagines from books, etc. The cottages were just the same inside as any of the Almshouses say at Knebworth, and they all had lovely fires in the grate, which made me think I wish to goodness my room was as warm as this.

(2) The excessive energy of the Church to persuade people to go to Church 3 times on Sundays and Bible Class in between whiles. I thought it all rather overdone and said, 'They don't go on at us like this. Why should they at the poor people, who are much less likely to take to it even than we should be?'

On Sunday we went down Petticoat Lane, the place with all the shops in the streets, and lots of Jews tried to sell me a second-hand overcoat. I saw the man from whom Daddy bought a thing to imitate birds with outside Lord's down there, and some of the hawkers from Henley.

The holidays began at Knebworth and ended in a ten days' visit to Mürren. Antony wrote to his mother after his return to Eton.

ETON.

Here I am again feeling rather flat and tired at regular life again after the marvellous irregularities of the holidays, but nevertheless happy. What a wonder it is that in England there is a school such that I have no more pangs at leaving home for Eton than Switzerland for home. . . . It's a wonderful place. . . . The holiday-task paper was frightfully hard in spite of my study—from London to Windsor; however, I managed to write a lot of rot on the 'Anglo-Japanese alliance' and 'Egypt a nation', which may pass me. Not a soul read the book! except the tugs!

Darling, I can't tell you what a wonderful holiday I have had, I think the best that ever was. I adore hunting, I adore dancing, I adore ski-ing, and I'm very fond of country life!! Every moment has been perfect from first to last, everything successful, everything exciting, everything worth doing again, and lots of delicious people. The things that stand out most are the Hertford ball, that wonderful Monday's hunt, and the run to Grindelwald—a queer mixture but all perfect, and oh, darling, how I have enjoyed it all. Thank you so much for everything and for making such a wonderful family and such great life. I am indeed lucky beyond all imagination. . . .

There's no news, everything is the same and why shouldn't it be, wasn't it always perfect? isn't it still perfect? and won't it be perfect for ever?

Towards the end of the half he was laid up with a bad arm and wrote on March 10th:

Darlings, both of you, all of you,

I am very nearly mad, I am quite slowly turning wuzzy. I see four people instead of one, and I have an irresistible longing to eat the fire and beat my door-handle. The reason is briefly this—that I am perfectly well and itching to box, etc., only my arm still prevents me from taking *any form* of exercise (other than writing) as it has not yet healed up and the skin (I am told my skin is very sensitive, as after having knives dug into it, boiling water poured on it, iodine flung at it, and being excluded from the fresh air by black bandages it shows a tendency to come off!) all round the wound is red and rather inflamed.

The result is necessitated inaction, in the face of the most vicious temptations. So there is some reason for this exasperation.

Added to which the boxing competition comes off next Wednesday, Thursday, Friday, and I shall probably have to go to Bedford to box on Saturday. I am badly in need of

practice and am not in good training. In the Light Weights
there is someone who I think will beat me, and if he does I
shall never get over the shame of it, quite apart from the
fact that I shall lose the cup; on the other hand, if I box in
the Welters I have to give away a stone, which is a lot, and
it looks rather bad. I feel perfectly fed up about everything
and without any hope, so I am entering the whole show with
a bad grace and a worse temper, not to mention a form of
dangerous insanity. Saturday next is a whole holiday and
I think it is improbable that I shall be able to be active, so
could some of you come down and spend the day? . . .

I hope you will some of you appear for luncheon on Saturday—until then I remain your dutiful obedient and devoted
little offspring,

EDWARD ANTONY JAMES BULWER LYTTON.

P.S. My supper experience this evening may amuse you.
I went down hungry and asked of my neighbour 'Is the soup
good?'—'Yes'!!! I fainted—on coming to I asked the maid for
some. 'There's no more, sir.' I fainted again. . . . 'Will you
have some bread and milk, sir?' But as I was feeling well I
would not. 'Have—or rather—'ave a cheese biscuit then?'
'I will', and I did, but it had to be taken away as I had not
brought a hammer. 'Water, please.' I drank and went to
bed.

His letters made us anxious lest he should not be well
enough to enter for the Public Schools Boxing competition,
but on March 14th he wrote: 'From everything going wrong,
everything is now going right! The weight for the Light
Weights is 10 st: and under. I weigh exactly 10 st.! The one
fellow who was likely to beat me, and whom I was afraid of,
weighs 10 st: 8 lbs: added to which my arm is quite well. I
feel quite well, and it has stopped raining!! What more
could one want? Such is life. From despondency to happiness is but a step (philosopher!). . . . The boxing here begins
at 6.30 p.m. on Wednesday and Thursday, and the Finals are
on Friday. I may not get into the Finals, but I ought to. I will

let Daddy know for certain later. About Bedford (where the
Inter-Schools competition is to be held) we leave here at
6 a.m. on Saturday, and box *all day* as far as I can see, as
there are several other schools competing. . . . I am quite all
right again now, so don't worry about me. I have been as
hearty as anything all day.'

Antony won the boxing competition, both at Eton and at
Bedford. He and his friends dined with us in London on his
way back, and we had all his news at first hand. But in a
letter to me from Eton after his return he wrote: 'Never can
I describe to you the misery before a boxing match, or the
exhilaration afterwards; it is too awful, so that one says "It
isn't really worth it" before, and "By God, it's worth anything" afterwards.'

He returned to Eton on May 6th, having had an
extra week for visits to the dentist. As usual, he found the
cricket boring, and wrote petulantly on May 11th, 'Oh, I am
bored with this cricket. I would like to take it all cheerfully
as fun, and not really worry about it at all, and yet there is
always that loathsome pride which makes one want to be in
Upper Club all the time and do better than other people.
How I hate it! There's nothing worse than having to play
cricket seriously, and I'm damned if I will! I wish it would
get really hot and then we could at any rate bathe. They say
there won't be any 4th of June, because of the strike, and if
there is I shall probably have to play in some damned 3rd
XI match. It's all too beastly for words, and I feel as if I
shall scream or die or something. I do loathe the summer
half, and its the longest too!'

His mother visited him on May 13th—his eighteenth
birthday—and he wrote to her that evening. 'Darling, what
fun it was seeing you today, I enjoyed it so much, and oh, I
hope you will be able to get a house near here. I am going to
write that story again, better if I can. I am determined to

try and write a lot and make a little money, but I don't expect it will be any good, do you? . . . Money is terribly difficult and I sometimes feel I simply can't manage; that's what I'm so afraid of at Cambridge—that I shall spend more than I've got, but it's frightfully good to *have* not to buy things '

As a matter of fact Antony was always very good about money matters—though not naturally economical, and with a taste for spending, he yet had a good money conscience, and as he was without any expensive tastes he always managed to keep within his income. He never incurred serious debts at any time in his life. The possession of an allowance while he was at Eton helped him to acquire a knowledge of values and proved a useful experience. His only difficulty was in keeping accurate accounts. He used to send the statements of certain payments and say 'as I have only got so much left I must have spent the rest on sock'.* Later in life, however, when he entered business and found accountancy was important, he took great trouble to master this difficult subject. He went through a course of study in book-keeping and accountancy and got 100 per cent. marks in an examination at the end of it.

The half ended with a great disappointment.

July 24, 1921.

You wonder why I don't love Eton as much as you would imagine. Here is the reason. I write it while the full force of the thing is in effect. When I came I looked with wonder at the great almighty tremendous ones, and I wondered if I should ever be like them—and I determined to be—and I've failed. *Voilà tout!* I have, of course, always longed for colours and I've not got many, and I always feel I've had bad luck. But this is the crowning blow. I've not got my XXII and I've not got into Pop—two things which though I may have hidden my feelings I was certain were going to happen. I thank God that I got over any regrets I might have about

* Food.

them before I knew I had failed, and so I am even rather
surprised with myself that I have not been more bad-tem-
pered and unhappy. But I am really rather depressed about
it. I am not quite the kind of chap ever to really go down
here, and I haven't got enough real friends who would believe in me whatever I did. You can't get colours without
trying, and I hate taking games really seriously—it spoils
them utterly, in my opinion.

Nicholas and Maurice have both got into Pop, and I really
thought I should, but if there are some people who like me,
there are as many who don't.

Damn, it's annoying, but I don't really mind very much.
I have got some friends whom I really do like and who I
think like me, but I hate and despise failure and I've failed
utterly. It's just because I can't be natural and dull. I'm
always acting and either sulky or maddening. Poor wretches
who have to put up with me!

Still, you can only worship a thing if you get the plums,
and I've got nothing but myself to help me.

It's almost incredible that anyone can write such a lot of
rot, so entirely egotistical, and I'm awfully sorry. Tear it all
up, it's complete rot from the beginning, but I feel like poor
Carpentier—'I am a failure'. Never mind, it's all over now
and we'll just pray that next half may be grand with success.

I answered on 26th July:

I am so deeply sorry for your disappointments and I can
sympathize with you the better because I went through just
such a disappointment myself. I was never in the running
for the 22, as my cricket was spoilt by Dentist visits two or
three years earlier, when I was in the running for sixpenny.
But at the end of the summer half, when I was just 18, I did
hope and expect to get into Pop. There was the usual sum-
mer-end exodus and many vacancies. At the first election I
was considered to be very near, as I only received 2 blackballs
(the excluding number) and some of my friends congratu-
lated me as if I were already in, as they considered my election certain. But those 2 blackballs remained constant not

only at every election at the end of that half, but throughout
the whole of my last year. Others who had received 8 & 10
blackballs at first, & some who were not then up for election
at all, subsequently got in; but my two enemies kept me out
for ever, and of course I never discovered who they were!
You have one consolation which was denied to me. You can
speak freely of your disappointment and pour out your feelings to parents who can fully understand and sympathize
with you. I had no father, and my mother did not understand
anything about Pop. So I had to keep my feelings to myself,
and the disappointment was therefore the harder to bear. It
made me rather hard and morose and more reserved than
ever. I loved your letter, because you were able to say exactly
what you were feeling, and I was proud to know that you
could count on our understanding and sympathy.

I always thought that you were over sanguine about getting your 22, and I was dreading your disappointment. But
getting a colour is not a matter of luck or favouritism, it is
the reward of achievement, and your keenness for cricket
was not quite enough to secure real proficiency. To reach
the highest standard in any games or sports, there must be
some touch of passion—you have felt it in boxing but not in
cricket—not even quite enough in football. Try and remember this at the *beginning* of next half. These words of Browning are worth remembering in this connection:

> Do your best, whether winning or losing it,
> If you choose to play!—is my principle.
> Let a man contend to the uttermost
> For his life's set prize, be it what it will!
> And the sin I impute to each frustrate ghost
> Is—the unlit lamp and the ungirt loin.

Don't sit among the ashes and talk about being a failure, but
gird up your loins and make up your mind to profit by the
experience. Next half you will have 2 'set-prizes' before you—
the Field and the Scholarship. Make up your mind to 'con-
tend to the uttermost' for both of them, and if your thoughts
are concentrated upon winning these you won't need to

worry about not being in Pop. It's a damned bitter pill to
swallow, I know, but it is just these bitter doses in life that
test character. So cheer up, old man, and don't brood. You
have very jolly holidays before you, and what it is still in
your power to make a very successful last half. Don't be a
'frustrate ghost'—whatever that may mean!

Chapter IV

ETON: IN POP

1921-1922

'So my career at Eton closes. Never was anything more happy, never can anyone be more thankful.'

ANTONY RETURNED to Eton in September 1921, for what he believed at the time was to be his last half there. Before the end of the year circumstances occurred which changed all our plans, but we were as yet unaware of the big events which were to break up our family unity for the first time. This Michaelmas school-time was to prove the period of Antony's greatest achievement at school.

He wrote on September 22nd:

. . . Once again Eton life, all the same old jokes, all the same places, but not all the same faces. I am the only one left in the house of my generation. . . . The old order changeth giving place to new, and I feel almost that I would rather be back in the old days when I was nothing, and Ral used to cook potato soup on his fire, and we ate it with blackberry jam under a pink lampshade! It sounds silly. Ah, Romance! Outside the house it is rather wonderful to find oneself at the top, all one's friends running the school in Div. 2 and afraid of no one. I think I would rather there were huge-looking seal-covered creatures who made one tremble to look at them, still patrolling the streets and suggesting dreams of future glory. Never has Eton seemed more changed. It is almost ordinary, a thing of the past with nothing but memories and no present. And yet it is the same—divine and wonderful.

Everyone exclaims 'Good God, Tony, you do look ill!' and my boxing man, in heavy black & white shirt & stick-up collar (for mourning—made me roar) said:—'You don't look well, Mr. Knebworth. What's the matter? Too many fast women and slow horses?' Comment needless. . . .

On the 25th Antony announced the momentous news that he had been elected to Pop in a characteristically casual manner:

In great haste as I have a lot to do. . . . David and I have got five fags each! ten to the mess! and are completely supreme, both in Pop!

You won't think too seriously about the scholarship, will you? Because I am not expected to get one, and haven't really any chance. I'm only going in for the sake of experience and I don't want you to be disappointed. *Of course* I shall try. . . .

On September 29th he wrote his first letter to his mother on 'Eton Society' paper!

. . . All my love to you all. I can't tell you how divine it is being in Pop or how happy I am. The great fun is that we are nearly all new and are consequently awed by no one and have no feelings or intentions of propriety! We are incredibly officious, fearfully bumptious, and entirely selfish, absolutely screaming with joy all the time.

To-day was a holiday and we spent the morning sealing our hats. Nico set his on fire and it is now spattered in sealing wax all over! I long to see you all, it's such fun and you must share it. . . .

His letters continued to be uproariously happy, telling of the fun of being in Pop with all his friends. A letter to me of October 6th contains a passage which reads curiously in the light of subsequent events—

Mother says that you suddenly think perhaps I ought to go to Oxford. I agree with you that I am not at all scientific, mechanical or radical, in fact plum the opposite, but I have

lived so long for Cambridge and thought about it that I feel
as if I had been there and I couldn't possibly change now.
Also most of my friends are, I think, going to Trinity.

Ten months later he telegraphed to me in India that he
had made up his mind to go to Oxford, as all his friends were
going there! In the same letter he said:

We are reading the *Ring & the Book* with the Vice-
Provost for 'extra studies'. I think it is most awfully good.
I hope to do Julius Caesar in the Shakespeare Society, which
I really love.

As the half progressed Antony began to suffer from his
usual complaint—inability to play a game well when he was
thinking about colours. He wrote that he had completely
gone off at football and was quite sure that he would not get
his Field. 'It makes me too miserable', he said, 'not so much
that I shan't get my Field, as that I can no longer play my
favourite game!' Fortunately, however, his fears on this
occasion were not realized, and he did get his Field before
the end of the half.

The subject of Antony's staying on at Eton or leaving was
discussed in many letters at the end of this half. Mr. Ramsay
begged me to let him stay on, and Antony after much waver-
ing was finally emphatic about his wish to remain. Here are
some of his arguments on both sides of the question:

I. In favour of leaving.

. . . I am beginning to feel that I long for greater freedom
and more of the world and less of school. In fact, to put it
crudely, I don't want to be a schoolboy any more, and it is an
awful wrench not to be one any more. I should have things
so much my own way next half and I am very much afraid
of an anti-climax. It has been such a glorious half and such
fun that I think I should rather like it to be a wind-up.

I am beginning to get a little tired of school life and long
to see more of the world and people not solely Etonian. Be-

cause, though I think Eton is the most wonderful and most adorable and happiest place in the world, one does get very narrow staying here for ever.

II. In favour of staying.

I've changed again and want to stay. I think that it was quite natural that I should have felt like leaving, when I had just come back from Long Leave and was feeling still a little homesick. Furthermore, I was depressed and not very well, and therefore feeling rather like home and comfort and quiet. But to-day I have been alright again and have thought of myself leaving and can't do it. I can't make this last crowded month, with a week at Cambridge, the last of my Eton life. When I have suggested that I might be leaving to any of my friends, they've looked at me as if I was mad, and after all, though one may say it's a bad thing to vegetate at school, I've never come across anyone yet who said they wished they'd left Eton sooner. I feel quite certain that as long as I am well and happy I can never want to leave, and after all, wherever one is, if one's depressed one wants a change. . . .

I should so love to see you about it. It's so difficult for me to do anything, because you know what I am for moods, and if one changes every two days it's rather hard to decide.

To these letters I replied:

I quite understand all your difficulties and uncertainties about leaving at the end of this half. It is inevitable that you should feel them. Don't worry about it any more, but leave the decision to me. I will talk it over with you when I come to Eton on Sunday. . . .

I can't tell you anything definite as yet about India, but I may know more by the end of the week. If I were to go to India, I think you would have to give up the University and come with me, but it will be time enough to discuss that when I know definitely whether or not I am going.

This means that I was being pressed to go to India as Governor of Bengal, and could not make up my mind. The

issues involved in this decision were even greater than
those which were troubling Antony. When at last I decided
to accept the post, I hoped at first that he might come with
us for a year before going to the University, but after much
further discussion finally yielded to Mr. Ramsay's entreaty
and decided to let Antony remain at Eton till the end of
the summer. The decision to go to India was a difficult
one to make, and often during our long separation I felt
cause to regret it.

The end of the half was somewhat hectic. First Antony
was laid up for some days and could not play in the last
school matches. Then he went in for the Rosebery history
examination and came out triumphant, winning the prize
with a paper on Napoleon. Then he went up to Cambridge
for the scholarship examination, in which he did very creditably, and finally he had the great disappointment of being
beaten in the house football ties. This last he bore with his
usual philosophy.

Of Antony's achievements this half, Mr. Marten wrote
very appreciatively:

December 17, 1921.

Dear Ramsay,
        Both of us may feel very well satisfied with Kneb-
worth's performance this half. To secure one of the Rosebery prizes, to be 'on the list' for a Trinity exhibition, and
to get one's Field, is sufficient to satisfy anyone's ambition.

He has worked very well up to me this half. He prepared
his Text-book well, wrote interesting Essays and 40 minute
answers, and was quick to take points in School.

In the Rosebery he scored, of course, by having a paper
on Napoleon. Mr. Headlam Morley told me that he could
not give him less than 86 for it; and he was struck not only
by the great knowledge displayed, but by the way he made
use of it in his answers. And with his English style generally
he was very favourably impressed. . . .

                    yrs   C. H. K. MARTEN.

This was accompanied by the following covering letter from Mr. Ramsay:

December 24, 1921.

My dear Lytton,

You have good reason to be proud of Antony. He has done remarkable things this Half. The Rosebery result has indicated his powers as a historian, and has kindled his ambition into a flame which may burn very brightly at Cambridge. The more I think of it, the greater pity it seems to interrupt so promising a career; and I do hope you will decide on letting him take the normal university course, beginning next October. This I am confident would be best for him. If he takes it later, his keenness may have faded, and in any case the credit of success will be less. I need not tell you that his help in the house next Half will be invaluable. In every way his example has been admirable. His keenness and fine leadership deserved better fortune in the House Ties; and I wish we had won the Cup for his sake.

Yrs ever,

A. B. RAMSAY.

Christmas was spent at Knebworth, but the joy of being back there again was overshadowed by the thoughts of our coming separation. On account of our going to India, Antony got a week's extra holiday, and I took him with me for a last short visit to Switzerland at the end of January. We went to Mürren and had a very happy time there, making several good expeditions. Antony wrote to his mother on January 25th: 'We are having such a wonderful time here. I can't tell you how divine it is. Perfect snow and boiling hot blue sunny days.' At the end of this letter he said, 'I have finished *Wuthering Heights*. It is far and away the best book I have ever read in my life. I absolutely adore every line of it. Do you know it well? Heathcliffe so loathsome in character is entirely redeemed to my mind by his passionate love for Cathy, who must have been the most divine creature in fact or fiction. I simply love her and the whole book. What a story!'

On February 6th he wrote to his mother from Eton:

I am back again at Eton. It seems almost incredible after such wonderful holidays and it is not only incredible but it is also not true. My body may be here but my spirit (like Catherine Linton's in *Wuthering Heights*) is wandering far away. It is with you all at home. . . . Now it is jumping a fence on Flavia, the best hunter in the county, now it is dancing, now it is smelling the smoke of the banqueting-hall fire, now it is playing hide and seek and laughing and joking in every corner and cranny of Knebworth, and now it is in the snow and the sun, climbing the Wasnegg or doing a last glorious Half-Way-House.

I sat in Chapel, I sat at breakfast or at luncheon, or I walked and talked, but all unconsciously, for all the time my thoughts and my heart and my soul were living over and over again that glorious and never to be forgotten holiday.

The future is frightening, the present is ordinary, drab and boring; but the past is glorious, eternal, and happy beyond all dreams; and so in the past I have been living, and until it grows dim and far away, know that I am thinking always of you all and my home and my wonderful, wonderful life last holidays. Oh, darling, a thousand thanks for the most glorious and most heavenly time which was so divine that it happens not only in fact, but over and over again in the imagination.

It is terrible to think that it is over and that there is a year to fly by before it can happen again. But in that year new and wonderful things are going to happen. Enough of sentimentality and imagination; now for the present, the bitter, practical, hardworking present.

Our last days were very full with farewell ceremonies and preparations for departure. Antony came home for his Long Leave before we left. His last letters were very precious, and the parting was the hardest thing we had yet had to bear.

To his mother:

Feb. 24.   ETON SOCIETY.

I can't tell you how I am looking forward to your visit tomorrow. Do you realise it will be your last? We'll have the most glorious bust-up tea in my room and all be ill. I hope you're all coming. . . .

It has been a wonderful time, my 5 years at Eton. I have adored it all and really learnt to love lots of good things, and I've seen such a lot of different sorts of people and made so many friends and had such fun; it has all been too wonderful. It is indeed the greatest and most marvellous school in the world.

I can never thank you and Daddy enough for giving me such a wonderful life and making me so very full of happiness. I only hope that in the time to come I shall be able to show myself worthy of it all, and turn out a really grateful and good son to such a marvellous mother and father. Oh, thank you, thank you, darling, so much for all my wonderful life, and I do hope that you will all be happy and successful in India, and that it will be the greatest fun and the greatest triumph for Daddy and for India.

Goodnight now and remember that I am longing for you all tomorrow.

Tomorrow and tomorrow and tomorrow.   ANTONY.

His mother wrote after our last visit to him:

7 a.m. Monday, Feb. 27th, 1922.

I am afraid I spoilt yesterday a little bit—the rain and I together! But it has always been the same at 'taking leave' since you were little and first went to 'West Downs'. This time it is you who stay and I who go. I am glad you are staying, darling son, to have this English year, your last at Eton, where you are so well established with friends and interests. Then holidays brimming over with possibilities—and your new life at Cambridge—which I know you will find very absorbing. . . .

It is a great sorrow to me breaking up our Home—We have always had such good family holidays. But as you all grow up, this becomes inevitable—I only wish Daddy's 'Call' had been elsewhere. I feel very strongly that he will not stay away long. Anyhow this first year will be my longest time away from you. And when it is all over and done—the time will telescope up as we look back, and perhaps we shall wonder why it seemed so very hard to face.

I got your letter in London just before I started for Eton. Thank you for it—every word you say to me is precious. I love you so very much, not only because you are my son, but because you are good and gay, loving and brave and full to the brim of all the qualities I love best in a man. I know you will do your best for me, in work and play—and always remember to 'keep your colour'; we shall never be separated, although we are parting now for 12 months. The great thing to learn in life is to take things well. Old as I am, I have not *quite* learnt this yet, when the particular thing is leaving you for a bit!

We left for India on March 9th. Antony travelled with us to Folkestone. After we had parted I found this letter from him in my coat pocket:

I can't think of a present to give you. Everyone has given you a farewell present except me, but I don't know what to give you, and so I will give you my heart. It is going to be very awful for me not having you with me as my castle and my strength, but you know how I love you and how I will try to become a good, wise and strong man while you are away and be worthy of you and all the wonderful things that you have given me.

God give you his blessing and watch over you always in India, and may you be a great and wonderful ruler, loved by all and very successful.

Oh, I wish you all the most magnificent things and great happiness, and I pray that I may live worthy of you while you are away.

This half brought Antony further successes. In addition to getting his Rugby XV colours, the first letters we received from him in India told of his winning the Loder prize for declamation, the School hurdles in the sports, and the cup for boxing in the welter-weight class.

To his mother:

ETON SOCIETY,
Friday, March 10*th*, 1922.

My first letter. Thank God that awful Folkestone boat is gone. I was dreading that moment. . . . I'm so sorry I couldn't help you in the least. But I got back to Eton alright that night and went almost straight to bed. Eton's a wonderfully good place to come back to, just the same and no sympathy, so you simply have to laugh and be happy, and you are.

Nico and everyone are delicious, and I know I shall be as happy as a bird here—but I'm just a tinge afraid of the holidays, and that's partly why I should love Spain, but I'll have to see. . . .

I have ordered special wonderful notepaper to write to you on, so that the next letter you get will be like a book! . . .

Tuesday night.

The day began superbly. I had a wonderful mail from you all, the most divine letters for which a thousand thanks. I have the most wonderful posts in our days. Letters from everyone which I have to answer, so I am kept writing all day long.

The match with the Irish Guards was scratched. I nearly wept. You know I have become so absolutely wild about Rugger that I think of nothing else and look forward to nothing else. I'm completely gone on it (to use a vulgar expression), so I was very depressed about that and didn't know how to spend the afternoon, and so wasted it and was in a foul temper. . . .

However, I am in a better temper this evening and things have cleared up (let me get it off my chest). I won the Loder Prize. I'm so pleased. I'm sure it was all Daddy's wonderful coaching at Knebs, though I got Luxmoore to help me with it here.

A mail from Port Said! Such joy. I gave a great yell when I saw your writing on that old green board once more. I

can't tell you what joy it was, I have missed its familiar
shape for so long. I am so so glad you have been having a
divine quiet warm journey, though I suppose you have almost forgotten about it now. And I'm so glad you're happy,
because I am—very—and what is a year?—just that—O—
that's all! . . .

I can't tell you how I have enjoyed hearing from you all
today. Such divine letters too! How I wish I was with you.
I do miss you all so terribly. Its alright when I'm strong and
well and happy, and full of life and fun, but just at the
moment I'm ill and hurt and feel weak, and then I do so
long to see you all again and be all sitting round your sitting
room fire, just us and us alone, such a happy group. Eton is
a hard place to be ill in, just as it is the best place in the
world to be strong and happy in, but there is no sympathy
and help in Eton—it is great and strong and full of life. One
must live and be happy, or one's no good at Eton, and when
I can't play games and get exercise I become like a damp
rag, mentally and physically, in two seconds. Oh, how I pray
to get well again, and then I can run and be full of life, 'A
body of England, breathing English air.'

I expect you wish you were breathing English air (but
you shouldn't—it's awful unwholesome at the moment, hail
and snow and frost and wind) and India must be so wonderful and new and exciting and such a good life. I can picture
you all on ponies galloping over the Himalayas. . . .

Wednesday morning.

I won my boxing last night. Just sticking out a left and
hopping about till the 3rd round, when I let one right go
over and knocked him flat. He got up and was all dazed, and
I could have put him out then, only my shoulder hurt quite
enough the first time and I wasn't going to risk it again.
That was Welter-Weight. I get another cup just like the old
Light-Weight one.

Now for the hurdles on Saturday to finish up the half!
That's flying rather too high, I'm afraid, but if one's going
to fly high, why not fly very high? Tee Ta Tara Tata Totoo!

I've got quite a lot to tell you, as the last few days have not been entirely uninteresting. . . . On Wednesday I did practically nothing, except that I jumped all the hurdles (there are about four million) in just under two seconds and thus created the world's record. . . .

On Thursday I jumped the hurdles again. I jumped them all at once in one long bound in one second. In the afternoon the school played the Masters at Rugger and were beaten. That is to say the Masters won. . . .

Tomorrow is the final of the sports. I am running in the hurdles and getting beaten by Norman, who does them all backwards in half a second and then stands on his head for twenty minutes to recover. I shall win and then they'll erect another statue. Shut up! . . .

Saturday.

'Praise to the holiest in the heights'. I think I shall really have to have a statue put up to me, I've gone and won the hurdles, beating Norman by 2 inches! We both fell at every hurdle and all the others fell twice at every hurdle, so it wasn't much of a race. I have never run slower or jumped worse in my life, but I suppose it's a good thing. He was ahead over the last fence, but I passed him on the flat and *just* won.

We have had a divine day and a delicious party. . . . It was superb fun. I'm so happy tonight. I feel that this half, though I've done nothing and it has had bad bits, has been the greatest fun in the world and a huge success. Rugger XV, boxing, hurdles and Loder Prize. It has always been one of my ambitions to get a gold shield to hang on my watch-chain, and I always thought that I should never be able to achieve it. And now I have, Hurrah! . . .

We go home next week. I'm wildly happy and in great spirits, full of life and friends and joy and excitement and everything that I could be.

Dawn on Wednesday.

The sun is up and it is a divine day. I think of this letter speeding away through the world and the sun and the warmth to you all in far away India, like the poem of Grandpapa—which I can't remember by heart—called *The Love Letter*—with a very good bit about the letter going away across the mountains.

We have finished Trials. I am filled with life and sun and happiness and faith this morning.

Hurrah for you all, Hurrah for the holidays! Hurrah for Bengal and fun and joy and friends and happiness. I send you all my thoughts and all my happiness, and damn the sea between England and India.

Antony's letters during the holidays told of plays and cinemas in London, country house parties with friends, and settling in to the Manor House at Knebworth—all in the highest spirits and full of enjoyment.

He returned to Eton at the beginning of May for his last half—

Monday, May 7.

ETON again.

Your delicious letters have just arrived and I feel I would give my eyes to see you, if it is only for a moment. Life seems so different here in England since you went away. I think of different things and see different people and write different letters and see everything in a different light. It's all very wonderful and exciting and happy, but it's different and I must say I long to show it all to you. And yet if you asked me to name specified differences I couldn't, only there just feels a new atmosphere.

I am only two off Sixth Form this half, which is rather hard. I should have liked to have been in 6th form, and speeches on the 4th would have been fun, though perhaps it is as well that I'm not, as you would not have been here to hear. . . .

Tuesday.

Listen! Can't you hear the Chapel bells? I can and I should think you almost could. Do you know why they're ringing? Shall I tell you? 'cos it's Chapel time and I must go (I have to go every morning)!

Another good day. Cricket? *Mais oui, toujours le cricket.*

Oyes! Oyes! Oyes! I made seven runs all by my little self.
Now wasn't that just fine? I was in for six consecutive overs
without hitting the ball! I can't get into the Eton routine at
all. I am always sound asleep till ten and in great form now,
about 10.30 p.m., when everyone else is a'bed. I prefer the
night to the day. Strange! . . .

I have been trying to think out a good Swiss party for
next year. . . . I find myself often day-dreaming of skis and
mountains and turns. I don't believe there is any sport in
the world like ski-ing. I have been sticking photos into my
book and the ski-ing ones make me get so excited. I moan
achtung to myself and fall heavily on the bed. I even jump
off the ottoman and land in telemark position! . . .

How I disagree with

> 'Wonder 'tis what little mirth
> Keeps the bones of man from lying
> On a bed of earth.'

I feel so happy and so full of mirth and bones and so extremely removed from the bed of earth! Yet the quotation
seems to hang in my head just to aggravate. Don't you
think I ought to go to bed? Yes, I knew you would agree
with me. Goodnight for the moment, or rather for the
night.

Wednesday morning.

I think I shall go and try a little boxing for a change, it
may tone down some of my spirits a little. What a lot of fun
one can have in this jolly world if only one doesn't take
things too seriously. I do so love laughing and I adore that
sense of oblivion which one gets when one is really in good
form. One just doesn't mind what one does, or what people
think of one. Sounds like drunkenness and in a way I suppose it is a kind of drunkenness, only health and air not
alcohol. . . .

We've had rather an amusing morning. I could hardly
sit still in Chapel, I was so excited. Of course there was nothing to be excited about, as nothing was going to happen,

but if you had all been coming home the next day I couldn't
have been more excited than I was. That's just the wonder
of having that sort of temperament, which goes to both extremes suddenly. You can be wildly happy for no reason. Of
course, you can be utterly miserable as well for even less
reason, I know, but as a matter of fact I'm happy now, so I
don't care a damn about the other side! . . .

The world's worst boy wot loves you all so.

Antony's long weekly letters this half were mostly filled
with comments on our mails from India, and descriptions of
his own moods. These were influenced by two considerations,
the weather and cricket. During May the weather was hot
and sunny, and he was consequently in high spirits and
wrote happily. But the rest of the summer was cold and wet.
The continual rain got on his nerves. His letters described
fits of depression which had always been a characteristic
feature of the summer half. He began by making good
scores in 2nd XI matches and was disappointed at never
being tried in the first XI. Then he got bored, played badly,
and was vexed with himself. But these moods were never of
long duration, and his natural cheerfulness asserted itself.

Her is an example of one of his depressed moods:

One has to live on one's own spirits at Eton, and I reckon
I'm rather ill tonight. At best my spirits are very low. I miss
your letters pouring in almost every day, I miss your visits
and I hate feeling that you aren't in London, where I can
get at you easily. I must say India feels a very long way off
tonight and it's terrible lonesome without you. Once one
starts thinking things over everything always seems terribly
depressing. One can only get on by just not thinking and by
just laughing through every day and only seeing fun and
enjoyment. But once my spirits give way I'm right up the
pole, and I long for you tonight more than any living soul
has ever longed for anybody else in the whole world. My
Gosh, I shall have to be very happy or I shan't last out until

next year. I sometimes feel there are lots of people whom I love and who love me here in England who ought to make up for you all, but it's a damned poor substitute, because I can never love anyone like I do you, and I know there is no one who can really love me like I feel you do. It's a silly sort of feeling, but I do so awfully want you back, and I do wish I was little again and it was all beginning over again.

I loathe growing up, and I feel so grown-upish just now. Oh, I know one has fun alright, yes, the very best fun in the world, but that can't last for ever, and when it stops it's absolute hell. It's hell tonight and there seems very little to encourage me or cheer me up. It's strange how little one's friends want one, if once you stop being funny, and I think it's a good job too. How awful it would be if there was no humour, and things were as much fun when you are serious as when you are mad. Yes, it's a good thing we've got to be happy. To enjoy yourself you have got to be happy, and to give anyone else any pleasure you've got to be happy too. Well, then I'm just going to be happy, though tonight I think I'd rather be dead!

What an evil temper I'm in and how fussy about nothing. I'm very sorry. I wont go on depressing you with my nauseous opinions, but will continue when I'm feeling more cheerful. . . .

Yet the next day he wrote:

I've seldom had more fun than I'm having this half.

On another occasion he wrote:

If one's feeling depressed it's a good thing to go on making oneself feel worse and worse and not letting oneself be happy. Then one soon gets bored with it! Such a good cure!

After a Shakespeare Reading, at which he had taken the part of Antony in *Antony and Cleopatra*, he wrote:

I think Mark Antony as Shakespeare pictures him is a character with which I feel deep sympathy. Not only are our

names the same, but I feel I can understand all that he says
and does very easily. He loves terrific words and 'fighting
maliciously'; he loves Cleopatra so hard, and is so torn between his love for her and his love for his own health and
manliness. He is very scornful, and expresses his scorn for
Caesar so well, and heaps his rage on Cleopatra with equal
venom. He likes a real good temper now and then, and his
sentiment in despair is very human. Above all, he appreciates valour, sees his own faults and dies like a gentleman.
I think he is a very wonderful character. Not too good, like
some heroes. Plenty of human nature, and yet not an odious
brute like Othello. A fine ordinary man, above the average,
who appreciates manly qualities, is a good soldier and yet a
gay young man, who can walk with Kings 'nor lose the
common touch'. Yes, I love Shakespeare's Antony; and of
course his oratory is unsurpassed. 'This was the noblest
Roman of them all'—good enough?

In games and sports it was speed that most appealed to
Antony's taste. Cricket was too slow for him, but rowing was
worse. Here is an amusing description of his last visit to
Henley, which he found 'dreary':

In the first place it is bitterly cold, and the only day in the
year when you feel unequal to the river. Then it is terribly
crowded by aged men with sombre faces and thin white
moustaches, clad in the shortest of shorts which meet nowhere and inadequately cover any portion of their anatomy.
They are made of flannel rescued from the dustheap of fifty
years ago and worn yearly (without a wash) for fifty-two,
which may once have boasted the title of white. On their
heads they wear caps just too small for them, which when
they started their careers had been the pride of their owners.
These had once been the aristocratic 'blue' of Eton, or one
or other of the Varsities, or the pink of Leander, but now by
time's rude hand are all reduced to the same colour—a
dusty mud brown! They wear blazers which in their prime
had both fitted and looked gay, but now fail to function entirely. Lastly, they one and all wear a little pink tie to show

G

their membership of that very exclusive Club—the
Leander!

The racing itself is such as to sicken any heart accustomed
to associate racing with speed. To watch the race you mani-
pulate your boat against a cold, wet, slippery pole, to which
you cling desperately. The next thing that happens is that
scores of the old men just described appear on the bank
(without their pink ties) evidently trying to run and shout
at the same time, but actually failing to do either!

Then two boats filled with half-naked miserable suffering
individuals row past *very slowly* with a cox in the stern of
each trying to excite them by exclaiming at intervals 'Well
done, 1, 2, 3, 4, 5, 6, 7, 8, 9, 10, well rowed, keep it up'.

If the boats row past together it is called a good race; if
they row by one behind the other it is a bad one. In neither
case does either crew appear desirous of getting to the end,
or aware of the fact that there is a race!

In the same letter he said, writing two days later:

There was a second XI match today against the I Zingari.
We had to stop on account of the rain, but I made 57, being
dropped early on, but after that playing well. I think it is
rather a shame that I have never been given a try for the
XI, because I have made a good many runs, and never failed
to get less than 20 or 30 all the first part of the half. My
average in 2nd XI matches must be 25. But the fault is really
entirely my own. When the moment came that I had to play
seriously I found myself in good spirits, ragged and got out.
If you want to get your XI in the face of popular opposition,* you have got to go at it tooth and nail, and I found
that I preferred to enjoy myself and play cricket as a game,
rather than get my XI and play cricket as a profession. What
is more, I do not regret it, for I have enjoyed my half immensely and my cricket for the first time for ever so long.
I am not disappointed, because I have been and am too
happy to mind. And I thank God for it. . . .

*As at West Downs, he thought the Games Master was prejudiced
against him.

His last two letters, of course, were full of the sorrow of leaving Eton.

On July 26th he wrote:

I am afraid that my next two letters will very likely be rather sad and depressing ones, because you see I have come to my last week at Eton and that is a very terrible thing. It has been hanging over me terribly these last two days, but at the moment I feel rather cheerful, and so I won't start talking about it until I can't help it. Only I thought I'd better warn you not to expect to be cheered up too much! . . .

'Old Eton places, old Eton faces.' I think of the thousands of people who have left before me, and of how very soon they are forgotten, and after all the great world of Eton goes on for ever and one is only a little speck upon the flood; generation after generation of people leave, and each generation thinks what Eton is to them, and can it be the same without them, and how can they bear not to be always there. And then in a year Eton is just a wonderful memory— they are immersed in new things, and Eton is immersed in a new generation, perhaps even more interesting, and certainly every bit as much, and they are forgotten. The old order may change and give place to new, but Eton—that most wonderful of names in the world—goes on for ever and ever, unchanging and unchangeable.

I think it is just the most wonderful thing in the world what Eton means to Etonians, and it is impossible not to appreciate the blessings which one has while one is here. Though hundreds go out into the world each year, and though the school apparently forgets them, yet they are always welcome when they come back—they always can and will come back and be remembered—and above all, they go out stamped for ever with the stamp of the finest school in the whole wide world. Yes, we are very lucky to be able to call ourselves Etonians, and there is something better than to pity yourself when the time comes to go, and that is to start determined to carry through life the name of Eton unsullied and undefiled. 'Keep the torch burning; hand it on.'

There is something to live for; there is something great to uphold in life, one may well say—one must say, when one leaves Eton, filled with her spirit—

> 'I will be treble sinew'd, hearted, breathed
> And fight maliciously.'

My old friend Mark Antony. He's always right!

However, this letter is more like a sentimental essay than a letter and it's getting very late, so I'll stop it for the moment and continue, I hope, in a more cheerful vein. . . .

My last letter from ETON.
July, 1922.

How I wish you were here to help me leave this place; it is like that awful Folkestone all over again, only it lasts longer and I don't think I can bear it much longer. I have just taken leave of the headmaster, which was a terrible ordeal. He stood up and shook hands and said, 'Goodbye, and thank you very much for all you have done'. My God, it nearly killed me, and I don't feel I have done nearly enough. I have been far too selfish and enjoyed myself far too much. I haven't given enough thought to things that matter. I haven't worked hard enough, I haven't helped m'tutor enough, it has all been just one long glorious, happy day from the moment when I walked through the playing fields for the first time in my new top hat with Daddy and you until today, when I have taken leave of the headmaster and been given a book AB ETONA DISCEDENTI.

The headmaster was very nice. He said:—'You know you've got a lot of fundamental donkey in you as well', which is, of course, too terribly true. Oh, if only I was more serious occasionally and a little less pleasure-loving and selfish. But I'm going to be—I'm going to be a man up at Cambridge. My old friends, whom I waste my time laughing with, won't be there, and so I hope I shall be able to work and do some real good, instead of rotting all day long. There is that to be said for not having one's friends. J. M. B. in his speech said that the wonderful thing was coming to

London and working without knowing a soul. Well, I mean
to work at Cambridge and not know people. Oh, God help
me to do it, that's all.

Nico and I had our leaving breakfast this morning, but
we were fortunately in rather good spirits and we had it out
of doors in hot sun, so that it was not as terrible as it might
have been. Well, after pouring all this out to you I feel a
little bit better and will go out into the air again.

Well, then comes Sunday. My last Sunday at Eton—just
think of it. It's a terrible thought, but somehow or other I
feel as if I had had my cry, and though speechless with depression I haven't broken down like I did saying goodbye to
Alington. He preached a wonderful sermon in Chapel about
Eton and leaving and love, and I went to early service in the
morning, which was rather awful too. But there is great
comfort in prayer and thinking of God, because the whole
idea of religion makes one feel how vast the world is and how
very small and insignificant little Eton really is. It does help
one a lot, if you feel that the world and God and Christianity
and love are the things that really matter—then leaving
Eton seems to dwindle almost out of recognition and one
doesn't mind nearly so much. . . .

They gave us a most harrowing last evening Chapel,
which was hardly bearable, with that marvellous last Sunday evening hymn, 'Lord, thou hast brought us to our journey's end', to start off with, then a fable from the headmaster, which really was very good, and most moving,
about the pictures of Eton which one carries away with one,
'Her sights and sounds; dreams happy as her day', and finally
we went out singing 'Onward Christian Soldiers', which was,
I think, perhaps the most moving of all. The evening, however, has afforded a little comic relief. First of all, I had an
auction of some old bric-à-brac, which would have been entirely dull but that one of the items for sale was a cash box.
Now, I couldn't find the key to the cash box, and so thinking
there was just an old silver pencil in it, I put it up for sale
unopened, saying that I didn't know what there was inside,
but there might be a gold watch or anything, and anyway it

was a mystery. Someone got it for 2/1d and then half an hour later found a key and opened it to find my War Savings certificates, value £16, inside!! Fortunately, being a decent chap he gave them back, but it was not a pleasant moment.

Then I went out to dinner with Marten, which was great fun. He was killingly funny and we played Donkey and vingt-et-un afterwards, which was fearfully funny. I roared with laughter all the time. Now then, there's only tomorrow left, and I have got such a lot to do that I don't know where to start, and I am quite vague and hopelessly wretched.

I can't think what to give either Marten or m'tutor, and I haven't got anything for m'dame. Well, anyway, I must stop tonight.

I long for you and for your help and comfort, but I know it is good for me.

Monday night.

I have just finished my packing for camp, and must finish this, the last letter you will ever receive from your Etonian son, before I go to bed. Last night I read two wonderful letters which you wrote to me just before going to India, and a letter from Aunty B. the day you went. They were very wonderful and moving, and made me think of bigger things than leaving Eton. Today has been spent in saying goodbye to everyone, which was rather harrowing. . . . Everyone has been speechless all day and quite unapproachable. There have been some bad moments, but on the whole I think that I got the worst over two days ago. That is a way with me; I am always fretting about things too soon, so that when the last moment comes I have got all the unhappy part over.

I said goodbye to Marten first, which was quite pathetic, but he is too mad to make me really sentimental ever. He gave me the *Dynasts* as a leaving present, and told me to work at Cambridge, which, as you know, I intend to do.

Luxmoore was perhaps the worst. I don't know why but it felt terrible saying goodbye to him. He said he was so happy to be able to continue his friendship with Daddy in me, and I told him he'd have to carry it on with my son! He got quite agitated and wrote 1992 in my leaving book, which was much too priceless to be called attention to. I felt quite a lump in my throat, shaking hands with him. It's an extraordinarily moving thing shaking hands, you know, much the most inspiring thing in the world when it means anything to you.

M'tutor was quite wonderful. I talked to him for some time, but he was so wonderful that he never made me feel sad, only proud and happy and thankful. He talked a lot about Cambridge, and we discussed everyone in the house, and who had done well and who badly, and he thanked me for being captain and said things would be very different without me. If only people would curse me and say 'Clear out', who would mind—but it's when you're thanked and appreciated that it nearly kills you saying goodbye.

We ended the day in the greatest of all Eton games—the Field game. A grand finale on the Field, in which we all got gay and young and happy again, and laughed and ragged and dreamt we were playing for our shorts.

Then supper, prayers, goodnights, and so my career at Eton closes. Never was anything more happy, never can anyone be more thankful.

> 'Unarm, Eros, the long day's task is done
> And we must sleep.'

is a good line from Shakespeare. All good things come to an end, and now Eton is finished. Goodbye, Eton, Goodbye, Mother and God bless you both.

> Your own son,
>
> ANTONY.

I will write to you from camp in a very different vein, but then I shall be an Old Etonian!

Mr. Ramsay's charming last letter about him was as follows:

> ETON COLLEGE, WINDSOR.
> *Aug.* 3, 1922.

Dear Lytton,

Antony's last reports, alas! I don't want to speak about them in this letter. The few little faults and possible dangers noted in them are known to him, and I have given him very full advice about the future. What seems to rule everything else out of order at present is my overwhelming sense of my debt to him in the conduct of the house. He succeeded an excellent Captain and has maintained the high tone and good discipline; but he has done this with a wisdom and a friendliness which have made him exceedingly popular as well as greatly respected. The splendid tone of the house is due to his fine example. But I look further back and recall his constant friendship in difficult as well as in easy times, and I am then aware of what can be done for a tutor by a single loyal pupil. He has taught me many lessons; and a few rough passages have only drawn us more closely together. He has just written me, from camp, a letter which brought tears of joy to my eyes.

I have told him that I claim the privilege of being his tutor and friend in all the future. He will, I know, come and see me from Cambridge and elsewhere, and his interest in the house will still be effective. I have urged him to make his education a great success and to be very ambitious on the intellectual side; if he will do this, he may become highly distinguished and a fresh credit to Eton.

I think he had a little bad luck in not getting a place in the Eleven. He took his disappointment very well, and I am sure he understood the special difficulties there were in choosing the side this year. He has been very prominent in school life generally, and his influence has been most wholesome. At the end of the half he scored a triumph by his rendering of Antony at the reading of the play by the Shakespearean Society. This was a really noble performance, and everyone who watched and heard him felt that he was born for great things. That is what I believe myself.

I feel I cannot write anything worthy of my theme. I can only thank you from my heart for your son.

Yrs ever,

A. B. RAMSAY.

Chapter V

OXFORD: A DIVIDED FAMILY

1922-1923

*'Life is good, and it is so hard to make the best
of it and not waste it.'*

AFTER LEAVING Eton, Antony went into camp with the
O.T.C. at Tidworth, where for the first time he was an
Officer.

While he was there he received a charming letter
from Mr. Ramsay, and wrote to us about him: 'He is
such a very nice man and such a real friend to have in life.
There were times, of course, when he was aggravating, but
all his tiresomeness was only part of his extraordinary
straight and wise nature, which sees absolutely no turning
whatever under any circumstances from the "straight and
narrow" (that's spoilt quite a good sentence!) Well, you know
what I mean. I love him and am very grateful to him, for he
has been a wonderful tutor.'

Every week brought us a bookful of entertaining news,
but Antony's letters were not confined to news. Throughout
the years of our long separation he wrote regularly and fully
on every conceivable topic. He discussed his friends, his
social activities, his work, his feelings, his dreams and ambitions, and the books he was reading. The tone of his letters
changed with every mood, sometimes gay—sometimes depressed; his opinions also changed as his character developed,
but his affection was unfailing and unchangeable. Considerations of space only allow quotation from a small proportion of his letters in this book.

An example of his delightful fooling about nothing is a
letter in which he gave samples of the letters he would soon
be writing from Cambridge:

Monday.

Letter from Edward Antony James from Cambridge,
Nov. 1922 (as he hopes it will be)—

PITT CLUB, CAMBRIDGE.

Darling Mother,

This is such a good life. My new hunter (Daisy) is
a great success and I had a real good day yesterday. She
jumps like a bird and I think ought to do well in the 'chases
next term. Pat offered me £150 for her, but I love her much
too much. I had such an amusing argument with Michael
Goodchap last night. It started over the rival merits of my
terrier and his and eventually developed into a heated discussion regarding the foreign policy of Louis XIV. We sat on
the sofa, drank port, and stormed at one another, till we
suddenly burst out laughing and went round to Archie's
rooms, pulled him out of bed, and asked his opinion. He
damned us both & went to sleep again. I have been reading
about Mazzini all the morning—what a fascinating character—I should love to have met him.

Oh, by the way, I'm being given a greyhound by Lord
Kindman, isn't it thrilling. Rugger progresses twice a week
with much effect & I am playing half for Trinity tomorrow
—rather a triumph, etc., etc.

(As it will probably be):—

Darling Ma,

This is a perfectly top hole place and I am having the
world's best time. No work yet but that will come. I went
to London yesterday on my new m'bike, 50 hp. Indian, goes
like blazes, a perfect topper. I saw that adorable thing Kitty
Katchem from the Gaiety and we had tea together. She's
such fun and a perfect gem. I'm dining with Bertie Blas-
temwot tonight at the Athenaeum. I expect we shall get
tight and have a bloody good rag. Awfully good fellow,
Bertie. Such haste—love to all, etc., etc.

or:—

Darling,

    Everyone is horrid—this place is horrid; work is horrid—games are horrid (there aren't any) friends are horrid; I'm horrid. Damn.

Yr horrid son,

Ugh!

or:—

Darling,

    I am so enjoying myself working all day & all night. I read Gibbon's 'Decline & Fall of the Roman Empire' this morning & Motley's 'Dutch Republic' this afternoon, and I hope to get through Macaulay's 'History of England' this evening. Such a good life, Winstanley says he thinks I'm doing too much. I tell him 'Rot'. After all I've only read 15 books in the 10 days I've been up, its nothing!

Love,

JAMES.

or:—

Darling,

    This is a great life. I played tennis for Trinity this morning & I'm playing rugger for the Varsity against Blackheath 's afternoon. In the evening I'm having a fight with Blacki for the welter-weight championship of Cambridge. Hunting tomorrow and a game of squash before breakfast, and if I have time in the evening I must do a bit of training for the Varsity ping-pong.

Love, etc.

I wonder which it will be, perhaps none of them, but just:

Darling Mummie,

Goodbye,

Yr loving ANTONY.

While Antony was staying with Sir James Barrie for a cricket week at Stanway, with a large party of his Eton friends, most of whom were going to Oxford, the feeling came over him that he could not bear to be separated from them, and accordingly he sent me a telegram saying that he wished to go to Oxford and asking if I had any objection. I thought that the grounds for this sudden change of plan were altogether inadequate, but as it was impossible either to ask questions or to argue the merits, I could not do otherwise than leave the matter to his own discretion. I therefore replied, 'Have no objection provided Cambridge is willing to release you and Oxford to receive you'.

Writing to his mother from Stanway in September, after speaking of the girls of the party, he said:

However, this is really a party of boys as far as I am concerned, and I love all these wonderful Eton people. I feel quite broken-hearted when I realize that it can never be again. Next year we shall all be men and in two years we shall have forgotten each other, and Eton we shall vaguely remember as rather fun, and society and the world and grown-upishness will be our lot. No more happy-go-lucky laughter and fun and that wonderful fellowship which Eton gives. This is really the very last bit of Eton life, and it is quite quite supreme. . . . I feel strangely contented, and yet strangely restless. I find real happiness and friendships that must last for ever, and at the same time I have a deep-rooted, almost subconscious knowledge that it is the meeting-place of two ways—that here in this very house, this very hour, manhood begins and boyhood passes away into a thing of the past. I dont know why, but I feel that very strongly. There is something new and awful that wants meeting and fighting coming into my life. 'The old order changeth, giving place to the new.' Here, even here at Stanway, in the month of September in the year 1922, a great change is occurring in the life of Edward Antony James Lytton, Viscount Knebworth!

To the same:

THE MANOR HOUSE, KNEBWORTH.
Sept. 13, 1922.

The real thing that is exciting me at the moment is the possibility of going to Oxford, which is such a wonderful thought that I am intoxicated with anticipation. I have really always wanted Oxford, but my own obstinate nature has hitherto made me stick to Cambridge, and now the moment has come when I have said goodbye to all my Eton friends and I have got to face Cambridge alone . . . and I suddenly realized I couldn't.

I pray that Sir Herbert Warren will be able to get me into Magdalen. He's the only Oxford man I know; he wrote such a nice letter about me to Daddy; I think he took rather a fancy to me at Eton . . . so I feel that there is hope. My letter went this morning and your telegram came. Thank you so much for letting me do just what I like about it. A far harder thing, of course, will be writing to Winstanley,* but I am sure it is worth it, because almost anything is justified when its a question of three of the most important years of one's life, and I know that my heart would be always at Oxford. It is the finer place; the nicer people go there and—well, I want to go there with all my heart and I pray for it very hard. Magdalen is perhaps not the place I should have chosen, but it is good, and I feel it is the only chance. Will it disappoint Daddy? I dont think it will at all somehow—the only thing that I should mind would be Winstanley, who cannot but be hurt. . . . I shall send you a wire directly I know. . . .

Mr. Winstanley wrote most considerately, 'I do not wish in any way to hold you to your promise to Trinity, and if you are quite clear in your own mind that if you came to Cambridge you would always be wishing you were at Oxford, I think it is better that you should go to Oxford. . . .'

As Sir Herbert Warren agreed to accept him at Magdalen, the matter was finally settled, and Antony went up to Oxford in October.

He wrote to me from there on October 14th:

MAGDALEN COLLEGE, OXFORD,
Sunday, Oct. 14, 1922.

Darling Father,

　　Here is your own son seated boldly in the Junior Common Room of Magdalen College, Oxford University, writing

*His tutor at Cambridge.

his first letter to the family as an undergraduate. Hail, all hail, and yet again hail!

I dont know anyone yet, I dont know what I'm expected to do and I cant find anything to do! I have spent the last two days seeing various men, Deans, bursars, tutors, junior Deans, junior bursars, junior tutors, presidents, junior presidents, senior Deans, senior bursars, etc., etc. They have all asked me:—

1. My name.
2. Date of birth.
3. Address.
4. What I'm reading.
5. Why am I?

I have told them to the best of my ability; then they have said, 'Oh, just before you go fill up this form, will you?' I take it wistfully, for I'm getting to know it quite well; it asks four questions & leaves a blank space for answers:—

1. Name (in block letters)
2. Date of birth (in small letters)
3. Address (in Greek)
4. What you are reading (in hieroglyphics)

Then they send me on to another man. Occasionally one shows a spark of originality, and asks what sport I am going in for, or how my father is doing in India, and occasionally one suggests a lecture I should go to, or another wants to know if I like Abraham! All the President likes to hear is either that my ambition is to be Pres. of Magd. or that I have been staying with the P. of W.! So far I have done nothing but loaf, except yesterday, when I played a little heated and mild Rugger. . . .

I think it is a mistake not being in College, & though Nico and I have splendid parties away in Abingdon Road & live in the lap of luxury, one gets to know no new people, and it is more home life than College. . . .

I'm going to Hall tonight for the first time, which is another rather alarming thing, I imagine, & we have had a sentimental address from the President there this afternoon,

exhorting us to be great and informing us of all the fine
people who were at Balliol with him & hinting (darkly) that
he was the best of the lot.

Well, you may or may not gather from this letter that I
am immensely happy, but I certainly am. Also rather
amused at my own timidity and behaviour. I have but two
regrets:—

1. That I am not in College.
2. That I have not got a single other chap from Eton that
I really know. Sam's coming next year, but all the others are
in different Colleges.

However, its a bloody good College & I'm playing in the
Fresher's match on Tuesday!! Stuff!

AN.

Although he went to Oxford determined to be happy, and
thought at first he was going to be, yet he found the life
there very boring at first, and his letters became more and
more discontented. This was inevitable, as no one who has
enjoyed to the full the sweets of popularity and power at
Eton, as Antony had done, can fail to be rather lost when he
first gets to the University, unless he is sufficiently distinguished at games or scholarship to pass at once into the élite
of his College. Antony found, as so many others have done,
the difficulty of making the best use of his time. He missed
the regular school hours and the regular games. He tried to
concentrate on the more difficult and unfamiliar subjects of
his studies—political economy, and the set books, Erasmus,
Rousseau and Saint-Simon; but it is one of the disadvantages
of class work at school that it is a poor preparation for solitary
study, and Antony found it difficult to keep his mind on the
subject during the long morning hours of reading, or to keep
awake in the evenings. In the afternoons he played Rugby
football whenever possible. It was his favourite game, but at
the University he found himself quite outclassed by men

who came from schools where that game was played regularly, and not merely occasionally, as at Eton.

'The Rugger is rather fun', he wrote to his mother, 'though I find that practically speaking you can only do one thing. I should like to hunt, play Rugger, Soccer, Eton game and box, but it doesn't seem at all possible. I naturally want to play for Magdalen, but it is obviously going to be very difficult, especially as there is an International Scrum Half in the College!! I shall have to play somewhere else.

' I cant tell you what an extraordinary place this is. I am really quite bewildered by the enormousness of it, and the number of strange faces. One could so easily feel entirely lost in this wilderness of strangers, and even the people I know always seem to be doing something, though I never quite know what. As yet I feel by no means happily settled in.'

The sense of strangeness gradually wore off, and he soon became more at home, but he could not get happy. Several visits to Eton revived all his glorious associations with that place and made him long to be back there:

'Eton has a most exhilarating effect on me,' he wrote. 'In whatever mood I go down there I feel at the top of my form in no time. Oh! how I love that place. There is not a thing about it that isn't absolutely perfect. I dont wonder that people live on and on there and get duller and narrower, and more boring, and care about nothing else in the world, but, by God, its the most wonderful place in the world.'

When playing football at Eton he got a bad kick, which produced water on the knee and more or less incapacitated him for the rest of the term. He wrote gloomily on November 26th:

I don't really think much of this place. It's not a quarter as good as Eton, and though I suppose one will get to like it eventually I cant say that I've got to that stage yet. There are no real games to make it fun. Its incredibly hard to work, and having nothing to live for as one did at Eton, life loses its interest. I cant be happy & well without games, and at the most you get two a week here, which are dull & lifeless played with people you dont know & mostly people you dont like.

I think what is at the bottom of my depression is the absence of you. You see with five of you gone clean away, the love which I gave to you is set free. I have no one near at hand to love as I could you all, so I have to keep on trying to find an adequate substitute to my family and this is terribly difficult. All my boy friends dont quite fill the gap. They're wonderful when one is gay; they're splendid people to have fun with, and they'd do anything for you when you're down and out, but when you're just depressed you dont really want sympathy or help. Its nothing serious; it'll pass, one must just wait. . . .

I dare say Oxford is a good interesting place for old men of 40, but for boys, why I'd rather be at a girls' school for knitting. It would be better exercise. I'm sure its my own fault that this term has been such a failure, and I pray God I shall know better next term, but I miss my Eton games of football and boxing and fives even more than I miss you. . . . The whole place is asleep and has been for years. . . .

In another of his letters, while in this depressed mood, Antony wrote:

Darling, I cant tell you how queer I feel. I've got nothing in life to aim at—nothing to give, I dont know what I want to do, I feel old & yet not old enough, I feel small & insignificant & not wanted—just part of a dull useless machine which goes on for ever and does no good to anything or anybody. Hopeless is the best word to describe what I'm feeling. I have been reading one or two war books and they make me wish I was just 8 years older. Then everyone knew where he was. He had a definite thing to do. It was a big thing & a creditable thing. It was something to be proud of doing, and in between whiles one could be really happy, & happy as one can only be when there is something big hang-

H

ing over one. You enjoyed your leave, you had your fun &
you went back to the real natural bare side of life in France
& you died. I know its silly to feel like this, but there
don't seem to be any boundaries anywhere. Everything is
one vast vague mass.

There's nothing hanging over me, there's nothing that I
must do. There's no great work here for me to do. There's
no real pleasure because everything's pleasure. I just go on
from day to day, work, play, joy, sorrow, all mingled into
one great indefinable mass of nothingness. What is there in
life? What is there to do? You may say that there's God and
right to live for and fight for. But thats so vague, I wont say
its imaginary, but it needs imagination to realize it. Its not a
physical fight, its a mental one. It deals with one's beliefs
and thoughts, but it doesn't give one a cut-&-dried line to
take in life. And after all the Christian ideals aren't the
things that really appeal to man. They are too big. He cant
understand them. What man loves is strength, bravery,
passion, revenge and cruelty. Love in the real deep lasting
sense of God's love & Christ's sacrifice and forgiveness are
too high, they're too wonderful. They dont inspire him. He
nods & thinks 'Yes, that's very wonderful, & a very fine
idea, but it wont really work. It isn't practical. Besides, its
not what I want. I dont want to die for my enemy and let
him know it, I dont want to love him. What I want to do is
to kill him, & by God Almighty I will.' And God looks on and
smiles and wonders what a lot we have to learn. I can see
what God thinks, but I cant feel the same. Why is it that the
things I love are pagan ideals and fierce heathen passions? I
admire the love of God, but I cant really prefer it. I am
thinking all the time of the things of this world and where
God comes in. There's no Christianity in the world as God
meant it. It doesn't exist. Men preach & men pray & men
shut themselves in a cave & die, but no one goes into the
world giving & loving & forgiving & helping. And why not?
Because it is not what mankind admires; it is not what he
wants. If we read in the paper about a great international
thief, who has murdered many men, who always wins, who

is brave, indomitable and fascinating, we think what a wonderful man. But we shouldn't even trouble to read through
the story of a man who gave all he had & who died innocent that others might live. We might think him fine, but
we should inwardly believe him a fool.

I dont know why, but all these things have been going
through & through my mind lately, perhaps because I
haven't been well, perhaps because the time had to come
when I should think about them.

But I long to go round the world alone to see everyone and
everything, how men worked & lived and died. What they
cared about & lived for—what they killed for & what they
were killed for and why? I want to *see* the real truths of life
as I can only picture them now, and understand the character of man as opposed to that of God. I know that Christianity has lived and spread because it is difficult, because it
is impossible, & because difficulty appeals to man, but today,
what is it? It just lives on, a monstrous sham, calm and un-
attended to, while we all go on with our lives contented &
happy & passionate & let it rip.

This is rather like a sermon. Dont you think I should
make a good parson? But I wonder if you ever feel the inadequacy of religion to meet your needs. I suppose you ought
to say your own inadequacy to live up to religion, & thats
the sham that we do say. But the fact remains—here are we
caring about this, influenced by that, & there is religion
miles away, not attempting to come any nearer or to meet
our aims. Its religion's fault, not ours. If it wants us to forgive, let it damned well come & explain why, otherwise we
shall go on killing and thinking it glorious.

As a matter of fact, all this religious discourse doesn't
really explain the peculiar things that I feel. I want an incentive to do something. I have ambition, but no goal &
therefore nothing to work for. Money? I want it, but it
doesn't thrill me. God? I dont understand him & he doesn't
fill me. Passion? Yes, but what does it mean? How do I get it,
what do I do? Strength? Yes, but what good is physical
strength? Power is perhaps the only light I can see clearly,

but that is very dim & very far & the obstacles are incredible, and the pleasures which distract one from getting it too good.

Oh, well, all this letter is a terrible muddle, but whether you get it on a peak in Sikkim or a palace in Calcutta, think of me here on a dull November afternoon, writing at a wee desk in the outskirts of Oxford, with my head going round & round quicker than the world, & an immense sensation of absolute nothingness all over me, and try to understand.

I must go & pack my box & put on my best clothes & become a bit of social machinery in a London ball-room all the evening. And I enjoy it—I love it—I feel it is the only thing in life, and it is really as worthless, useless and hopeless as it is to sit down & think of everything under the sun and say 'Why?' and then go to sleep!

You see, I don't care about the big things. I ought to prefer sitting here reading Mill's *Pol. Econ.* & saying to myself 'Read this & one day you may be Prime Minister of England', but I don't. I'd rather go to London & dance with P—— B—— & I'm not ashamed of it & I don't think I'm wrong. But I am, aren't I?

Heaven help me.

Yr loving

A.

To this letter I replied at some length:

. . . It is evident that you have begun to investigate for yourself some of the deepest and strongest emotions of life and to question the truth of the religious teaching which you received in your childhood. That is an experience which comes to nearly every young man who thinks at all seriously as soon as he gets to the University. Don't be afraid of this inclination. You have now arrived at an age when you are entitled to question every conventional opinion, in religion, in morals, in politics, in social ethics, and you should accept nothing that you are not able conscientiously to reconcile with your own convictions. My only advice to you is not to be disheartened and discouraged when your sheet anchors begin to slip, and don't be in a hurry to form new conclusions. It doesn't follow that ideas and beliefs which you have

hitherto taken on trust are necessarily wrong, because when
you first begin to examine them critically they fail to convince you. Our business in life is to search out truth for ourselves and to reject falsehoods whenever we discover them;
but the lesson which life teaches as we grow older is that
many apparent falsehoods are in fact half-truths, and that
new truths are not so much corrections of old falsehoods as
the completion of old truths hitherto only half recognized.
I, too, began the process of looking all conventional beliefs
squarely in the face and testing their sincerity during my
first year at Cambridge, and I have been at it ever since.
Every year I find myself readjusting values, correcting impressions, fortifying some convictions and abandoning others.
But on the whole I find myself coming back to most of the
points from which I started, only with wider knowledge,
deeper insight, more understanding.

Your chief concern at the moment seems to be a restlessness caused by the absence of any definite purpose in life.
You have no rudder and are drifting with wind and tide.
This is the inevitable accompaniment of the disposition to
challenge conventionalities, but it won't last and you must
not let this depress you. Just now you can't quite make up
your mind what is your goal, or what your motive. Is it to be
wealth or power or distinction? What is to be your profession
—the army, politics or business?

It is very depressing at times. I can only recommend to
you the course which I have adopted myself—namely, to
concentrate on the job you have in hand and leave the
future to take care of itself. . . .

The next point for you to decide is what do you mean by
success at Oxford. What do you mean to achieve there and
how are you going to do it? You must have some rudder to
steer by, and the best guiding principle I can suggest is the
pursuit of happiness. Happiness is the one form of wealth
which you can spend with the utmost prodigality without
overdrawing your account—the more you spend the more
you have. Some would call this demoralizing advice, and
argue that the pursuit of happiness was a false ideal. But

that would be an example of what I have called describing as a falsehood what is only an imperfect understanding of a truth. The pursuit of happiness is only a false ideal to those who have an imperfect conception of happiness. Man is a composite animal with physical, mental and spiritual desires. He can only achieve happiness if he satisfies all these desires, and all the unhappiness in life arises from the gratification of one set of desires at the expense of the others, or from the conflict between these three in their struggle for satisfaction. And here is the difference between pleasure and happiness. You derive pleasure from the company of your friends, from playing games, from a jaunt to London, from a ride across country, etc. But none of these things can bring you happiness if the price you pay for them is failure in your exams or loss of self-respect. Success in an exam, on the other hand, or in any intellectual achievement, will give you pleasure but not happiness, if it means the starving of your physical desires, or the loss of your physical health. And finally even success, both in athletics & exams, will not bring you happiness if your spiritual desires are starved by the neglect of others and the satisfaction of a merely selfish ambition. Full happiness, therefore, can only be obtained by the exercise of all your creative faculties in the service of the community to which you belong, and the problem of every day is to reconcile all the conflicting impulses of your nature. . . .

Antony's fits of depression were always of short duration, and the rest of his letters during his first term at Oxford were cheerful enough.

His life there was thus summarized in a letter to Hermione:

This is a very queer place. You can get every type and variety of person and class you can possibly imagine. I only see the best in all of them, so that I long to know all. I feel excited in the political set—ambitious, eager. I feel much the same with the clever people. I love the sporting side— hunting and checks and dogs; and I am slightly ashamed to say that I am terribly happy with the society set. The mechanics alone don't draw me at present, nor do the aesthetes! But there you are—you have them all to choose from, and a hundred more beside. What a place! No wonder one feels bewildered and at a loose end sometimes. . . . It's a great life —a little world all on its own, and just as bewildering and bewitching as the real big world outside.

Before going down for the Christmas vacation, he wrote to us all with Christmas greetings:

OXFORD, *Dec.* 4, 1922.

Darling Father,
    I am afraid that this is rather a moderate mail from me this week—but I want to try & write to all of you, as I believe this will get to you about Christmas time. First of all then—

'The Governor of Bengal
coupled with
The Lytton family.'

and the very happiest of Christmasses to you all. 'Cheerio' I feel would be the proper Varsity way of putting it, but I am far from the proper Varsity man & so I will spare you the pain! And talking of Xmas, what about 1923? Well, may it be a happy and gorgeous year. . . .

I do long to come out to India and see it all; your descriptions are so awfully alluring that I'm dying to come too. Is it an easy country to work in, because if so I'd better come there pretty quick. I do find it awfully hard to do work here. Did you never find it difficult to work? There must be something wrong with me. It's not that I don't try, but I can't be interested in the subject, and so of course my thoughts start wandering and I don't get very much forrarder. . . . The atmosphere of this place is not very conducive to work too, it's very easy to say 'No, I'm working to-night', or 'I'll work tomorrow morning', but when the time comes I either go to sleep or sit and stare for an hour or so scoring imaginary tries or otherwise amusing myself. I'm a very poor son, I'm afraid, terribly gut-less (to be rather crude) and quite unworthy of your 'in whom I am well pleased'. Someone said in a book I was reading the other day 'Oh, it's easy to laugh at death; lots of men can do that, but it's to laugh at life that I can't face.' Ought one to laugh at life, do you think? I think not; it's dirt easy. The hard thing to do is to drink deep of it; make the best of it and fill it.

'I warmed both hands before the fire of life;
It sinks; and I am ready to depart.'

Silly ass! Why didn't he poke it?! I'm getting quite a philosopher, aren't I? But life is good and it is so hard to make the best of it and not waste it.

Goodbye, darling, a very Happy Xmas and all my love and thoughts. I wish I could live up to you, but it's awfu' hard.

Yr. son,

A.

Sir H. Warren asked me if you and I were good friends! Damned cheek! I said 'Of course not, we were father and son and naturally hated each other, and never spoke in each other's presence!' But we're not in each other's presence, so I can speak. God bless you!

I replied that I also had found work difficult at school and college, and he wrote on December 20th:

Your letter last week cheered me up more than anything has ever done before. I was afraid that I was a gross degenerate beside my father, but when you say that you did no work at Eton and found it damned hard at Cambridge, it is wonderfully encouraging. I always imagined that work had been second nature with you. But you did find it hard once? So perhaps there's some hope for me yet. At least I'll be optimistic. . . .

And so ended 1922, the first year of our long separation. Antony wrote to his mother from the Manor House on January 1st, 1923, on the eve of his departure for Switzerland:

Darlingest and most beloved of all mothers,

 I wish you a New Year as full of joy and happiness as the last one has been unhappy. May the most wonderful things happen to you; may everything go well with you and may you be very greatly blessed. We have something very wonderful to look forward to in this New Year, haven't we, darling? and I believe the pain of parting will turn out to be well worth the joy of meeting again. . . . Randal* came over here last night and we drank the New Year in as we did last year, but there seemed more welcome in this one and less of dread. I didn't feel solemn as if something was going to happen, I just felt happy as if it had happened. Well, anyway, darling, we've got to meet before we can say goodbye again, and so we can always look forward to that meeting. Oh, my God, how I yearn for it.

Your mail arrived this morning in answer to my letter about religion from Oxford. You mustn't feel unhappy when I write like that. It only means a mood, and it is really very wholesome that I should think about things.

I do really see that forgiveness is a finer thing than revenge, because if one was really thirsting for revenge, it would be so much harder; but I should feel slightly ashamed if I forgave someone, but almost a hero if I got my revenge. I think that the standard of Christianity is so high that man has ceased to aim at it or regard it as practical. How can I sell all I have and give to the poor? What happens then? It isn't reasonable.

These are the natural things one says to oneself, but as the headmaster always said: 'Have you ever tried them?' There are perhaps only two known instances of this being tried—St. Francis of Assisi and the Bishop in *Les Misérables*, and they were hardly failures. However, the fact remains that we are most thrilled by a story of relentless revenge and unforgiveness. Are we though? Oh, I don't know, I never know quite what I do admire. . . .

I wonder if you will think me at all altered. I dont mean facially, but more grown-up. I believe I am a little, at least some people think so, and I do a little bit too. . . .

  *The night watchman at Knebworth.

Antony's next letter to me was written in the train on the way to Gstaad:

. . . I am on my way to London, from there to be on my way to Switzerland.

Your letter about the pursuit of happiness was a wonderful one and I quite agree with you. Happiness is a big and great thing, well worth achieving, but one must be careful not to muddle it up with the pursuit of pleasure. They are very different things and yet appear to be much alike. I started to pursue happiness at the beginning of last term with moderate success, but then something went wrong and I switched off on to pleasure with singular failure. I worked a little, played a little, and was sociable a little and I was happy. But then I chucked the work and the play chucked me (knee) and I pursued pleasure and in consequence I dread next term. I have made up my mind to work, box and play Rugger next term and nothing else, and I don't know whether I most dread the thought of work or the possibility of failing to do it. I find it very hard indeed to work.

His visit to Switzerland this year was not altogether a success. He had deliberately eschewed Mürren—a place we had so often visited together, and where he would have found ski-ing friends of his own standard, because he thought he would be more conscious there of the separation from his family, and he had chosen a new place in order to be in the company of friends whose standard of ski-ing was not up to his own. The weather was bad, and he only stayed a week.

He wrote from the Manor House, Knebworth, on his return: 'I have an idea that I wrote you some very depressed and unhappy bits of letter from Switzerland. I won't read them through but just pop them in the envelope, as there is interest even in the devil, but I will write this to take away the taste.

'Is it Knebworth? Is it the Manor House? Is it Aunty Beryl? or is it just home that makes me always blissfully happy in

this place? I don't know that I have ever felt so happy or so
contented as I do to-night in my life. Perhaps it's 5 grains of
aspirin, or perhaps it's because I have had 3 teas!! It's wonderful to be at Knebs. I adore the place.'

As had happened so often during his last years at Eton,
Antony, during his second term at Oxford, found in boxing
the best remedy both for boredom and depression of spirits.
This form of sport enabled him to work off his superfluous
energy; the exercise and the training which it imposed kept
him fit, and consequently able to make good use of his time
for work. Although his work was uncongenial and done
against the collar, he stuck to it conscientiously, and so his
letters were generally quite happy in tone, and interesting
as regards his mental development. But the sadness occa-
sioned by the separation from his family, and the eager expectation of the joy of meeting them again in the Spring,
found expression in every one of them.

To his mother:

OXFORD,
Saturday, February 3rd, 1923.

I feel rather happier to-night. I am getting back to
my old good health and strength, and always through the
noble art. They are trying to make me go into training to
box against the Army, or some similar opponent. I have got
to get down about 4 lbs. The man at the gym told me this
afternoon the best thing to do was to drink nothing except a
glass of water (as hot as I can bear it) directly I get up and
before I go to bed. Can you imagine anything worse than
drinking a tumbler of hot water directly you get out of bed?
It's bad enough at any time, but at 8.30 in the morning, the
limit!

But at the moment I'm crazy about boxing again. I think
my rest has done me a lot of good, and I have grown much
stronger and developed a harder punch. In a way it's more
fun here than at Eton. You don't get the same people every
day, and you get hit about much more, which is good for one

and for one's boxing. So far I have only had my jaw knocked crooked and my lips cut up, but I shall soon have my face cut up and a couple of black eyes, I expect. I boxed with a divine man called Albert Lloyd this afternoon. He is going to fight Soldier Jones in about a fortnight's time, and is a real good man. He was awfully nice and helpful, let me hit him like hell and never demanded reparation. It is the test of a really nice and good boxer to be able to let some insignificant person hit you about without ever hitting him back, except quietly. Wonderful I call it. He taught me a good deal. They get all the funny stuff out of me here. Little tricks and graces aren't the real thing. What one has got to learn is to hit and be hit, both hard. I'm full of it all to-night! I have not done quite so much work this week, but have been finishing off odds and ends and have written what I think quite a good essay on the Rise of Prussia—Frederick William, the Great Elector, Frederick I, and Frederick William I, the father of Frederick the Great—an impossible man and entirely German (his favourite dish was cabbages and bacon in quantity and without quality!) I read Carlyle on them all three—the first time I have read him. What a queer man! At first his style reminded me of an illiterate Japanese journalist writing for an English paper in Australia! but it rather grows on one and I got quite to like his queer ways and tricks. But he writes in the present tense, which is rather a bore. I must get down to Saint-Simon next week, which is in very difficult French and I find very hard to read. . . .

The time flies quickly, thank God, and I think that in about 4 or 5 years I might really get to like Oxford. I see that it has its possibilities, provided one pretends to be a man and if possible a dull man. Then with work, independence, and dreary luncheon parties one might become quite attached to the place. But for the young, the high-spirited, the spendthrift and the sociable dependent type of humanity, which Eton is wont to send up to this seat of learning, most things would be preferable. Spring is already beginning to move in my veins, and it has the effect of making me

long to revert to nature. To live half-naked in a tent with
hot sun and cool water and scented air. However, this is not
either new or original and I have said it before, so let's forget it. After all, I have to sit indoors and read books or jump
about indoors and box, and many people are worse off than
that. Cynic! Goodnight, darling.

Later.

. . . I have been boxing Dick Smith this afternoon, the
Varsity Welter Weight and Middle Weight, and good old
Albert Lloyd, with a sack and a punch-ball thrown in, so I
am rather tired this evening. Dick Smith is a relentless man
who pursues with a determination which I can accredit to
nothing else except Nemesis. But I succeeded in making
him laugh after he had told me that I shouldn't laugh in the
ring, so I felt I had won a moral victory at any rate!! . . .

I boxed to-day, lunched at the O.E., worked in the morning, played bridge after tea, and shall work this evening.
While working I thought about boxing, while boxing about
bridge, while playing bridge about work, and all day long
about you, and if I couldn't day-dream a bit I should become
a damp wet cloud!

Mon dieu!

Goodnight and God bless you always.

Yr. loving son,

A.

To his father:

108, ABINGDON ROAD, OXFORD,
February 13*th*, 1923.

I had to run hurdles for the College this afternoon.
I was told the ordinary hurdles, but I found I had to do 220
yds. of low hurdles, which I had never done before and so I
was rather ruffled. Of course, I couldn't do them at all, and
there were only two in my heat and the other was the
champion of America! That's what I'm always doing in this
place—doing something very amateurishly and finding myself up against the world's champion! However, it was so
ridiculous this race, and I was so unable to do these silly

hurdles, that I burst out laughing in the middle. This startled the champion of America, so that he looked round, knocked down 4 hurdles, and all but fell on his face. My mirth was further increased at this, but I didn't win!

I read *Sohrab and Rustum* last night, which is a wonderful poem, I think, and have got a rather good book on the Court of Louis XIV by a woman called Pardoe, at least I think it's a woman, What a time they had, it's quite amazing! Is it better to be openly immoral or to pretend you're not, I wonder? I find the history between 1713 and '40 very difficult and the diplomacy entirely bewildering, but it gets better after that, I think.

To his mother:

108, ABINGDON ROAD, OXFORD,
Friday, February 19*th.*

Darling,

I must write. For once in a way I feel like it! How queer life is. I came back here bored stiff and I have worked like a nigger all the term. Now I feel suddenly happy and can't work. Always reaction. I went to London yesterday with Nico and went to 'The Cabaret Girl'. I fell in love with an actress there. So sad, because I don't suppose she will marry me! but she was divine! To-day no longer the silent man with his pipe, his training, his work and his boxing! I feel flashy, rowdy, excited, passionate. I want to dance and drink champagne and smoke cigarettes and go to the 'Cabaret Girl'. Always reaction! Oh, dear, how difficult everything is and I so agree with Stevenson over Dr. Jekyll and Mr. Hyde, though I don't feel as if I had a Hyde or was a Jekyll, but I've got two natures—only they're both so nice! One's a bit cheap and bounderish, perhaps, but then the other's dull. One—given a free hand—would soon send me to Chinatown and the bankruptcy court, the other might shut me up for life in a small room with one book and smoke and confine me to the company of faceless great athletes. But both combined—ah, there's the rub. Prime Minister? What a queer letter! I must have luncheon.

To-day's Sunday and everything's different. I'm back in
the usual mood. Bored and miserable. I want and long for
only one thing in the wide world and can think about nothing else, and of course that's you. Oh, I do so awfully
badly want you back and I'm almost dead with longing for
you. You can't imagine what a great gap there has been in
my life this last year. At first it all went pretty smoothly. I
had Eton, which was the same, and the summer holidays
were full up with good things. Since then I have had to pretend to be older and braver, and I have been acting one immense part ever since then. I suppose it is what a man does
do always—act. When he feels he wants to break down and
cry, or just run amok and kill everyone and break everything, all he does is to laugh and make polite conversation
and resist every feeling. It's only the men that can't act that
one hears about, they're the ones that go wrong or perhaps
become famous. All this time I've been seeing heaps of
people, and not one of them has a notion of all the queer
things I feel. It's getting worse and worse and harder and
harder to bear, because you see I am not quite a man yet.
I'm only still in the chorus, so to speak; one day I may become a great actor! You know I write everything to you,
darling, and so you mustn't be offended by anything or take
anything seriously, only just read and try and see my outlook
at the moment. Then I come here, where I get no female
society and only my men friends, and then all I want to do
is to dash off to London and fall in love with an actress! I
have met so few girls who I *really* think anything of. I
sometimes get attracted to them, because they're pretty, but
the attraction is always accompanied by a feeling of deep
humiliation at caring about anything which is so worthless
—which in my heart of hearts I feel infinitely superior to.
That idea, of course, has exceptions. I should feel no humiliation in grovelling in the dust before you or Hermione,
that is because I really love you. With most others it is
different. I can't express at all what I mean. But I feel at the
moment that women in general are just the plaything of men,
and that there are just a few exceptions. This is a beastly thing

to say and not, I know, true. I suppose it is just the mental
attitude I have got into by reading Louis XIV history, etc.

I have just finished a very good book on his Court which
makes me feel quite sick. I love aristocracy, monarchy and
big things like that and I don't mind immorality at all, so I
have always felt that Louis would be rather a man after my
heart, but I find nothing in him that I like. He clung to all
the worst things in life; he believed in all the worst things in
monarchy; ritual, pomp and show are wonderful things, but
where they are the only things and are based on nothing
at all they're sordid. I adore a Roman triumph, or the
Tuileries during the first Empire. There's pomp and show
for you, but real proud and deserved triumph, which is
fun. Louis could only be a great King because 15 men
dressed him every morning and because he never forgot
that he was a great King. Napoleon was great because he
did something which commanded respect. Louis had Kings
at his feet, because he had more diamonds than they and
because his throne was built so high up that they were inspired by his presence. He looked and acted like a God and
it was all due to powder and jewels. Napoleon's ante-rooms
were full of Kings because he had marched triumphantly
into all their capitals. He was a little man and had no throne,
but his personality was as great as Louis', because it was
Napoleon and not the work of the barber and the tailor. If
Louis is really what the world means by monarchy, give me
the bourgeois Napoleon every time. I hate the man. What
fun they might have had at that Court, and how they just
missed it by going in for etiquette instead of pleasure. Of
course, it was better in the early part of the reign. They
married their daughters at 12, which was so silly, and they
did all kinds of things which just spoilt the romance of it
all. Madame de Maintenon I think the most monstrous
woman, and it was really all due to her that the Court was
so sordid. She tried to purify Louis and everyone by the
Church and religion—all her efforts were directed against
immorality, and she substituted things which were so much
worse. I don't think anything is worse than boredom.

Something dull is far worse than the worst crime in creation. Crimes are far better than blunders; the immorality of Charles II far better than the dreariness of the Pilgrim Fathers.

I suppose all this is a monstrously immoral view for me to take and quite wrong, so I won't exploit it more. . . .

Religion is so obviously a thing of imagination and faith. If you start to consider Christianity logically, it at once becomes an absurd romance. It can only exist in people's minds. It cannot be made a science of. The Church is always trying to make concrete one of the most glorious abstracts in the universe. Just look at Christianity to-day. If there is any in the world, and I doubt if there's much, it is certainly not in the Church. Very few people go to Church, except because they have to or because it's a habit, or because the music is good. No one will go to Magdalen Chapel, because it's such a dull and dreary service. Eton Chapel is always packed because everyone has to go and the service is wonderful. No one goes to either because it's part of their religion. Going to Chapel every day at Eton has entirely destroyed any respect I ever had for Church services. They mean nothing to me unless I can sing loudly. But I do believe in prayer and I do feel that it has a force which one cannot get on without. But why not pray in your armchair in front of the fire? It's just as good as on a red stool in Church. Church is only a show, and I have at the moment such hatred for shows unless they're very good or entirely deserved. Church is a bad show with nothing behind it. I don't feel quite the same about Holy Communion. I do feel that is a wonderful thing, but it is only because it's a fine show—because there I want to pray and don't want to sing or look at the people, and the people there are not just there because it's Sunday morning. But it would be just as effective in this room here on a Monday as it is at 8.0 on Sunday morning in St. Paul's, I think.

I feel that all through history the Church has gone wrong. What does it matter if I stand or kneel to pray? Why should I be burnt because I say my prayers in Latin instead of English? It's still the Church's attitude, though the burning's

I

finished. They will have you orthodox, mechanical and dull. It's always dullness that kills everything. I can't see how any great believer in God or lover of God *can* become a clergyman.

Well, this is all a very queer letter and just what prompted me to write it all I don't know. I feel dull myself to-day and that, as I've said before, is the greatest crime of all.

Later.

Well, a little practical regard to fact, in the form of a man with two hands both eager to hit me, has brought me down from the pedestal of the cynical critic to the position of an Oxford undergraduate. . . .

Long for Marseilles passionately. I hope I can get someone to come to Paris for a bit first. As you say, nothing matters except this History exam. I wish it would happen quickly. I'm ready for it! What fun when it's over, if I pass. I shall.

I just long for you such a lot that I can't write no more. God bless you all and keep you well and happy. Forgive this very strange letter, but I feel it is nice to give vent to one's feelings and from your point of view it's better than nothing though foolish.

Loving,

A.

Antony rather regretted this letter, and wrote the next day:

I wrote you a horrid letter yesterday, for which I apologize a thousand times. I think it's too beastly of me to write letters like that, and I'll try and never do it again. I hate myself for it, especially as it was all such absolute rot. I'm afraid I have got my Mr. Hyde after all, and I shall see that he doesn't write you any more silly offensive letters.

I wrote to him in reply:

I was very interested in your long letter to Mummy which you afterwards attributed to Mr. Hyde, and regretted having sent. You need never disapprove of your Hyde nature—it will do you no harm to give it free vent. Jekyll is as often wrong as Hyde, and if properly understood they are both always right. I long to discuss that letter with you, but I shall never get a chance, worse luck, and it is impossible to do it adequately through the post. What you say about Churches and Clergy is fully justified and quite true—yet not the whole truth. The fact is that religion is an ideal of human conduct, and Churches are only community organizations. The doctrines of a Church are no more religion than the rules of the Carlton Club are politics, yet both Churches and parties have their uses, for without them religion and politics could not be continued. The real meaning and practicability of Christianity is a subject which I should like to discuss with you some day—I cannot attempt to do so in a letter. I am glad you have a 'hatred for shows'; that is quite a healthy frame of mind. Go on hating all shams, and look for the truth everywhere, but don't assume too readily that it doesn't exist just because you can't see it. When you are inclined to doubt the truth of something in which you have believed, or wish to believe, let me know, and perhaps I may be able to put you in the path of finding it. But don't be afraid to look everything fairly and squarely in the face and demand to see the truth that resides in it. I have no time to write more this week, but I wanted to let you know that I like what you call your 'Hyde' side and want to know more about him! Don't hesitate therefore to give him a run now and again.

His mother wrote: 'I will not answer your Mr. Hyde letter now—it will make such a good talk when we meet. I think it is right for Mr. Hyde to write all his feelings down, and equally right for Dr. Jekyll to tear them up!'

Antony's letters during the rest of this term were filled with reports of his work, descriptions of his moods, and a crescendo of excitement over the coming meeting.

To his mother:

OXFORD, *February 28th.*

My own darling,

    I have lots to write to you about and a world of things to pour out and no time to do it. Last night, just back from

London, I lay long awake in bed thinking, thinking, thinking. I feel thoroughly ashamed of myself—I haven't been
worthy of you and your love all this time. I have been always grumbling, always selfish and terribly spoilt. 'Be
thankful', you say in your letter this week, and it has hit the
very heart of the matter. I have not been thankful or humble, always selfish and self-centred and conceited, and I
haven't faced difficulties and things as I should. I feel terribly penitent and ashamed of myself. I was so angry last
night that I nearly broke the bed in my rage. The 'don't
care' attitude is really monstrous affectation, and yet what
I hate in others I practise myself. Oh, I feel so small and so
ashamed; it is good for me. You see I haven't had anyone to
tell me off, to say how spoilt I am, how selfish. Everyone has
been so sweet and just said, or looked, 'Poor darling, how he
misses them', and I have just said or looked 'Yes' and then
held out my hand for the sugar, so to speak. If it comes, it
seems quite natural—if it doesn't, I get depressed and say
'No one loves me, I want my Mummy and Daddy again'.
Just a spoilt baby. Thank God I have realized the situation
though. I must brace up. The finest things in the world can
be mine for a little trouble, it is surely worth while to take
it. I'm sorry I have written you horrid depressed or idiotic
letters, but it can't be helped, it's done, only I am sorry. I
don't want love and sympathy really, good heavens, I've got
enough. What I want is a little difficulty, a little trouble.
Someone or something to stand up and hit me.

'I'll learn ye', is what people should say; what they do say
is 'I'll help ye'. I'll do better in future, I owe you such a lot.

If I was Erasmus, I might write all this up and call it
'Apologia pro vita sua'. Thank heaven I'm not. But I felt
very apologetic last night and so I must write and say I'm
sorry, darling, that I'm always grumbling.

I also thought a lot about the future, about what I would
do. A man owes so many things. To himself—happiness; to
his family, his name and their name to make great; to his
country, his life; to God, everything.

It is all very difficult. I don't feel like being a clergyman and I'm not sure that that's the best way of serving God. For pure selfish happiness I believe the South Sea Islands is the thing. A small income, a little work, few needs, the most wonderful climate and beauty in the world, perfect contentment and perhaps a black wife!

But that's hardly good enough, is it? One would not be happy oblivious, contented, but a failure. And yet, why a failure? What has one to do in life? Is the Prime Minister of England or the richest man on the Stock Exchange, with all his fame and power and money, a happier or a better man than the outcast, who lives half naked half in and half out of the lagoon on a little island in the Pacific? Why be discontented with nothing? Perhaps it's the greatest thing in life!

Travel appeals to me tremendously at the moment. I should love to start round the world with a fiver—work my passage—really see and understand the lives that men and women live—I believe it would be the finest education in the world. I believe one would come back wise—knowing what the *real* things in life were, what the greatest virtues, what the worst vices, what was worth doing and what wasn't. In England it is so hard to tell. There is so much convention, so much acting, so narrow a view and so orthodox an outlook on things that one feels bewildered. I'm alone here just now, so I have to think a bit. But I have thought my last. To-morrow I begin work again in earnest and after that *le déluge*!

I had a heavenly letter from Davina this week. We have a great deal in common, I think. She seems to have grown up a lot. She says that you are a 'celestial jewel', which is too sweet. How I agree with her. You are too wonderful, darling, and to have such a mother as you is greater happiness than most men achieve in the whole of their lives. How I wish I felt I deserved you more. . . .

Such love as must make the world go extra fast I send you. Keep it till Marseilles.

Yr. loving son,

ANTONY.

To the same:

> 108, ABINGDON ROAD, OXFORD,
> *March 7th.*

I wonder if you realize the situation? A week to-morrow the schools begin; a week on Saturday I go down, and after that there is nothing but joy ahead for years. I am so excited that I hardly know what to do. I am glad that I have worked this term, and it will be worth it if I get through and have the summer free from care. I'm afraid I shall never like work, at least not mental work. I'm not born with that kind of temperament, but everything seems quite supreme now.

I have got very little time, as every moment of this last week must be packed with things to revise and learn up. I did seven hours yesterday and seven the day before, and have been steeped in the letters of Erasmus for about a week. They are not very exciting and I hate Latin, and above all I hate Erasmus, a most objectionable man in every way, except that he was sensible and said 'I like leading this kind of life and so I'm going to. To hell with your monasteries, fasts and ceremonies'. That was all right—but he as good as added 'Anyway, I'm a much better Christian than you', which just spoilt it all.

However, I've finished with him now. I've done every-thing—2 centuries of European history, the *Contrat Social*, the memoirs of Saint-Simon, and the letters of Erasmus, is not really a bad 7 weeks' work, and now there remains a week in which to look it all up, and then—Oi!

As a matter of fact, I think perhaps it would be better if you stayed in India, because it is rather 'unsettling' to me the thought of your coming home. It interrupts me when I'm working, and I have to go and put my head under the cold water tap before I can go on. Also I'm afraid I shall get a weak heart from excitement!! That is the pernicious argu-ment which, if I was a schoolmaster, I should put forward in all seriousness, but I'm not. I go absolutely crazy every now and then with the excitement of just the one second at Marseilles, when I first see you.

To his father:

108, ABINGDON ROAD, OXFORD,
March 12th, 1923.

Darling Father,
    I think I might spare a minute to write to you, as it is only tea time and I have already done about 5 hours' work today. I feel just like a champagne bottle that someone has been shaking for about 8 weeks, only the wire is still holding out. On Saturday at 12.30 precisely the wire will be removed, the cork will go God knows where and the champagne will come out with considerable force. In fact I am just ready to burst. The strain of thinking about nothing except Dean Colet, *la volonté générale*, Thomas More, Alberoni, Catherine II, an inconvertible paper currency, the sovereign, the Duc de Lauzun, the Duchesse de Bourgogne, Mme de Maintenon, the Thirty Years War, the Treaty of Kutchuk Kainadji, Ferdinand of Brunswick, and about fifty Archdukes, John, Charles, Frederick, Bernard, Ferdinand, Stephen, etc., etc., is absolutely terrific. I didn't know that so many treaties, wars, ministers, mistresses, battles or Jesuits existed in the world. And the worst of it all is that I get interested in some entirely irrelevant little question like, who the father of Philip III's second wife was, and why, and spend two days finding out; entirely forgetting that all I have to know for the schools is the date of the Treaty of Teschen.

    Well, it will all be over now in less than a week, thank God, and then as I say, the wire will come off and the cork will come out. The worst of it is that I have suddenly got the wind up about the exam; having thought that I had been working the whole term like blazes and that I should pass quite easily, I now find I know nothing, and everyone says it's no good thinking of passing unless one has read everything three times! I have only done so once!! It's too awful. But one can only hope for the best and try and do it all over again in two days.

    I'm afraid when you get this you will be feeling horribly like an empty champagne bottle (to continue the metaphor) as Mother and all the rest will just have left you. It will be too awful for you and I do so sympathize with you. I hope you won't be too lonely and that you will find things to do to while away the summer. But I'm afraid it will be ghastly for you. I will try and write long letters every week all about everything, and at any rate you will have the fun of a more replete mail each week like I have been getting. Perhaps it will hardly be fun, as yours is probably so vast already.

To the same:

10, EMBANKMENT GARDENS, CHELSEA,
March 25th, 1923.

Darling Father,

. . . I went up to Oxford yesterday for my viva with T——. They first of all had us all in. Then read out a few names (me included) and said 'You come back at 11.0.' This I was told meant we were on the border line, as they take the certain 'passed's' or 'failed's' first. It was rather terrifying to think that it depended upon my ability to remember things which I never knew—(you see they ask you the things you got wrong). I thought that my Rousseau and my Latin unseen were my weakest. So I was trying to think of all the French and Latin words I had misconstrued. I went in at 11.0 and sat down to listen to other unfortunates getting it. It was really very funny, especially as there was one bullying man who *crushed* his candidates by laying traps for them to fall into, and then when they'd fallen—laughing. It was most amusing.

I was called up by a nice man. He said 'Now you can draw very good maps. This map of Frederick II's territorial gains is excellent and shows a thorough grasp of the situation. Then why on earth do you draw things like this?' And he hurled my map of Alsace-Lorraine at me. I had drawn it very tentatively, not knowing it all, and I hadn't looked it up since. I knew Alsace alright, but nothing about Lorraine. 'What's wrong with that map?' he said,—Lorraine was underlined and anyway I knew that it was that that was wrong, so I said, 'It ought to be south of Alsace'.

'No.'

'It's much too big.'

'No, which is the bigger of the two?'

'Alsace.'

'No.'

'Oh dear', I thought, 'I'm doing badly'. I *only just*
stopped myself saying 'it ought to be on the other side of the
Rhine'. Then he asked me a tributary of the Rhine. I
promptly said the Ruhr. He laughed and said 'I meant on
the other bank'. Long pause. Me, tentatively, 'You can't
mean the Moselle'. He, 'Yes, that's right, have you got it in?'
Me. 'Yes.'

He. 'Sorry. Well, what's the principal fortress of Lorraine?'

Then it suddenly dawned on me, and bursting forth as if
I knew and always had known everything about Lorraine,
I said, 'Of course, how silly of me. The Moselle flows through
Lorraine and Metz is the most important town in it. How
careless I am!' Then I held forth most fluently and perfectly
correctly in answer to his questions on the capture and
strategical position of Strasbourg and the *chambres de ré-
union*. He then suddenly jumped on to Political Economy
and my heart sank, but rose again when he asked me the
only thing which I thought I thoroughly understood. However, everything I said was either untrue or incomprehens-
ible, so I left the room feeling dead sick, quite confident I
had failed. T—— had had a very short viva about his maps,
which were not thought good and which the examiner
agreed with him were beastly things to draw.

We then returned to London, and T—— got a telegram
while we were lunching at Paddington—'Failed'. It was an
awful moment and he had done masses of work, so I felt
sure it was the end of all things. He was nearly sick. I
couldn't bear to go home, so I went to a cinema and saw the
National being run. At five I struggled back to Embankment
Gardens and crept into the house. It was the most agonizing
moment of my life when I opened the door and picked up
that telegram. My heart stopped. I opened it—'Passed'. I
went mad. . . .

In a letter of April 3rd, written from the Manor House, Knebworth, just before he started for Marseilles to meet his mother and sisters, who left India at the end of March, Antony said:

Your thrilling letter about your tiger shoot has just arrived. It makes me long for camp and sun and sport again —in fact for India. It must be marvellous fun. I have a terrible longing for that kind of life. I want to go to the South Sea Islands, or East Africa, or India, or anywhere where the sun shines, but I'm fed up with England. You can have immense fun in England and you can spend lots of money. Dances and plays and girls and hunting and shooting are all good fun and all worth doing, but I don't feel that any of these are worth living for. I'm not sure that I feel business or politics or law or the army are really worth living for either. But I do feel that health and the sun and an open air life, with perhaps a touch of danger, are worth while. . . . I don't feel that I am made to be a genius, but I have got it in me to be immensely happy and fairly healthy. . . .

To this I replied:

You say you are not sure whether business or law or politics are worth living for. They are not, of course. No man lives for his profession. The only thing worth living for is life itself and that is made up of many things—work and holidays and exercise, love and companionship and service, joys and sorrows and trials, disappointments, achievements, anticipations, realizations, memories. We all have these materials, and out of them we can make ourselves happy or otherwise. Your happiness will not depend upon the profession you choose, but upon the life you lead. Travel and sport and adventure and physical exercise and the open air will always provide the spice of life for you. They will give it flavour, like salt, pepper and mustard, and you need never be without them, but don't mistake them for the meat itself ! . . . I am so glad that you have got a home and a family again. I don't grudge them to you for a moment. I feel that **it is my** turn to be left, and I am much better able to be alone than you are, as I have plenty to do and lots of people to look after me. So don't any of you have any regrets on my account. The time is passing very quickly.

From Beaulieu, where he was staying for two days with Mr. Somers Somerset, while waiting for his family to arrive at Marseilles, Antony wrote to me on April 12th:

Last year is over. It has been far the most interesting year of my life. I have been a man, entirely on my own with no one to stop me doing anything. I don't say I have managed it entirely well, but it has been a great experience. Now I can go back to being a boy again and have Mother's wing to hide under, but I don't expect I shall find that I can. One may go forward with a big bound, or by gradual degrees, but I rather doubt if one can go back at all. I do feel that I have changed enormously in this last year. I don't know if Mother will notice it at all, but my whole outlook on things is different and my tastes are different and everything seems to have changed. I can hardly remember your leaving England, and Eton seems ages and ages ago. Even Oxford is practically a dream. I shall write to you next week from the *Mantua*, when we shall have met, which will be incredibly exciting.

Somey and I sat up and talked for hours last night, just like two old men in a club, of how the world was going to the dogs. We couldn't remedy it, but we saw it was inevitable! I think the most fatal thing of all is the general tendency everywhere to be good. It is such a mistake and so unnatural. I mean by 'being good' things like disarmament, upholding the integrity of smaller nationalities, prohibition, League of Nations. They're awfully nice ideas, but no one is good, at least not for more than a fortnight. Look at France and the Ruhr. Everyone is down on her, and I agree with them she's not playing the game. What game? The 'good' game, of course. She's not so foolish as to play the 'good' game. She's sensible enough to play the real game, and it does her diplomacy credit that it is based on the sound unarguable doctrines of Frederick the Great. Old-fashioned, perhaps, but unanswerable and therefore sensible. If France believes in the possibility of everyone being good, she is quite frank in saying 'I can't be'. If she doesn't believe in that possibility, then her policy is justified. It's these drivelling idealists like Woodrow Wilson and Bob Cecil (is that libel?) who want to try and make people do everything for the peace of the world at the expense of nationality. It is fundamentally communism and is a fatal thing for everyone.

I daresay I'm talking rot, but it's rather fun to be able to say what I feel about everything to someone who won't mind. I never dare discuss things with other people, because I always forget my arguments and always get angry, so that they always win! ...

To this I replied, though he did not receive the reply till June:

GOVERNMENT HOUSE, DARJEELING,
May 2nd, 1923.

Darling Antony,

I got your letter from Beaulieu this week and I noticed in it the influence of your talks with Somey! But you are right, the moralists have spoilt the meaning of the word 'good' and the poets have spoilt the meaning of the word 'love'. We shall have to invent a new word, therefore, before the world can be got to accept Christianity as a workable philosophy. But for all that, hate remains an odious as well as a disastrous policy. Wherever there is hate there is fear, and fear is the one thing in life which always breeds mischief. The French are still afraid of the Germans, although they beat them in the war. If they did not still fear them in the future, they would no longer hate them for the past. And because of their hate their policy—which you call 'the real game' as opposed to the 'good game'—is the surest way to retain the enmity of Germany and to perpetuate the German menace. A victory is no victory which leaves you afraid of your defeated enemy. You say that French diplomacy 'is based on the sound unarguable doctrines of Frederick the Great—old fashioned perhaps but unanswerable and therefore sensible'. But the doctrines both of Frederick the Great and of French diplomacy today are far from 'unarguable' or 'unanswerable'. They are, on the contrary, highly debatable, and though there may be much to be said for them, there is also much to be said against them. You may not agree with 'idealists' like Bob Cecil, and you are fully entitled to disagree with them, but if you call them 'drivelling' you betray a want of confidence in your own case. . . . The French are right in thinking, 1. That the Germans deserve no consideration; they wantonly attacked France, destroyed her towns, killed her people, and behaved in a cruel and brutal manner, for which they ought now to pay the penalty of their defeat. 2. That the Germans could be made to pay—if all the Allies were united in bringing pressure to bear.

They have the *right*, therefore, both of the conqueror and of the injured party to exact the utmost reparation, and they would have the *power* to obtain it if we were to support them.

They are wrong, however, in my opinion, in thinking that the permanent and ultimate interests of France will be served by their policy of getting as much as possible out of Germany. The Wilsons and Bob Cecils—whom you consider 'drivelling idealists'—believe that France has more to gain in re-establishing neighbourly relations with Germany, and in the revival of European trade and commerce, than she has by obtaining forcibly a few milliard gold marks. It is simply a question of whether you take a short or a long view of the matter. The French want money today, but they will have to spend in future years more than they can get in protecting themselves against a bitterly hostile neighbour. It is a matter of interest, not goodness.

Antony's next letter was written from sea, after the great and long desired meeting had taken place:

S.S. Mantua.

Darling Father,
        It has happened at last. We have met. They are all just the same, not one atom changed, and I feel as if I had

never been away from them. So many things have happened
since last year. They are all far, far away in the distance, but
it just seems as if we had always been together for ever and
ever. The *Mantua* got into Marseilles some amazingly early
hour in the morning. They told us at the P. & O. Office that
she would be in at 7 and that we probably shouldn't be
allowed on until about 9 or 10, as there were 360 people to
get off. I was with Somey who motored me over the day
before from Beaulieu. We got down to the quay at 8.0. and
found the boat almost deserted. We had been told that there
would be an awful difficulty to get on—that we should
write a letter to Mother to show at the gangway, that we
should get hold of the 'agent', etc. but of course there was no
difficulty at all. Hermione and David and John rushed down
the gangway and welcomed me on the muddy quay. It was
simply pelting. Then I rushed up and found Mummie with
tears in her eyes. It was really a very wonderful meeting,
but I have forgotten it now and just can't remember either
parting or meeting. Somey was a perfect angel and looked
after me all the time like a father, motored me to Marseilles
along the most awful of roads in the world, in pelting rain,
and filled Mummie with happiness and fun all day. She is so
cheerful and full of laughter and wit and quite, quite adorable. I can't get over none of them having changed one tiny
atom. It's too, too marvellous. . . .

Somey took me along to Monte Carlo one night. We had
an excellent dinner at the Hôtel de Paris and then went to
the Salle Privée and gambled a little. I imagined the rooms
to have an immense air of tension. I thought they were
smart and flashing and one saw wonderful men of all nationalities immaculately dressed flinging gold coins and
notes and things about, calmly raking in millions, calmly
losing thousands. I dressed up immensely to try and look as
if I felt as grand and rich as the Greeks, the Argentines, the
Dukes and the Counts. I imagined the croupiers as devilish
grasping fiends with sinewy clutching hands and diabolical
moustaches, Oh, how wrong I was. There was no atmosphere at all, unless it was that of a middle-class boarding-

house parlour. There were a few very old, very fat women
working out systems and playing in 5 frs. There were a lot
of dingy men in dirty, soft shirts sitting looking bored, betting on red and black—there were one or two Americans in
day clothes betting fairly high and losing. There were no
vampires, no visions, no fortunes, no wonderful men, and
everywhere a feeling of ineffable boredom. The croupiers
were kind, simple, sweet men, eager to help you, longing
for you to win, putting on your money for you and paying
with a painful willingness. They whispered the winning
number, swept in the money and paid out the winnings, and
everyone sat and looked as if they were listening to a cinema.
I lost 300 francs and was very amused and went about singing and dancing, but everyone was horrified. It was quite an
amusing evening, but not half so thrilling as 'the Casino at
Monte Carlo' sounds and looks from the outside. . . .

About plans; it's all awfully difficult to know just what to
do. I shall be able to write more about it when we have seen
various authorities and talked it over again. What I should
like you to tell me is this:—

1. Are you very anxious for me to get a degree?
2. If you are, are you content that it be just a degree (in
   which case I could come to India winter 24-25), or
   do you feel strongly that if it's worth doing it's
   worth doing well?
3. Do you want me to go into the army? (Mummie does.
   I don't—because I think in peace time the army
   consists of people who aren't capable of doing anything else, and also, like the Varsities, from a young
   man's point of view the army is *passé*.)
4. Do you think it would be a good plan to chuck Oxford
   and come to India and learn certainly something?
   You see in days gone by young men grew up, inherited money and property, married and settled
   down as the squire or big landlord. Then the university was wonderful. They learnt to make friends,
   'to hold their port', to spend their money and to
   waste their time like gentlemen. Ditto the army.

They made more friends, learnt a little militarism and received further training. But nowadays life is not like that. Very few young men can afford to spend money at Oxford and in the army just for fun. Very few inherit properties which they can just inherit and live in. Very few can afford Parliament.

The result is the Varsity is not what it was, the Government is not what it was, Parliament is not what it was, the army is not what it was, everything has gone to the dogs! The only thing for a young man to do is business, which like politics is just another form of unreality and just as unimportant.

Some people always have and always will get away from all these things and get down to realities—probably not in England. But then they're never any good for anything again. They're spoilt—and spoilt by truth, which seems a pity. They are probably very happy, but they're almost certainly forgotten. What or who is the man that makes the bridge? He is forgotten, he never makes his fortune, he has seen and has touched reality. It is the fat man in his office for whom the bridge is made, who has probably never seen the bridge, who rakes in the money and leaves a name to posterity. So it is always. That is my philosophy of life. It's quite hopeless. You must either be unknown, wonderful, poor and happy. Or famous, insignificant, rich, and if you have any love of reality, miserable. Consequently the problem is insoluble. . . .

His mother wrote by the same mail:

The most amazing thing was the climate—rain like a Monsoon downpour, only icy, icy cold. We watched the shore from about 6 a.m. and hardly dared to breakfast for fear of missing Antony. But it came off all right. It was 8.15 when they got out of their taxi in the rain and ran up the gangway. Antony was quite white with excitement, and we were all very strung up, as you may guess and feel. I do not think him the least altered. He is very, very happy, and we are gradually beginning to settle down and talk. . . .

They arrived at Tilbury on April 21st and went straight to Knebworth, where they all settled into the Manor House after receiving a great ovation from the village. Antony went up to Oxford the following week and had rooms in College this term. Although at first he was even more impatient of Oxford life with his family at home than he was with his family abroad, he soon settled down and enjoyed the term thoroughly. He wrote to me on May 1st:

I am back at Oxford—in College this term; miserable at being away from everything that I love, and longing to go down again quickly. . . .
Life up here is not the boxing, working life of last term, but the cinema bridge type and altogether a little gayer. . . .

In his next letter he told me about his previous exam.—

I find (he said) that the knowing one—the man who knew all about it—who told me I was on the border-line because I had to come back at 11, lied. I never was anywhere near the border-line. In fact, I nearly got distinction. They only send you away because they can't take you all at the same time. I have seen my marks, but of course they mark at Oxford differently to anywhere else in the world, and so I didn't understand what it all meant. They don't give marks in numbers, but in various letters. I was told my best paper was marked S?? + Do you understand? I don't. However, it was explained to me that I had done well, and that if I had got one more query, or two less minuses, or another half plus I should have got distinction! But it's all Greek to me.

The summer passed all too quickly, with cricket and boating and tennis and gay friends and parties in London. Antony's letters were full of gaiety and the enjoyment of life—'one bang of joy and fresh air and suppressed exuberance,' as he said to his mother.

He made the acquaintance this term for the first time of Gilbert and Sullivan's operas, and these remained with him

K

always as the only form of opera that he really enjoyed. He also read with delight Guedalla's *Napoleon III*—a book which he never tired of re-reading or quoting from.

His mother and sisters visited him at Oxford for his twentieth birthday, and sent me the menu of their dinner at the Clarendon Hotel, signed by themselves and Edward Jessel, Edward Woodall and Philip Guedalla:

I wrote to Antony on May 16th:

Owing to the late mail last week, I have two lovely long letters from you to answer this week—both very happy ones. I was delighted with your description of the gambling rooms at Monte Carlo. I have a very hazy recollection of them, but my impressions were much the same as yours.

As regards plans, I am quite certain that to take a good degree will help you more than anything else in life, and even though it means postponing the joy of seeing you for a year, I strongly advise you to stay at Oxford and get a first if you can. I am quite sure you can do it if you really try, as you have begun so well. When I was at Cambridge there was no examination in my first year and I wasted nearly two years before I learnt how to work. I don't agree with you that the Universities are played out. A man who gets a first at Oxford or Cambridge is just as much respected now as he ever was. It is rather early to decide definitely what you should do after Oxford, but I am against the army. The army for a few years is quite a good *alternative* to the University, but it is waste of time after the University. Regimental life is only a continuation of public school and University life, and when a man is twenty-two or twenty-three, it is time he started upon the profession which he intends to follow.

My advice to you would be to spend a year abroad and indulge your tastes for travel. See as much of the world as you can, which will help you to decide in what direction your tastes lie, and then if you have no other strong inclination, I should advise you to take up politics and stand for Parliament. It is the fashion to despise politics, but if you treat them seriously they afford, not only the most interesting life, but the best avenue into all the highest posts in public life. The successful politician who reaches Cabinet rank nowadays can obtain the best posts in almost any profession. Ambassadors, Governors, Directors of Business Companies, are all chosen from this class. The only disadvantage is that it is an expensive profession in the early years and the rewards do not come till late in life. It will therefore be necessary to consider whether you can afford to take up this life at once, or whether you will have to earn a living in some other way for a few years. You will know better by the time you leave Oxford. In the meantime concentrate on your degree and be assured that if you succeed in that other opportunities will follow. If you are thinking of business, there are several big business men who are already interested in you, and if you have taken a first they will be all the more anxious to secure you. Your alternatives of being either unknown, wonderful, poor and happy, or famous, insignificant, rich and miserable, are quite wrong and the problem is not insoluble. The real lesson to learn is the difference between being and doing. If Napoleon had only dreamed of *being* Napoleon, he would never have been anything. The man who wants to be famous will be miserable and probably insignificant. The man who wants to *do* things will do them—whether they are big things or small things will depend upon his capacity, but he will be happy doing them whatever they are. Don't bother then about what you are going to be, but try and decide what you want to do. Chance and your capacity will settle the rest, and in any case you will be happy. But don't *want* to do one thing and do another— that is the road to unhappiness and failure.

The following are some of the more interesting passages in his letters to me from Oxford.

I was amused at your spotting Somey's influence on my theories. He was very full of ideas and views which I was very ready to listen to, and I absorbed them all as if they had been my own. I entirely understand your letter. I quite realize that everything is defensible and that for everything there is an argument, and I also agree and accept your correction about abuse. Of course abuse is a confession of weakness, but like all confessions of weakness it is both human and pleasant. It weakens your case, that I understand. When I spoke of the unarguable doctrine of Frederick, I meant that from the idealist point of view they were not to be argued about, because there was no idealism in them. They were there, cut and dry and definite; might is right. Frederick did not believe in ideals, just as he did not believe in strategical victories. Like war, Frederick thought life depended on a pitched battle, and this doctrine was arguable only with the sword. Further, those on whom it was practised had not got good swords to argue it with. That was Frederick's business—and he would not consider ideals. That is what I meant by 'unarguable'. Of course, he may have been wrong, and that can be argued about. Personally, I like him because he was frankly offensive, frankly aggressive and frankly successful. There was no hanky-panky about his ideas. There they were—take them or leave them —but you damned well had to take them! . . .

I quite understand that it is possibly not a crime but a blunder that France is guilty of. It may be bad policy, but I don't know. I believe that the stimulant of defeat was sufficient in itself to reconstruct Germany and fan her hatred of France, and that this yearning for revenge would sooner or later drive the Prussians back into France. After 1870 the Germans were severe but not merciless, but that sore never healed. France believes that the sore of 1918 will never heal in Germany, therefore she must be merciless. I feel that too, and I believe that though her attitude is prompted by fear, it is also prompted by intelligible policy. . . .

OXFORD, *May* 30th, 1923.

. . . Have you read Philip Guedalla's book on the Second Empire? I think it is the most brilliant thing that I have ever read. It's so good that I can't digest more than a page a day. But the Bonaparte dynasty and family are to me the most wonderful and in many ways pathetic romance of the world, fact or fiction. . . . There is a bit about Napoleon after his downfall, when he is in England, which apparently has no value as good writing, or any interest at all, and yet every time I read it (I've read it about 50 times) I almost cry, no matter in what mood I am—

'One might slip over to Ostend, by Germany into Switzerland and then to Annecy' (here it begins) 'past the great lake where Eugénie had stood with him under a night of stars and by the dim hills above Aix, where Hortense had once sat sketching.'

It may leave you cold. But to me it is a vivid picture of the whole Napoleonic romance. I can see the long story of the Second Empire contained in that one sentence. Louis Napoleon's life lies before one—the whole tragedy of the thing....

It takes me back such a long way, and includes rather pathetically in one sentence two ladies whose names have been household words in two different and almost equally romantic generations. And the bitter irony—Hortense was sketching! Standing under a night of stars is certainly a little better occupation, but where was this place? Switzerland! Switzerland is the place, of all humble, uninteresting European countries, where Guedalla chooses to become for a moment sentimental over the great Napoleonic legend. Had it been Fontainebleau or the Tuileries or the Kremlin or even the Italian battlefields, you're all right. But it is typical of the 19th century. What an age! Malmaison, Osborne, Sandringham, Farnborough, Chiselhurst, and yet the most magnificent century in history.

Do you remember a bit in the *Ballad of the White Horse*, which ended up, 'the last cry of the Gaul'? That is the 19th century. The Gaul is the old aristocratic feudal tradition of tyranny, and it went out in the last century—it went out—how? Through Osborne and Farnborough! *Comme c'est triste.*

June 6th, 1923.

Thank you so much for your delicious letter and your wonderful philosophy. You are the most wonderful counsellor and always seem to understand things so perfectly. Unfortunately I am naturally rather inclined to be pessimistic about things. I love the past—it is my own form of sentimentality—and I take a morbid delight in sitting and thinking 'Ah, that can never be again', which of course is not conducive to success in life. I am naturally very conservative, and because the mistakes that people have made appeal to me more than the successes of others, I try and look at everything in a Tory light. I try and interpret things which I admire as reactionary, when they are really revolutionary, and I like to feel that my part in life is to die for some great cause (like the Stuart monarchy), which not existing any longer has destroyed the point of living. I want to live, as I say, in the past with only a horror of the atrocities of the future and the present. This is only what Philip Guedalla cynically describes as 'the fondness which all very young men have for all very old institutions'. I suppose it is human nature when young to neglect the future, when old to forget the past. . . .

You are able to convince me because I am sensible enough to understand that one must go on. That the thing which counts in life is to want to do things. Then we will do them. . .

June 13th, 1923.

I am having such marvellous fun this term that I hardly know how to sit down and write sense for two moments together. There is only a week more of term, then a marvellous month in London, a wonderful one at Knebs, and then Scotland, etc. I am so happy and everything is so, so wonderful that there is nothing in the world that I want and haven't got. . . .

I seem to enjoy every sort of life just now. The prospect of camp life and health and living in the open air is wonderful, and I enjoy dancing and night clubs and champagne just as much, and now and then I even take a pleasure in history. . . .

After leaving Oxford Antony stayed with his family at Manchester Square, in a house they had hired for the season, and the rest of the summer was devoted to the social activities of a London season, with continual balls at night, week-end parties, lawn tennis at Wimbledon, polo at Ranelagh and Hurlingham, etc. 'The London season is a more colossal affair than I had realised', he wrote. 'Life is very gay and happy, but I can't help feeling rather dissolute and idle. I think there is little doubt that health and country and fresh air and exercise are really better than all the dances and champagne in the world.'

In spite of dancing for many hours every night, he complained that he was not getting enough exercise in London! Of the climate he wrote:

We have all been a little amused by your describing the heat in India, and appearing to think that you are undergoing some sort of hardship! The temperature has been well over 90° here for weeks and about 102° at night. All the Anglo-Indians and men who have spent years in the Congo chasing monkeys are perspiring over every ballroom and street, crying to God to transfer them to the equable climate of the equator! Every industry is at a standstill, owing to the evaporation of its workers. Every ball is a failure, owing to the disgusting state of the dancers. Only the swimming baths flourish, and even there the water is so hot with the heat of the human body that one has to climb out to get cool. No, believe me, it may be warm in India, but the blackest nigger God ever made couldn't last a day in Piccadilly! With the usual deliberation of the British nation, we did, after three weeks' evaporation, realize that it was hot, buy cooler clothes and do cooler things, when with all the fury of a polar winter the snow was upon us, and we now shiver in our new tussore suitings, sit in icy baths and pretend that the heat wave is still on.

In one of his letters, referring to Sir Herbert Warren's question whether he got on well with his father, he wrote :

It's such a queer idea to me that some people should

quarrel with their fathers, but I expect it is that they don't all have such wonderful ones as I have. Oh, Daddy, you can't imagine how much I love you, and thank you for always being such a wonderful father to me. Such a wise counsellor and always so loving. I owe you such a lot for all that you've done for me, and God knows I hope that one day I'll be able to get square with you, but I doubt if it's possible.

To this I replied:

> GOVERNMENT HOUSE, DACCA,
> *Wednesday, July* 18, 1923.

Darling Antony,
    I got a beloved letter from you this week telling of the pleasures and fatigues of dinners and dances and your longing for a life of open air and exercise. I hope you will get this now during the holidays and soon recover from the effects of a London season. . . .
You talk of hoping 'to get square' with me some day, by which I gather you mean that I have given you so much that you are in my debt and hope some day to give me something in return. Please get out of your head any idea of being under an obligation to me. Everything which I have given you since you were a baby I have given as much to myself as to you. My love for you has made me want to make you happy, and the sight of your happiness has made me happy in return. As you have both been happy and made me happy for 20 years, I don't see any occasion to talk of 'getting square'. I don't think we could either of us be happy at the expense of the other, and therefore though I feel the sadness of separation and hunger for your presence, I have no anxiety about your conduct or habits. I have perfect confidence in you in everything. You have a healthy body and are not likely to enjoy for long any form of dissipation that would impair its health and vigour, and your love is strong enough to prevent you from seeking or finding happiness at someone else's expense. You will have trials and difficulties, of course, and there will be times when it will appear that

whatever you do you must hurt someone, but you will confide in me then, and I think I shall be able to help you. Only
don't let there be anything—*anything at all*—which you
feel you could not speak to me about, which you don't want
me to know. Never speak of getting square with me, or
think of me in that light. We are square now, always have
been, and all we have got to do is to keep square. It is one of
the glorious qualities of love that it automatically insures
one's every stake. What I spend on you I spend on myself,
and what you repay to me you repay to yourself. What
Shakespeare says of mercy is not psychologically true of that
quality, as mercy implies inequality and obligation, but it
is true of love—real love which produces absolute equality,
or rather maintains absolute equilibrium. The love that
wants to be loved in return is not true love—that is dis-
guised self-love, which is gratified by the adoration of the
adored. It is that love which is so often disappointed and con-
sumes its possessor in the flames of jealousy. But the love
which looks for no return, which is satisfied in merely finding expression, which derives its pleasures from giving, not
from receiving, is never disappointed, can never be disappointed, because it makes its own reward and introduces no
element of obligation.

But if I sermonize any more you will want to get even
with me with your fists!

Your loving Father,

LYTTON.

At the beginning of August they all moved to Knebworth,
and Antony wrote to me from there:

We are all at Knebs and absolutely, peacefully, blissfully
happy. I can't think more than a day ahead and so I don't
get depressed with worrying things out and wondering
what's right and what's wrong. . . . I just lie flat on my back
in the sun or walk through the bracken, or play tennis, or
sink in a boat on the lake—laugh and thank God that life's
so good. . . . And it's so divine being right away in the
country—just family—after all the turmoil and fun of

London. I am going to hire a horse for a fortnight and ride about the country-side rejoicing. . . .

KNEBWORTH,
August 14*th*, 1923.

I have got a wonderful letter from you this week, which is full of wisdom and good wise thought. I don't remember what I said about 'getting square' (which are the only two words you quote of mine) but I think you have misunderstood them. Your answer is wonderful, and giving and loving is so obviously greater than receiving and being loved. That I realize to be so great a thing that in my selfishness I hardly can understand it. But I disagree with you about there being no obligation. Every man who is born into the world owes his existence to his father, and though that very existence is in itself sufficient repayment for anything which his father has done for him, I still argue that there is obligation (in the nice and right sense of the word— not the haggling sordid sense).

Every man has his duty to do, not only to his father but to his family and to his country. If he becomes a rotter and goes wrong and wastes his money and his brain and his body, he disgraces his family and is unworthy of his father. If he does great things in life and makes a great name for himself, he also brings kudos to his family and more than rewards his parents for the care which they have taken of him. He justifies his existence.

Love is such a strangely great thing that it makes no distinction between the rotter and the success. 'He is my son', and that is sufficient, whether the person in question is in Newgate or Downing Street. That is a wonderful and mysterious gift which belongs only to God and which we cannot understand, but it is not for man to abuse it and say 'It doesn't matter what I do. My father will always love me just the same'.

That is what I mean by obligation. A son owes everything to his parents, and though, of course, it must not hang over him like a shadow and keep him thinking 'How can I get square?' it should be a thought to keep him straight, and an

ideal for him to aim at. It should be perhaps more an ambition than an obligation, but it should exist.

αἰὲν ἀριστεύειν καὶ ὑπείροχον ἐμμέναι ἀλλῶν
μηδὲ γένος πατέρων αἰσχύνεμεν

'All in all to excel and ever to rank with the foremost;
So to behave as ne'er to disgrace the long line of his
   fathers'

                                        HOMER.

illustrates my point.

But don't think I don't see yours. I appreciate it. Only I
felt that from what you said you hadn't understood me
(Though God knows what I said!). . . .

Damn it all, though I feel gloomy enough about everything to do with India, in all conscience, what is there to be
gloomy about? What is there in a year or two? We've got
lots of time ahead of us, and after all there are lots of people
who choose to live in India and never to see their friends or
children. It is quite true that a home is the most wonderful
thing on earth, and I have never felt that more than this
summer, but as it's got to be incomplete, it may as well be
incomplete to the power of two instead of one. After all,
what is the point, the interest, the fun of life, if one doesn't
have adventures and difficulties and heart-rendings? I don't
see that they should really matter. There can be nothing
that really matters in the world except birth and death. . . .

The subject of this correspondence was concluded in a
letter from me on September 5th:

You return to the charge and say that every man has 'a
duty not only to his father but to his family and to his country'. I agree with you, if you will substitute 'service to render' for 'duty to perform'. Duty has come to be regarded as
the antithesis of pleasure, and the two are always represented
in conflict. But service is not the opposite to pleasure—on
the contrary, the highest pleasure is the service of those one
loves. Therefore I would rather not talk of my duty to you
or your duty to me. I should hate to think that I had a 'duti-

ful' son, if by that was meant that my son loved me or
served me as a duty which was in conflict with his pleasure.
Rather let us talk of the pleasure which we each experience
in the service of the other to the utmost of our capacity because of the great love we feel for one another. Then there
is no obligation on either side. I expect we agree really. It is
only a question of how you put it. I like your Greek quotation. The Greeks were great artists in life, and had a rather
warmer sentiment than the Romans.

That is good enough, isn't it, or, as Bunny Hare says
quaintly of John Deg—'wishing quietly to do not less than
his best'. If my children live up to that, I am well content....

I hope you and Hermione are enjoying yourselves. I have
had to put off my visit to Ooty because there are some tiresome revolutionary societies which are plotting the murder
of my police officers and have to be suppressed—all due to
ignorance and misunderstanding. My police folk think these
men are wicked dangerous people—and so they are, for they
deal in bombs and pistols—but in reality they are very mild-
mannered, crazy idealists, who mean well, but because they
are full of ignorance and fear become dangerous. They in
turn regard my police officers as clever cruel tyrants—and
so they are, for they deal in jails and gallows—but in reality
they are kind, brave men who love their wives and children
and want only to be at peace with all men. And I sit like God
above it all, and see the glory and the mischief and the pity of
it all! I wish they would go and shoot tigers together instead
of shooting each other.

At the beginning of September Antony went with his
mother and sister to stay with Sir James Barrie at Stanway
for a cricket week. All his friends were there. 'It is all the
most glorious fun', he wrote, 'even better than last year.'
He returned to Knebworth on September 7th, and wrote to
me from there the next day, before going to Scotland:

Stanway was quite the most divine party. All my best boy
friends in their best form, Mother and Hermione, and wonderful golf, tennis and cricket. A little too much of the last

to suit me, I'm afraid, but great fun, even the cricket. . . .
On the last night Sir James and Hermione acted a wonderful
charade—Scene, a railway carriage. Sir James a Scots student
going to Edinburgh, and Hermione a 'designing young
woman' against whom he had been warned as a class by his
Aunty Jane, and who of course caught him. They were quite
supreme and Hermione acted brilliantly. Gloucestershire is
the most lovely county in England. It is all beautiful, but
the view from the golf course beyond all words lovely.

Monday. Tonight Hermione and I set out on the long
trail for Scotland. . . . She and I have had a delicious week-
end together here. We get on terribly well when left alone,
and each understands the moments at which the other considers it sacrilege to speak. So we seldom communicate, but
do our own jobs. When we've finished we have supreme intellectual talks (a good deal more supreme than intellectual).
I love doing things with her, and I love being here alone
with her too.

Antony paid visits in Scotland to the Wallaces at Kildonan,
the Colquhouns at Rossdhu and the Dalhousies at Invermark,
and wrote me very happy letters from each place about his
sporting activities. He got back to Knebworth at the beginning of October, and wrote to me from there on the 11th.

I hate the feeling of leaving Knebworth and going back to
Oxford, because it revives the old school-time feeling, and
because it means the end of the summer, which I have lain
awake at nights thinking about for a year. But, on the other
hand, the more partings and the more goings back, the more
used one becomes to them, and also I am really looking forward to Oxford. I don't feel this next year in England will
be nearly as bad as last, as

    1. I am older, and
    2. I shall know what not to do.

In all his letters during the winter, he wrote hopefully of
coming out to India in the following autumn. These hopes
were never realized, but they helped us both to bear the long

separation. If I had known when I parted from Antony as a boy at Eton, in 1922, that I should not see him again for 3½ years, and that when we next met he would be a man who had finished with Oxford, I don't think I could have borne it. It was necessary, therefore, to make plans for earlier meetings, and to discuss them in our correspondence. This helped to make the time pass quickly; but looking back now the only thing I find to regret in the story of our perfect relationship is the decision which caused so long a separation between us at such a critical period in his life. That is the only thing done I could wish undone in the past, but my consolation for this unceasing regret is to be found in the letters which this separation called forth, and which are now such a precious possession.

This term, of course, was overshadowed by the return of his family to India. I had foreseen this, and written to him from India—'When you are feeling particularly depressed at the thought of parting with Mummy, will you try and remember the letter you wrote to me last March or April, describing your feeling like a champagne bottle which was waiting to be uncorked. Well, I am feeling like that now, and I doubt if the wire which restrains the cork will hold until Mummy and the girls arrive! It will be some time before your champagne bottle and mine both explode their corks simultaneously, but when they do—what a loud pop there will be!'

Antony responded nobly, and his sturdy philosophy and high spirits enabled him to face this ordeal cheerfully: 'I love Oxford,' he wrote to me, 'I love life, I love the sun, and I am full of things to look forward to. What more can one want? I am going to be happy all this next year, and I hope that I can make John so too. You will have Mother back, so you will be happy, and we shall all have a roaring time till we meet next year.'

In his last letter to his mother before her departure, he wrote: 'This has been a delicious bit, this summer, hasn't it, darling? I don't mind the parting half so much this time. Perhaps I am older, perhaps it does not feel for long. Perhaps it is just the second time. You must not mind it either. I will look after John for you as best I can, but I am a bit young to be more than a brother. And you must think that it will soon be next summer when you can see him again, and then I will come out to you in the winter. I feel India is not so far after all, and it is only for a few years, so why should it matter? There are much greater tragedies in the world than ours. In the meanwhile this summer has been heavenly. I have enjoyed every minute of it, and I'm sure you have. . . . And now you have got a great thing to do—you have got to make that Father of mine happy for a year, until I can come and have a go at him. Give him such love from me as I cannot send in a letter, and tell him that I love him with all my heart, and will soon see him again.'

They all left for India on October 31st, and Antony wrote to his mother the next day from Oxford:

'The Gods make this a happy day to Antony', as was said on the morning of Actium. And the Gods make this a happy day to me too—though they didn't to the other Antony! I don't feel anything this morning except happiness. I am thankful with all my heart for our wonderful summer in England—I am thankful that I have such a family to love and that I mind parting from them—I am thankful that Daddy will be happy and I am thankful that I have life before me to do what I like with. We are very blessed, you and I and all of us, with all the good things of life, and we have but to stoop and pick them up. By being unhappy, by crying, by grumbling, by lamenting our lot, we leave them lying there untouched for the next person to pick up. Personally I am out with a couple of baskets at the moment, and I expect good results.

You won't get this letter for years, when the memory of yesterday will be only a dream—to me it is still very vivid, but it was just the same a year and a half ago, and now—well, it is a year and a half ago, so that I have got the two muddled and any moment it may be a year and a half hence!. . .

Antony's next letter described a thrilling adventure that might have been very serious, and filled us with dread as we read it:

Well Mother darling,   *Sunday, November 7th.*

Quite a lot of things have been happening to me since you left. In the first place I have been practically killed by Nico. We went down to Eton on Thursday—the day after you left—to play football against the school, and drew with them love all. It was a real splendid hard game and the first I have played in which I haven't been hurt at all. It's divine because it means that I have reached that age when football no longer hurts.

Well, we started to motor home about 6.0 and the fog was so thick that you could have sat on it. When we had gone about a mile out of Eton, we came to a bridge over a small stream with white railings on each side. Nico took the left hand railing on his right and the car took to the water. By the grace of God he went absolutely dead straight into it. Otherwise we should have turned over and all been dead. We stopped almost immediately on reaching the bottom of the ditch, and then followed a long pause in which we all tried to make out if we'd got a broken leg, and all thought the other three were unconscious. Then a breathless 'Are you alright?' from Nico, then a hushed 'Yes, are you?' from me. Then a long pause—and then we all four burst out laughing! The front axle of the car and the wheels and mudguards were completely smashed up and we couldn't have got the thing out with 15 horses. I regret to say that I bumped my knee.

My other adventures are that I played Rugger yesterday against Radley and played very well, and that I concluded a

healthy and delightful day by losing £7.10 at vingt-et-un
—though at one time the situation was even more serious
than that—That took me till 12 p.m. I then played bridge
until 3 a.m., never held a card above a 9—lost £5. I cut my
creditor through the pack double or quits and lost—and then
tossed him for four times or quits, and won, thereby saving
the family honour and the quarter's allowance. So my life
has not been destitute of incident.

We were rather shocked at the tale of losses of money at
cards contained in this and other of Antony's letters at this
time, and we both wrote to remonstrate with him. 'Your
gambling troubles have my sympathy, but not my encouragement,' wrote his mother, 'for I know of no more aggravating reason for being down at heels than vingt-et-un.' I
also wrote that it seemed silly to lose so much money at
bridge and poker, considering how little money we all had
to spare, and that to win money from friends who have
equally little to spare was no more satisfactory. But before
our letters could reach him, he received rather a rude shock,
which proved no doubt a salutary lesson. The College Dean
discovered a party, of which Antony was one, in possession
of a roulette table, and they were summoned before the
authorities. The facts were frankly admitted and the justification pleaded that it was a harmless amusement. The
authorities took a serious view of the matter. The owner of
the roulette was sent down for a term, and Antony and the
others were sent down for a fortnight.

Antony went to Knebworth to spend his enforced holiday
with his grandmother. He wrote from there to his mother
the following entertaining description of a party with Lady
Desborough at Taplow.

    . . . I have had a most amusing week-end at Taplow
—A. J. B.* Maurice Baring and Linky Cecil†, all in killing

    *Rt. Hon. Arthur Balfour.   †Lord Hugh Cecil.

L

form, and Edward Rice, who was at Nuneham—Elizabeth
Gathorne-Hardy—Mogs.* Ettie† said that she had never
heard of anyone being sent down for an adequate reason,
and cited the instance of Guy Charteris, who was sent down
for throwing a duck in the Dean's face and then kissing
him!! Also two brothers, one of whom was sent down for
not reading a book of Xenophon before an exam, and the
other for reading it during the exam! We played the two-
people-talking-and-having-to-guess-who-they-are game, and
she was quite, quite brilliant, knowing exactly who you were
after two words. Linky said he was going to discuss an event
with her and she was to guess who she was meant to be. He
said 'I think you were so wonderful under very trying circumstances', and she answered 'Yes, I minded the smell
most', and then the conversation went on for ages. She was
meant to be Mrs. Noah and guessed it at once. I did the
Empress Eugénie to Maurice B.'s Baldwin, neither of us
knowing what the other was, and that did stump Ettie for
about 2 min: she thought I was the Queen of Sheba! Doesn't
say much for my grasp of my subject, I'm afraid. Linky told
a divine story about Eugénie and Queen Victoria at the
Opera. Eugénie before sitting down looked to make sure
the chair was there—Queen Victoria sat down, knowing it
was!!!

Ettie was very excited with that toy that you look through
and turn the wheel and it makes pretty patterns. She showed
it to A. J. B. who remained with an absolutely unmoved
face. Ettie didn't think he could see anything, and asked
him, saying that he should be emitting cries of delight.
A. J. B. said he never did that and that he was not impressed, as it was only a cheap form of a well known optical
toy which he had played with in his youth! He was absolutely
killing about it for half an hour. . . .

This sort of thing went on all the time. It was too wonderful. Every now and then someone would talk about someone
and Ettie and M. B. sitting together would try and guess
from one sentence who they were talking about. M. B.

*Imogen Grenfell.　　　　　†Lady Desborough.

always guessed right immediately, and so brilliantly that it quite took your breath away; Ettie always capped it by guessing someone to whom the description would apply so far more funnily that the genius of the correct guess was at once eclipsed by the brilliance of the incorrect one. It was killing to sit and listen to, and I thought I must write it all down to you, though on paper it is probably neither interesting nor funny. . . .

The political situation is really rather exciting and I don't know what to think. I wish Daddy were here to be in the thick of the *mêlée*. The speeches on Tariff Reform—Birkenhead—Robert Horne—Baldwin—A. J. B.—Austen C. and Derby—are all concise, interesting, easy to understand and thoroughly convincing, while Asquith, Lloyd George and Winston propound the most magnificent rhetoric, but say nothing. Winston says 'Britain without Liberalism is Britain without a soul', and everyone cheers, but he doesn't even hint at the reason! L. G. says the Government are going to the country with tin-cans on their tails, and everyone laughs, but it doesn't mean anything, and Asquith says Baldwin thinks he's discovered something which was dished on the head 20 years ago and that the Conservatives must all be imbeciles, but he appears to have nothing to support his statement. I have always been brought up to regard free trade as the soul of British industry and the backbone of our existence. Daddy is a free trader and free trade sounds so wonderful. I have never really understood it, but I have always felt on the side of free trade.

Now the question has come again. Every day one hears the case for tariff reform brilliantly put—perfectly explained, argued till it is unanswerable, and absolutely proved to be the only possible policy which can save or help Britain at all. All the Liberals do is to abuse the Conservatives and call them half-wits. On the strength of that one must be entirely pro-Baldwin. If there are any good arguments for free trade, one would like to hear them. It is not convincing to be told by the most brilliant men in the world that Britain without free trade is like a flag without a flagstaff. They never say why.

Unless there is a change of plot altogether I don't see how
the ordinary person can fail to vote for reason against abuse,
and it seems that the Government must come back with an
overwhelming majority. I wonder what will happen? . . .

Well, I must finish this letter off now. I am going to be
here with Granny for a week working, and then I go back
to Oxford again and am to be received with acclamation and
a dinner by the undergraduates, and tears of penitence
(apparently) by the authorities. It is all so very funny but
cannot be helped. I do hope you won't fuss about it and
think it awful.

Antony returned to Oxford at the beginning of December
and wrote happily about his work:

I do about 8 hours reading a day and spend the rest of the
time reading the paper, sleeping, eating, walking, and yesterday I went to the Cinema. Melancholy? Well, oddly
enough, no. I am quite oblivious of everything but what I
am reading, and I am full of thoughts and things which keep
me happy as a bird all the time. . . . My life is very dull and
I am more or less immersed in Henry V at the moment. He
seems to have been a charming man, with a delightful wife
and an angel for a son. Do you think it is possible to be good
and successful? Do you think that people like Henry V and
Chatham and Alexander the Great, who were all so successful in life through war, were good? If there is a Judgement
Day, will the blood of the dead soldiers at Agincourt be laid
to the charge of Henry V?

Does the use of gas in the war by the British get atoned
for by the fact that they won? Wouldn't it have been better
to go under playing straight than to cheat too? In a game, if
your opponent cheats, you don't cheat too. You get beaten
and feel a hero! Well, had we any right to cheat in the war?
Has anything big ever been accomplished in history except
through cheating? St. Francis of Assisi, I suppose, and one or
two others did great things and were real saints, but no
national hero has been anything but a cheat. Again I ask, is
it possible to be good and successful? If not, which is the best?

At the end of the term he wrote:

John came home this morning, because there was a case of German measles in his term at Dartmouth. He is taller than ever and more God-like. Absolutely happy as a bird, full of spirits, strong, well and valiant. He is really a wonderful boy. I am quite certain that he has done superlatively well at the R.N.C. His whole soul is in the job, but there is not one atom of 'side' in him. I think he must be as nearly perfect as God can make a man, for he has all the virtues, and with no vices is as wonderful as it is possible for anyone ever to be. I do so love him and have had a feeling of being with something inexpressibly perfect all the afternoon. There never was such a creature, and he is only thirteen!

Chapter VI

OXFORD: UNIVERSITY LIFE

1923-1924

'I do love just living.'

THE TWO brothers went to Switzerland together for their Christmas holidays, and Antony wrote us many long and entertaining letters from Mürren, where he enjoyed himself to the utmost. His ski-ing achievements this season were remarkable. Hitherto, though he had enjoyed ski-ing as a pastime, and had done many delightful expeditions with me, he had not taken up downhill racing seriously, and had not made any particular mark in the ski-ing world. When he arrived at Mürren this December, he had not even completed a third class test, though he had passed the first part of it as a child. He found himself with a group of runners of the very first rank, yet much to everyone's surprise he won the Roberts of Kandahar Cup, and competed creditably in the race for the British Ski Championship. In this season, therefore, he passed at one bound into the class of international runners. He was not able to devote sufficient time in later years to reach the front rank, yet when I returned from India in 1927 he had become so great an expert that I was not able to keep pace with him, and my dream of a long holiday in which we should do all our favourite expeditions together was never realized. Antony had become a racer, and I could never again get him to show any interest in mere expeditions.

The following letters tell the story of his principal achievements.

To his mother:

The Kandahar race is to-morrow, and I went over the course this afternoon. It is down the Schiltgrat, but on the north side, and finishes in the same place as the last year that I ran in it. I don't think I have got a chance, as there are several awfully good runners in for it, but it will be great fun, I expect. The weather is cruel and monstrous. It does nothing but snow all day long. We've got from 6 to 10 ft. of snow about.

The race is described in his next letter to me:

Kulm Hotel, Adelboden.
Thursday, January 10th, 1924.

Darling Father,

Does not the address cause you some astonishment? No, I haven't been chucked out of Mürren! And if I had I wouldn't be here. The story is a long one but here it is, *en projectile de noisette* (nutshell!)

Yesterday I won the Kandahar at Mürren, and being a bloody fool with a much swollen head and too much ego in my cosmos I have been prevailed upon to come here and go in for the British Ski Championship. We are feeling a little happier to-night with the arrival of some of the Mürren people, including D'Egville, who is such supreme fun. Our contingent consists of Angus, Ford, Johannides, Dowding, Arnold, D'Egville and another R.A.F. man called Robinson. We had a foul journey in a lorry from Frutigen, packed with Germans, French, Swiss, two Poles and a Czech! . . .

To-morrow is the Slalom race, and the day after the Championship race. There are no trains and we have to climb about 3,500-4,000 ft. and race down, which is unpleasant and almost intolerable. Also there are many good runners to compete with, and I wish I had stayed at Mürren, but I always was damned conceited! We have also spent the evening pouring money into a 'Loyal' machine, shaking it, turning it upside down, kicking it and not getting much forrarder at all, at all. But I will go backwards, (as when climbing a steep gradient on skis) and tell you about the Kandahar.

The course started at the top of the Schiltgrat and ran down the whole length of the ridge at the top. Then dropped over the cornice at the end facing the Jungfrau and turned left-handed over a neck called Parson's Shoulder. From there it ran straight down to the bottom of the Blumenthal and along the valley to the wood by the topmost of the two bridges which cross that little stream, through the wood, and finished at the same place as last time I ran in it.

There were some quite good runners in for it. Angus was favourite, a very strong man and strong runner, with a lot of dash, who got his 1st class last year. Ford, who is only 17 and is the ward of one 'Boulton', who says he was in Room 40 at the Admiralty with you, is also a very good 2nd class runner. Arnold said he thought I should be 3rd, and like a fool gave me 10 to 1 in francs the night before! There were several other good steady runners, and one or two people from Cambridge who ran in the Inter-Varsity race and didn't mind running straight. But ickle Antony beat' em. The snow was powder, but very deep—up to one's knees, very fast in tracks, but otherwise nice easy though heavy running.

We went over the course the day before, and it seemed to me that the chap who got down into the Blumenthal first had got the race. The running along the valley was just the fast pace one likes to go, ski-ing ordinarily but not racing speed, and I didn't think anyone would catch anyone else after that. But it turned out otherwise. I ironed black and white wax well into my skis just before luncheon, and we started up at 1.30 from the Allmundhubel. At the top of the Schiltgrat we had to make tracks, so that the deep snow should not hinder the people on the wings. But I drew No. 7, and rather luckily got in the middle on the fastest track of all. I rubbed more white wax on at the top, and got well away on a very fast pair of skis (I haven't been able even to walk on the flat with them since!) I was about 20 yds. ahead by the time we got to the cornice, but I took God's own crash coming into the soft snow after the tracks. However, I was first over the edge. But I fell at the bottom of the first steep slope, and two people passed me. Then I took the steep side down to the Blumenthal straight, and took one purler in the middle (doing a telemark—my skis got crossed and I ran 50 yds. with the left foot on the right side of the right and came over at last!) That undid the buckle of one ski, and doing a Christie at the bottom of the valley my ski came off and I fell again. While I was clipping it up Ford passed me and I swore like hell, because according to my reckoning one wouldn't catch anyone up after that point. But Arnold had had a wide path trodden out by running down four abreast, so as to make passing possible, and for the second time the wax told. I caught Ford in about 10 yds. going 3 times the pace, and came down the valley faster than I have ever run in my life before. I was dead beat with falling, and the path was so bumpy that I was in the air most of the time; but by the grace of God and an effective crouch I didn't fall. I got through the wood and across the path, where all the spectators were. I heard John and Nanny yelling, and then Mrs. Lunn yelled, 'Well done, Antony!' I took one look at her and just fell down from fatigue. I didn't feel I could go an inch further, but someone yelled 'Ford's just behind you', so I got up and went on, only to fall down again at once. Then I saw the flags and ran through them, collapsing completely at the end in a heap. My time was 5 min. 20 sec. and I won by just over a minute from Ford, who I think never got over the pace I passed him out on the path.

It was such fun, and quite a good standard year to win the race. It just shows how waxing pays, because it got me right away at the start and enabled me to catch up Ford in a flash when we both had to run the same gradient. But, my God, I did come a pace down that valley! I have never been so scared! Angus was only 5th, and got stuck by the crowd at the top—drawing a bad place and not having skis as fast as mine. I don't think anyone ever has had such fast skis in the world before. By God, they did slide and I felt quite the little hero—so much so that when Arnold suggested coming over here for the Championship I said I'd have a shot at it. I might stand a chance if (*a*) I can stand up a bit more than I did in the Kandahar and (*b*) I can stand the strain of the course, which is twice as long!

Anyway the Slalom will be interesting. I must go to bed now as it is late. . . .

I am so happy and entirely absorbed in ski-ing which I simply adore and can do much faster and straighter than I used to. The crouch with knees bent and one ski in front of the other is the ideal position for running fast or over blind country, I'm sure. Arnold is so nice to me and sends his love to you, or rather asks to be remembered, or whatever people do! . . .

Goodnight,
Your loving son,
ANTONY.

The British Ski Championship race is described in Antony's letter to his mother:

THE PALACE HOTEL DES ALPES, MÜRREN,
January 7th.

Darling,

Mother—(You see I'm rather silly or I shouldn't have written it like that). It's absurd trying to write letters in Switzerland. The weather has changed—the sun is so hot that we ski in our shirts and just scream with happiness all day long. I have never enjoyed a holiday so much. Ski-ing is just too divine for words, and there are some very nice and very good ski-ers here to do it with, all of which is divine. I got back yesterday after the British Ski Championship. I was second in the Slalom and third in the race. I should have done much better in the latter, but it was such a lovely day, and such a lovely run, that I couldn't race, but just came down quite quietly singing! So, of course, I couldn't really win it, because I was never reckless or out of control.

I did the best time in the hard snow Slalom, but unfortunately fell over one turn for which the penalty was 10 sec.

I made an awful mess of my telemarks in the afternoon—
got my feet crossed, missed some flags and had to climb back.
But I got a second on the day. It was like coming home getting back to Mürren. There are some awfully nice people
here and I adore this place. Wild horses will never take me
anywhere else again. . . .
    I can't write. I am too happy. Life is divine. Sun and ski-
ing, it's all too perfect, but there's only a week to go now.
Oh, how I have loved it. . . .
    Well, darling, I love your letters and will write to you
more when I get back to Oxford on seriouser things. But for
the moment think of us both laughing, singing and ski-ing
in the sun. Six years old and wild with joy. . . . Oh, but life
is good!

    Visitors to Mürren to-day are familiar with a field called
'Martha's Meadow', at the end of the course of the Kandahar Race described above. How this field came by its name
is told in a letter Antony wrote to his mother after his return
to Oxford:

                    MAGDALEN COLLEGE OXFORD.
    . . . Do you ever see the 'Daily Mirror'? There is a
wonderful picture of me in it to-day (January 23rd) dressed
as a girl on skis. I can't remember whether I ever told you
about that, but I have an idea that I didn't. It was so funny.
There is a ladies' race at Mürren for a cup given by Lady
Denman, and I thought it would be such fun to dress up
and enter as the girl from St. Moritz *très chic pour le ski*,
so I entered my name on the list as Martha Mainwaring,
and asked Arnold if he minded. He said No, but eventually,
on the evening before the race, seeing a nasty glint in my
eye, said I'd better not! So I got up very late the next morning and met Mrs. Arnold just leaving the hotel. She said
'oh, Antony, I thought you'd gone back ages ago with the
other competitors'. I said Arnold said I wasn't to, but she
said that was rot and that he was expecting me to and
thought it was going to be the most marvellous rag. I hadn't
got anything ready at all then, but they dressed me up any-

how in a skirt and jumper and scarf. The only hair we could
get was a beard, which I put over one ear, and the hat over
the other! I looked the most poisonous sight, but it was
snowing so no one could see very well! I hid behind a rock
half-way down the course, and, after the first two had passed
me, dashed out and pursued them and passed them. They
were puzzled to death, wondering who this strange lady was,
though with true female eyes they knew they hadn't seen
that jumper at the start! All the anxious mothers waiting
for their daughters at the finish were awfully fussed too
when this scarecrow arrived first. It was quite amusing, but
unfortunately the lady who was first when I passed them
ended up second and said I'd put her off, which was quite
idiotic, as I passed her 20 yds. away and didn't run on the
course at all (it was much too steep and frightening!) but she
made the hell of a fuss all day, so I thought the least I could
do was to apologise, which I did. I don't suppose I shall ever
be forgiven! . . .

In a long letter to me which came by the same mail, he
expressed the feelings which all sportsmen feel on returning
to work after a perfect holiday:

OXFORD, January 20th, 1924.

Darling Father,
    It is pretty bloody being back here again, after such
a marvellous holiday. I didn't know it was possible to be so
happy as I have been in Switzerland this Christmas, and of
course it makes the coming back here feel so unnatural and
beastly.

I have done my glacier trip at last and was extremely disappointed in the ski-ing, though the party was great fun.
We went with Fritz Fuchs, the man who took you up, and
was very anxious to be remembered to you—he is such a
sweet man and made us roar with laughter all the time. A
man called White from Wengen was responsible for the
party, which consisted of Mac (the great Mackintosh, who I
must have written to you about. He's far the nicest chap in
the world and miles the best skier) John Carleton—an

American who is up at Magdalen—the second nicest chap
and the second best skier—myself and Sandy Irvine,* who
rowed for Oxford last year and is going on the next Everest
expedition—he was out at Mürren to learn about snow and
ski-ing and do a little climbing if possible. We went up to
the Joch, down to the Concordia, and then climbed up to the
right to the Egon von Steiger hut. We were all terrified of
falling through into a crevasse or something, and roared
with laughter all the time. It's an awful sweat up to the hut
—but you've done it, haven't you?—and we found it 10°
below zero when we got in. However, we eventually managed to thaw the damned place a bit and had a wonderful
supper there. Fritz had quietly made away with half our
brandy on the way up. Mac made some wonderful cheese
soup which we devoured, and it started to snow. We had to
catch the 3.15 at Goppenstein next day, so as to get back to
England.

We were going to get up at 3 a.m. and climb the Ebnefluh
next morning, but thank God it was snowing and blowing
a blizzard, so we were allowed to sleep until about 7.30. We
ate a huge breakfast and tidied up the hut, and eventually
got started down about 9.5. The weather was clearing up,
and though it was bitter when we started the sun came out
about 11. We ran down to the first village (Plätte or Blätter,
or something—we called it Blotto) in 2 hrs. and found a
marvellous pub there. The village gossip refused to believe
us, and said the best time ever done was by him 2½, and we
couldn't have done it in 2 hrs. But Fritz said he was a bloody
bad skier, and he must have been, because we came quite
slowly. Before I go on, I will give you my views on glacier
ski-ing. In the first place, the snow is probably bad because
it is either crusty from the sun or wind-swept, and even if
it's powder it's very slow, because it's so cold. With us it was
a bit of everything, but mostly wind-swept crusty stuff,
which we didn't go wild about. Fritz said it might have been
much worse. In the second place you don't know where you
are, or what you may fall into. You've got to follow the

*He and Mallory were both killed on Mount Everest a year later.

guide and not deviate from his line, or you may hit a 60 ft.
drop, which is an infernal bore. You can't just run down
doing telemarks, because you catch the guide up at once,
even if you wait until he's out of sight before starting. So
that I feel there is no dash about glacier running—it's all
kick turns and 'daren't fall down' sort of running. We all
agreed when we got to the bottom that we'd much rather do
Tschuggen, and that is the opinion of at least two of the best
ski-runners in Switzerland.

Well, when we got to the first little mountain village, we
found the pub very quickly and all got completely tight for
2 frs. on *vin du pays* and a kind of home-brewed brandy. We
entertained the village, and sang songs to them for about an
hour—in fact had a real good orgy, and then went on and
tried to ski. It's the funniest feeling in the world trying to
ski when you're blind. The snow comes up and hits you in
the face! Old Fritz went off first, waving one ski round his
head, and sitting down every few yards. One had no idea of
the contours or the bumps or anything, and it felt too queer
for words. I got down to Goppenstein at about 1.30. Mac
and John Carleton at 1, Fritz about 1.15 and the other two
at about 2.0 or 1.45.

The whole run is supposed to take 7 hrs. at least, that's
what is generally allowed, and we did it in 3½ hrs. Fritz said
he'd never done it so fast before, and he was sweating like an
old hog when he arrived! We could have done it twice as
quick if we'd hurried on the glacier and been sober down the
path. Have you done that run? I think it's a rotten one, but
the whole expedition was enormous fun. We got to Spiez
about 4, and had baths and tea, and found our boxes and
changed, and then caught the 9.35 back to England with
heavy hearts and a feeling that we shouldn't do it again for
a year. . . .

I have never enjoyed anything so much as Switzerland
this year. Did I tell you that I went over the big jump? I am
going to take up jumping next year. I can only count the
days until next Xmas. How I wish you had been out there
too! It is all 50 times as attractive as it used to be.

Having just come back from Switzerland and being consequently in the mood for it, I am now going to burst some more of my introspective complaints upon you. In a letter which you wrote to me once, but which I can't find because I haven't looked for it (I don't believe in looking for things you can't find, especially when they may be in one of three houses) you said that the object of life was the pursuit of happiness, and that one must learn to discriminate between pleasure and happiness. Now I'm going to disagree with you and whine for a bit. You may say, like an American said to me at Spiez, when I said the beer was nasty, 'Quit your crabbin', Tony', but you'd much better see how absolutely right I am.

If you are not miserable or unhappy or discontented or fussed or worried, then you are happy. You are supremely happy when you are drunk. You may argue that it isn't real happiness in its true ethical sense, in which case I can only say that if my whole life I was to be as happy as I am when I'm blind, I'd have nothing to complain about. Is there, on the other hand, some duty which one has to fulfil in one's life, and by duty I mean something unpleasant? Am I here for a purpose, or can I just enjoy myself? If I'm here for a purpose, what the hell is it, and how do I set about it? But if not, then why, when the only thing that I want to be doing is ski-ing, am I sitting in my room at Oxford writing to you? By being at Oxford when I might be in Switzerland, am I fulfilling the job which God has given me to do?

Why should I go into the city when I leave Oxford, if I'd rather go and ski? Why should I work if I'd rather do something else? It surely isn't God's work I'm doing, selling shares on the Stock Exchange. But your answer would be twofold. Firstly, you'd say a man is only happy when he's working; 'tis work that fills a man's life and gives him interests. Secondly, you'd say you've got to work or starve. Well, work may make *you* happy—it does, I know. But it damned well doesn't take me that way! When I am no longer happy without work, then I will go and work. But why should I go into the city or read history at Oxford, when

I want to be ski-ing in Switzerland or travelling round Europe? Can't a man morally do what he likes? The cash argument is a much better one, I admit. But you've worked like a black for years and you're not half as well off as I am. I know you've worked so that I can be well off, and you'll say that that is exactly what real happiness is—the joy of giving. But I'm afraid I don't really believe that. I'd much rather have my £600 a year than give it to anyone else. In any case I don't see the point of making money. People go on saying that it is not the most important thing in the world, and I am almost beginning to believe them! The rich are all broke. If Labour comes in, what's the good of having money? Nobody's got any money, and if they have someone else gets hold of it, and when all's said and done, what do you do with it when you have got it?—only get rid of it. I don't see that money is a thing to concentrate on at all, and I've no intention of fussing about it. If you do fuss, you fuss to death. It's much better just to live, and trust to the money to turn up somewhere. You can always work if the alternative is starvation.

What I really feel is that, if on a pair of skis in Switzerland I forget everything except the joy of living, and the moment I get back here I sit down and write a long morbid letter on the object of life, well, why in God's name not stay on skis? Perhaps if I stayed on skis long enough I might begin to get morbid and think about the evils of the world, then I'd come back here and forget them all. But what, if any, is the point of tearing oneself away from a situation in which one's only thought is how wonderful it is to live? I don't believe anyone has ever tried to live on this theory. At least if they have, everyone has always said, 'Oh, he's a rotter, he doesn't work'. Well, I think that's just rot. For God's sake let's be happy, and the thing that makes me happy is ski-ing. So I am going to spend the rest of my life ski-ing. There's an ultimatum. I won't work till I want to.

I've never wanted to yet, and I've always been told, 'You ought to take a real interest in your work in another year or two'. I don't believe it. Call me a rotter if you like; work is not in any way a thing which will ever go hand in hand with your son. When I leave Oxford I'm going on the ran-tan, so you'd better cut me off with a shilling right now, and let me try my system! But I'll get a first for your sake first before I go down.

Well, what do you think about it?

Your loving son,

A.

Antony found it impossible to settle down at Oxford for some time. His letters continued to dwell on the joys of his recent holiday and the boredom of his University life. He wrote to me on February 5th:

Darling Father,

Although I have been back from Switzerland for ages, it is only just beginning to dawn on me that ski-ing last holidays was different from anything it has ever been before. It is all so wonderful that I must try and explain what I mean.

The whole thing can best be explained like this. We always used to look at Arnold or Caulfield as the goal of a skier's ambition. We were excited to go out running with them. We wondered how they did their turns, etc., etc. They were our idols, roughly speaking. Now my idols are Mackintosh and John Carleton, both at Oxford. Mac is 20 and Arnold is about 35 (?) You see what a difference it makes to one's whole outlook. . . . Instead of rejoicing to go through Caulfield's wood with Arnold in a quarter of an hour one afternoon, and come out tingling with pride and satisfaction (like an old man after his 3rd glass of port) we now run from the top of Tschuggen glade to the bottom of the valley in 4 min. and arrive breathless and exhausted, but with one's eyes flashing and one's heart too full to speak. Instead of watching the Swiss jump 30 metres, and thinking them Gods, you try and jump 35 yourself! The Swiss are brought down to your own level, and such things as lifted stems on the nursery slopes and 3rd class tests become incredibly inane. John Carleton can jump 49 metres, and run as fast as

M

any Englishman in Switzerland, but he had never done a lifted stem till this year, when Arnold showed him how; but there's not a first-class English runner who wouldn't look a novice beside him!

Mac was so furious at being beaten by a 'Swiss guide' in the ski race that he drank 4 glasses of grog for tea! Instead of starting off for the Scheidegg with a rücksack and spare clothing, and regarding it as a day's expedition, this sort of thing happens:

Up to Wengenalp by the first train, back to Wengen, back to the Scheidegg, down to Grindelwald, up to Alpiglen, back to Grindelwald, and then race the train to Zweilutschinen— that's an ordinary day! . . . Mac and John's best day consisted in climbing from the Water Station to the top of the Lauberhorn, running from there to the Scheidegg in 2 min. exactly, down through the wood all the way to Grindelwald. Then they climbed back from G. over the Scheidegg, and ski-ed down to Wengen in the dark. You see, there's a new spirit altogether which makes it all wonderful. Instead of plugging seriously along with earnest old men loaded with rücksacks and hats and coats and skis and luncheon and tea, etc., you just rush off suddenly with a friend and a pair of skis, and go the whole day, just roaring with laughter, and like hell all the way—arrive at your destination, find you've got no money, so race the train home and beat it! It's all so new and so wonderful that you must understand I feel excited about it. It's the Caulfield style as opposed to the Lunn, but it's developed to such a degree as would make Caulfield blush, and it's all just done for the sheer joy of the thing. Nothing that has been done on skis is too difficult; it's all worth trying, and you can do most of it. You don't gaze in wonder at the Swiss and Norwegians, you imitate them.

Well, I've tried to show you the change—as much for my own satisfaction, for I have only just understood it, as for yours—but I think the whole situation is best described when I say the best skier in Switzerland is now an attractive and reckless young man of 20 instead of a reliable and cautious old one of 35 or so. . . . And I must say you feel inclined to laugh at the Test theory a bit when you see Dowding—a first-class runner, and Mac who hasn't passed his 3rd.

By Gosh, you'd love Mac, Daddy, he'd make you roar with laughter, and simply thrill you to watch him ski. You'll meet him one day. I think I shall very likely make a great friend of him, because he is one of the nicest and most interesting people I have ever met. He's the finest athlete I've ever known. Plays rugger for Scotland, runs for the Varsity, a good cricketer, plays tennis wonderfully, can do anything on skates or skis, very clever with amusing theories, can speak French and German and Swiss like a native, lives in Paris, completely mad, and never does a stroke of work. It's my idea of a perfect character—high moral standard too, at least I mean what I think just right.

I wonder if you remember his father. He used to be a very fine skater at Wengen when I was tiny—and was killed in the war.

All this is a very peculiar letter, not really calculated to amuse you, but huge fun to write. I am very likely going to Norway for a fortnight with Mac next vac just for the skiing, and we think we're going to shoot wolves, but that is as it may be!! . . .

Your loving son,

A.

As in the previous year, boxing was his chief resource. Though the training was irksome, it helped him to keep fit, and doing something at which he was really good kept him on good terms with himself.

To his mother:

MAGDALEN COLLEGE, OXFORD,
February 6th.

Darling,

. . . I am rather fussed what with one thing and another, and life seems to stretch rather gloomily into the future. I don't think I am sufficiently keen about anything to make training feel worth while, and I hate the idea of stopping doing things I like so as to be able to box better.

But it is the same old story, which I have written about
thousands of times. I was just wondering what I really do
care about at Oxford, and the answer is obviously only people.
They are, of course, the whole point of University life, but
they're so bloody expensive and I feel absolutely broke to
the world just now.

What an awful person I am. I can never get any self-
absorbing interest which will carry me through 8 weeks of
my life anywhere in the world. And I know I'm writing depressing and boring letters. I'm so sorry, but I think I ought
to have been born with God's permission never to stay
longer than a fortnight in the same place—(Switzerland
omitted!!) and a permanent income of £10,000 a year. What
an amusing chap I should be then, and how generous! How I
hate Banks and cheques and allowances and bills, etc.!! I
shall certainly have to live most of my life in Honolulu or a
South Sea island, where the only possible exercise is swimming, the only possible thing to do—sleeping, and the only
possible interest—dreaming. I should be so happy there—
for a fortnight! Isn't it fun just going on talking endless rot
like this? I don't know what to do anyway, either now or
ever, but I have changed my mind about money, and entirely disagree with the cinema-producers who maintain
that some things cannot be bought with money and write
films called 'The bird in the gilded cage', which always ends
up by the hero throwing his cheque-book into the Missis-
sippi or the Ohio or the Potomac, and the heroine, with true
feminine instinct, secretly buying him another. The 'fade
out' is always a little cottage way down in California, with
roses round the door and perfect peace and quiet on all sides.
'A haven of rest when life's battle is done', but you can see
at a glance that it's going to cost them $100,000 a year to run
the place in the style they're used to, especially as the hero
doesn't seem quite such an adept at chopping wood as he
should be for the job. So on the whole I sympathise with the
girl when she got the new cheque-book. She was right.
Well, I feel you've either got to have £10,000 a year as I
have already rather impractically suggested, or else you

have got to behave as if you had £20,000. But then your family gets fussed and father starts selling the plate.

So I don't know what to do (but I wish Father'd sell the plate!!) Isn't it difficult? Meanwhile I continue to refrain from smoking cigarettes, on the ground that I shall be able to hit someone harder in a fortnight's time. I continue to read about how Edward I paid for his soldiers, as compared to his son Edward II, and in comparison with his grandson Edward III, in order to bore some unfortunate don with my views upon this particularly uninteresting subject in two years' time. Then occasionally I spend 10/- giving someone dinner, and go to a cinema for the evening to see all the things I have already described. This I may say signifies the height of a day's happiness at Oxford. I can then go to bed happy, feeling much more interested in Lilian Gish and her Californian cottage than any of the blasted Edwards' damned soldiers, or whether my stomach muscles are as strong as they should be and my weight going down nicely. No wonder people get drunk at Oxford! It *is* a silly life! But it's just as silly sitting in the City all day and wondering whether rubber is going up or down, as it is writing an essay about what might have happened if William the Conqueror had conquered Africa by mistake for England. And I don't see that it's much better saying in the House of Commons every day that you would like to know whether it is proposed to build another Dreadnought. I'm damned if I can see what the point of living is, unless it's to be happy, and I entirely disagree with anyone who says that happiness is not pleasure. But this is my favourite ground of dispute and I won't enlarge on it now. I know that whatever better and older and wiser people tell me I am damned well not going to waste my life doing what I don't like and don't believe in, simply because they say it's what I ought to do and point to its many advantages. Here's a whole whacking great world hundreds of thousands of miles round, which there is conceivably some object in living in. That object is not—called 7.30; breakfast 8.30; office 9.30; luncheon 1.30; leave the office 5.30; Club till 7.30; dinner 8.30; bed 12.30; called 7.30;

breakfast 8.30, etc. But that appears to be the privilege
which man has acquired by growing as to the forehead instead of the jaw. I'd rather stick to the jaw and be a monkey.
But then all young men feel like I do at this age! Oh, yes, I
shall get over it, that makes it all the bloody sillier, because
I am so right.

Bless you, darling and forgive this blasphemous letter.
But don't you think I'm right really?

> Your loving son,
> ANTONY.

To the same:

> MAGDALEN COLLEGE, OXFORD,
> *March 3rd.*

Darling,

Thank you so much for a wonderful letter which I
have just received. You urge me to go and see John at Dartmouth, and as it happens I have just this moment returned
here from two nights with the Meades. The place struck me
very differently than it did you. It is, of course, entirely
naval and I have always very mixed sentiments about a
collection of sailors. They are so concentrated on modesty,
ignorance and manhood that they are almost unnatural.
They can't believe that a sailor ought to know the most
elementary academical facts—they seem to live continually
in fear of a Cleopatra descending upon them and making
them 'soft', and they are so modest that they can scarcely
speak, especially in the presence of a senior officer. It is no
doubt a very fine training, and manliness and modesty very
fine qualities, and the sailors with character and charm are
really wonderful people. But one doesn't quite know where
one is with people who are proud of the fact that they never
heard of William the Conqueror, who refer to the floor as
the 'deck', and whose carriage drive is ornamented with a
notice demanding that cars shall not exceed 10 knots!! I suppose they are very wonderful, these sailors, but I always feel
that they carry things a little too far, and they certainly all
hold exactly the same views about everything (except perhaps nautical technicalities, which it is their business to hold

views about). You always know what a sailor will say if you mention Winston, or *vers libre*, or individuality, or Nelson, or the Battle of Jutland, and you're generally right. Well, I'm sure that the particular part of Henry Ford's factory responsible for the manufacture of carburetters could learn a great deal by watching the process by which sailors are manufactured at Dartmouth.

As a magnificent factory for the yearly production of so many sailors, my admiration for the R.N.C. is unlimited, but otherwise I think it is narrower even than Eton, and yet terribly convincing withal. As a school I consider it beneath contempt. It appears to me to have everything that was worst about the system of schools in the last century, with a few of the most idiotic ideas of a 'modern education' attached. It is an incredibly hard life for a boy of 14, but an almost absurdly healthy one, and it is as narrow and as simple as men who have spent their lives among barnacles, binnacles and compasses, in a continual state of abdominal unrest, can make it. But then every year it turns out the finest specimens of the finest service in the world. Men who are ready to swear throughout their lives that there never lived a man more virtuous than Nelson, that Winston ought to be hanged, and that Robin Hood shot Henry VIII in the New Forest!! Well, that's how I feel about the R.N.C., though I never had the courage to say a word of it while I was there—so the navy does impress me in spite of all this. . . .

Really, what I feel about it all is—put crudely—that I wouldn't be at the R.N.C. for the world. That if I were there I should be mad about it all. That it is very easy to laugh at the mechanical nature of the whole place, but that there is nothing to touch the service—that I agree with a great deal the sailors say about mothers, aunts and nannies, and that even if I didn't I should let them have their own way because they run their show pretty well, and it isn't supposed to be a human one. Leave the Navy as it is, and you can't grumble. You can go on laughing at it, but it will win your battles and never give in. Try and humanise the navy, try and introduce a natural touch and individuality, and you will make it a troupe of girl guides. . . .

The chief event of the end of this term was the Varsity boxing. Antony was selected to box for Oxford against Cambridge, and though he succeeded in winning his fight he broke his thumb. This necessitated a setting under an anaesthetic and keeping it in plaster of Paris for a fortnight. He was therefore obliged to give up his projected trip to Norway, and instead went to Paris for a few days at the beginning of the vacation.

In one of my letters at this time I returned to the well-worn theme which occupied most of our correspondence this year:

Your letters (I wrote) are delightful and entertaining and I adore them, but I wish I could help you to get a little more solid satisfaction out of life. You want something to get your teeth into—Let us go back to our favourite theme about happiness and pleasure. You still think they are the same—that is only because you have never yet tried a life of uninterrupted pleasure. If you had you would find it is like a diet of sweets, which becomes nauseating in time. Happiness is a state of enjoyment, but one cannot be really happy unless one is enjoying the realities as well as the frivolities of life. You don't like being hit on the nose or punched in the jaw, but you enjoy boxing which includes these experiences; you don't like being kicked on the shins or trampled in a scrum, yet you enjoy football which involves them. So one does not like the labours nor the knocks of life, but one cannot enjoy a life that is without them. Oxford does not seem to be giving you enough of either at present, and you are right in objecting to being bored. That is the one unforgivable mistake of life—to let it be boring. A bored man can be neither happy nor well nor kind. You write as if you were bored stiff, but I doubt if you are really as bored as you make out, as I gather that you are both well and happy. But I think you could be happier still if you could come up against some-

thing tough—something to stretch you—something to call
out all your reserves of both mind and body. Oxford seems
to be boring because the mental and the physical exercise
are separated. You box at one moment, and read history at
another. The two are separated and are therefore in the
nature of 5 finger exercises on the piano. What you want to
complete your happiness is to be allowed 'to play your piece'
as Davina would say—that is to say, a job which requires
both mind and body and stretches them both!!

Antony replied on March 24th:

I so agree with you that what I want is to get my
teeth into something, but it is very hard to make 'a piece' out
of boxing and history. I feel it wouldn't be harmony. I had
what I call a conscientious term last term. I worked hard,
boxed hard, trained hard and spent very little. Also I broke
my thumb, which was a bore and still is a bore (it's in a
splint). But directly the Varsity boxing was over I let myself
go, and have been 'going' hard ever since. And herein lies
the sad truth. That I have enjoyed the last fortnight in
which I have been celebrating the end of the 'conscientious
bit' much more than any of the hard work and clean living.
Now they always say that what makes a man happy is a
healthy, regular, energetic life with plenty of work and lots
of friends and a packet of laughter. That's what sounds so
lovely. That's what makes you as happy in a way as you can
be. Exercise, health and work. Now I am happiest when I'm
up all night—in bed most of the day and generally dissipated. I admit that I want exercise too, but with this thumb
I can't get any. But I never seem to want work, though
again I am beginning to get a bit tired of dissipation, but a
day's rest will put me as eager as ever for it! I am quite sure
that it would do me a world of good really to come up
against something, but what? I do so crave for happiness, and
to me that *does* mean pleasure.

I believe that the real point is this. At present I am living
entirely selfishly. I love you enough to do just a little work
occasionally, but otherwise I have nothing to live for except

myself. If I was to fall in love or to get married, or suddenly to be visited by some higher motive which would cause me to be ambitious for someone else's sake—it would be different. I don't want money except to spend myself, and so I've got no desire to work for it. I don't want position because it doesn't interest me—all that I want is just pleasure—because that does interest me. This is because all my affection is concentrated solely on myself, in fact I am quite intolerably spoilt. Now this is not likely to be a permanent situation, because I shall one day fall in love. Then I may be a better man. Otherwise, I'm not much good.

Well, I went to Paris for two nights the other day with another chap and we had such fun. It's a marvellous place at night, though I didn't see much of it by day. What impressed me most was that walking home at 10.45 a.m. in evening clothes with no hat or coat, looking very dishevelled, no one even turned to look! I liked Montmartre enormously! In fact I am quite wild about Paris and shall never be able to enjoy myself in London again. I long to go there again and I long to see the Quartier Latin and also a little of Paris proper by the more sober light of day. Also there are about 4 night clubs which we didn't have time to go to!!!

Now I've got to be in London for a week getting my thumb massaged—then Taplow and then Knebs, where I intend to be healthy and to work a little and take some exercise. I can only think of Paris.

His mother wrote in reply:

Some day you will want to be married, because you will love very deeply. Then you will feel that all you have done in life, and all that you are, is your offering to your wife. This will never seem quite enough. But be sure and let it be your best. Don't lay up for yourself too many regrets when that sublime moment comes to you.

I always knew you were ambitious without being competitive—keen to win, but too bored by competing to practise enough! I am sorry for you, because it must produce so many quarrels with yourself. When you say you are keen about nothing, and see no reason for living except pleasure, I just realize how sleepy you must be as you write! What is the use of pearls without a string? You cannot wear them.

You who love life and can turn stones to laughter, must needs get hold of life, and shape it finely. Where is the use, or the honour, or the fun, or the satisfaction, of letting life get hold of you? God has given you so much, darling son, do not spill his gifts by the way and render them valueless.

Antony spent the vacation at Knebworth, and returned to Oxford at the end of April. His letters during the vacation were all very happy.

To his mother:

KNEBWORTH, *April* 10*th*, 1924.

Darlingest,

Here I am in the nursery at Knebworth writing to you. And such a Knebworth too! Bathed in the most glorious sunshine we have seen for years and looking beyond words lovely—as it does in June, although there are no flowers. I think of you all so much and do so wish you were all here. This place has the call of home so much more strongly than even I had ever imagined. Everything else is forgotten but that wonderful feeling of home. Sad one must feel, of course, everything is so different, and the house is shorn of all its treasures. There are little things missing everywhere, and it all looks bare and unlived in, and even decaying. . . . Every now and then one comes up against a very old friend. A picture that one has brushed one's teeth in front of for centuries! A corner that one has never failed to knock one's head against, a smell that has always haunted one, even one's dreams, and a broken pot that one remembers breaking when it was the size of a giant. How can one help feeling sad? But not miserable. There is no feeling of unhappiness— the very atmosphere of home destroys that—the very air of Knebworth is nectar, the sound of the garden in the sun (do you know it?) goes to one's head like wine. It is a smile of sadness, not tears, that haunts me. A kind of inexpressible joy just tempered with something that makes it feel alloyed.

Here is the nursery—the same as ever with familiar furniture—the Easter eggs over the dresser—the white hen on the cupboard, the cuckoo clock not going—the little blue tables and chairs, but where are all the little china ornaments from Eastbourne, Brighton, Birchington, Westgate, etc., etc? Where is the picture of Peter and Wendy flying over the midnight village? Where is the toy-box? But above all where is the smell of damp clothes drying on the fender? It's funny what absurd little things one misses. I have been more fussed because the bootjack was not in the corner of Daddy's bedroom than anything, and John's only comment has been that the towel-horse in the bathroom has grown a very great deal smaller! But it is all wonderful, and waiting for you with a longing and a desire that makes Penelope like a puppy waiting for its bone! (poor Ulysses! how upset he'd be). . . .

Knebs has twice the appeal and four times the attraction that the Manor has, only I can do nothing but sit in it and dream and laugh, when I remember incidents connected with that cupboard, or this door, or that corner, or something else. It is like a fairy-tale—a glimpse out of the past— but such a wonderful past that it makes me happy. The Manor House may one day be a home, but at present Knebworth, and Knebworth alone, has that intoxicating influence on me. I think my heart will break with bliss when I see the last stranger go, and we are all once more united and living here. But even then there will be somebody or something missing, which one will mind just a tinge. That I suppose is the glory of living. It is always new, it always changes, and one has always something to look back at and to sigh or rejoice over, and then one goes on again. . . .

I have seen quite a lot of Iain lately; he has been in London in a house in Berkeley St., and I have also had amusing talks with Dinah, whom I love. . . . Iain is still the only man in the world, and I think always will be. . . . It would be marvellous if he would come out to India with me. I feel I should adore the camps and the wild life, but perhaps not Calcutta.

It does one such a lot of good to sow wild oats for a few weeks, as I have been doing. You emerge with such much healthier thoughts and ideas and a longing for country and exercise and *real* things, which quite carries one away. Contrast is everything in life, isn't it? Work-time and holidays, dissipation and health, sunshine and rain. All necessary to help the other. I feel so happy now here at Knebs after a wild bit in London and Paris, and I never want to move again, which is perfect. Wine, women and song seem to have left me for ever, and I care about the really good things once again. . . . I do love you so and do so adore this place. Lift your glass and drink to the day when we meet again, all of us, in the picture gallery!

Your adoring,

YA.

Most of Antony's letters during the summer term were about parties he had been to and people that he had met. He wrote to his mother on May 6th, describing his delight in *Don Juan*:

I have been, and am still, reading *Don Juan*, for which you may think I am rather young. But Granny has also been reading it and says it's so wonderful that I thought I couldn't be outdone! Also there has been much talk about Byron lately, as it was his centenary.

I don't think I have ever read anything which gave me greater pleasure. As poetry, it is every now and then magnificent, and as a series of love stories it is most alluringly told, but far the best of it is its philosophy and comments on life in general. My word, what a man—it is almost incredible that anyone can be sincerely so cynical, but his wit is quite a thing apart from cynicism, isn't it? I've never read anything which poured ridicule on every convention of life more wholeheartedly, and yet made you feel that life was infinitely worth while—which gives you an idea of infinite happiness and all the wonderful and good gifts which the world has to give, even while it shatters all the ideals from which you thought that happiness emanated. I am simply

adoring it. I love the way he takes you to the height of sentimentality with four or five stanzas of the most beautiful and
sad poetry. Your feelings are being really harrowed by a
tragic and beautiful description of Don Juan leaving his
native land and his loves, and soliloquising on his eternal
adoration and faithfulness—

> '. . . or think of anything excepting these;
> A mind diseased no remedy can physic
> (Here the ship gave a lurch and he grew sea-sick).'

It's really priceless, the fearful crash from the most sublime
of sentiments and the most beautiful poetry to the most
practical and ridiculous of all ailments. And it happens again
and again. Just as you are getting sentimental and silly and
wondering about flowers and sun and beauty, you are suddenly brought—crash!—face to face with someone cleaning
their teeth! or something equally ridiculous.

And then after a magnificent description of a storm, when
the last boat but one (the cutter) is overturned and all in it
lost—

> 'They grieved for those who perished with the cutter
> And also for the biscuit-casks and butter.'

It makes you laugh for hours. They draw lots with Don
Juan's most precious love-letter as to whom they shall eat,
and the lot falls to his tutor! It's a good cynical-making start
for a young man in the world deeply in love, to have to eat
his tutor by decision of his most treasured and sentimental
possession! And yet it's all very merry and happy—

> 'Let us have wine and women, mirth and laughter,
> Sermons and soda water the day after.'

Who but Byron would bring soda water into a poem!! The
whole poem's philosophy seems to be, if unkind, at any rate
delightful. You feel above the world, and you can laugh to
see Byron tear the tenderest of human passions into shreds
by hunger or sea-sickness, or some idiotic but horribly sane-
making process. And then after all, when you think you've
lost everything in the world worth living for, you find it's

not worth dying, and there's something just as good comes
along.

> 'She thought to stab herself, but then she had
> A dagger close at hand which made it awkward.'

All this is old, and even if it was original when Byron thought
it, it is not now, you may say, but all the same it's too well expressed not to make me laugh. And then, God in heaven, in
the midst of all this cynical laughter and ridicule, suddenly:

> 'The isles of Greece, the isles of Greece!
> Where burning Sappho loved and sung,
> Where grew the arts of war and peace,
> Where Delos rose and Phoebus sprung!
> Eternal summer gilds them yet,
> But all, except their sun, is set!

> 'The mountains look on Marathon—
> And Marathon looks on the sea;
> And musing there an hour alone,
> I dream'd that Greece might still be free;
> For standing on the Persians' grave
> I could not deem myself a slave.'

It's too good for any man. But I am writing all this as if you
didn't know it. Forgive me; you see, it's all new to me, and so
I feel that it must be to everyone else too. Anyway, I've not
got much else to write about, and Byron is not a bad theme.
But I'm sorry for quoting all the old things as if I had discovered them. Gosh, but I think *Don Juan's* good to read. . . .

The next event of interest was the celebration of his
twenty-first birthday. As we could not be with him on this
great day, we had to be content with letters:

His mother wrote:

You have always been perfect to me, darling, and I wonder still at all the joy and bliss you have given me since you
first came to be.

> 'I know myself no more, my child,
> Since thou art come to me.'

This is what I copied from a poem of Æ when you were born.

So be glad and happy and strong and loving, my darling son. Go forth into the world of men equipped with those blessings.

I hug you to my heart—and know, like a voice telling me, that God is with you.

My message to him in the same mail was:

My heart is overflowing with tender and loving thoughts of you, and I long to sit up all night and talk to you of all the great changes that this imperceptible transition means. With the exception of Oxford we have shared all the other transitions together. We have passed each milestone as it were hand in hand, and it is cruel that we should be separated now at this most important of them all. But you are a great philosopher, and will know that it is unprofitable to waste time on vain regrets over what cannot be helped. So I must just try and say a few of the things which I should be saying to you if we were together.

In the first place, my heart is full to overflowing with thankfulness and gratitude for the past. At every stage in life hitherto you have been all that I could have wished, and much more than I could have expected—a perfect baby, a perfect child, a perfect boy, and now you are a perfect man. May your manhood throughout life fulfil the promise of these early years. My darling boy, I thank God for having given me such a perfect son, and I pray that I may never fail you as a father.

The next thing I want to say is that this experience of the past has given me complete confidence in you in all things, and I cannot tell you what a relief it is, when I am so far away, to know that I can trust you implicitly to deal with every situation in which you may be placed.

Owing to our absence in India, there were no formal festivities at Knebworth, but Antony entertained his friends to dinner at Oxford and wrote us a full account the next day.

To me he wrote:

I thought that on my 21st birthday I should feel rather a chap, but everyone has written me such beautiful things, and been so extraordinarily sweet, that I feel I am an absolute swine to be so unworthy of them and their trust and respect for me. Darling, thank you so much for your letter —it was a truly wonderful one, but I am really not all the good things you think I am. I'm afraid I'm an awful little rotter really, and I have never yet done anything that was really worth doing, or that was worthy of you and Mother. I'm incredibly selfish, very conceited and absolutely idle. I waste my time, and I spend your money, and do all those things which I ought not to do and nothing that I ought. And then everyone writes and tells me that they have faith in me, and love me, and think me charming. It's rather depressing, but now I'm a man I will try and be a bit better and do something partially to justify my existence. But I do love just living. Thank you ten thousand times for having given me the chance, and for being such a wonderful Father to me, and for writing such angelic things. May I never fail you.

To his mother he wrote:

My throat aches from yawning, and my eyes are heavy with sleep, so if this letter is as unintelligible as the one I wrote to Daddy this morning, I am too sorry. I got up bright and early after my very heavy dinner-party last night feeling so well, but when I started writing to Daddy after breakfast I found I could hardly write at all, so I didn't answer all the hundreds of letters I got yesterday, but went and sat in the sun in my window. I woke up at 2.0 p.m.! And having just had a little luncheon I am trying my hand again. It is a pity that I should be so enfeebled by my 'tipsy' dinner-party, because I have ten thousand things to write about and would like to write you the best letter ever written, but the hand works badly and the brain hardly at all! Since the reason is my dinner, I may as well tell you about that first. I sat between Nico and a divine American

N

boxer called Eddie Eagan. (I have a perfect passion for the
Americans—they are scrumptious people). There were 21
people at a T-shaped table. I had marvellous menus printed
with Lytton coat-of-arms (shield) in the middle, Magdalen
on one side and Eton on the other. Underneath a K, and
May 13th, 1924, and in the corner the initials of the person's
whose it was. Also little pencils, so we could all sign our
names. It went awfully well, but for a dinner-party like that
everyone must be more or less what Granny calls 'tipsy'
about just before pudding. I began to get frightened it was
going to be a frost. But then suddenly something went snap
and all was well. Another delightful American—John Carleton (a skier)—got up amidst yells and roars, told a funny story
about an Englishman in America, talked about hands across
the water, and proposed my health. That started us off and
everyone had to get up and say something. Far the best, of
course, were the Yanks! Eddie began by saying that he
couldn't make a speech, so he'd emulate Dempsey, who
under similar circumstances in England rose to his feet and
said, 'I can't make a speech, but I'll fight anyone in the
room!' This was well received and was followed by a wonderful speech!

We got noisier and noisier, until, when we had at last
drunk the college dry and were about to adjourn, Nico rose
and said that the first speaker of the evening had talked
about hands across the water, and he felt sure that however
deep or wide the water, however short the arms, one thing
was certain—that they would all stretch them out to me!
The first toast had been 'Our host', the last should be 'Antony'. Sweet of him, wasn't it? After that we made a noise
in the college, and then went back to the room (now cleared)
drank more, and danced. Here the thread of my narrative is
no longer visible or coherent, or indeed a thread at all. All
I know is that somehow or other I got into bed after falling
over twice in the effort of undressing at 12.0!

But I have begun at the end of a really marvellous day,
instead of at the beginning. I don't think I have ever enjoyed a day at Oxford more. Marvellous presents, wonderful

letters and nine telegrams, which came all through the day.
I got Daddy's letter at breakfast, and all your glorious parcels
about 11.0. As for the pyjamas being 'a tentative essay', all
I can say is 'Please keep on trying'. Thank you, darling, ten
thousand times for them, I adore them with all the passion
which a man is permitted to lavish on his pyjamas! . . .

Lastly, darling, before I finish—your letter. You are so
wonderful and I do love you so that I can hardly bear to read
the sweet things you all say about me. I feel so so rotten and
unworthy of you. Thank you ten thousand times for your
letter, though I wish I was a better son. It came on Monday
morning, when I was feeling very rotten after two hours'
sleep and a silly but wild expedition to London, and gave me
such an uplift. I felt a great wave of security and love come
over me, it was like an anchor to a tired ship. I greeted it as
Clytemnestra pretended to greet Agamemnon—

> '. . . as watch-dog of a fold,
> As saving stay-rope of a storm-tossed ship,
> As column stout that holds the roof aloft,
> As only child unto a sire bereaved,
> As land beheld, past hope, by crews forlorn,
> As sunshine fair when tempest's wrath is passed,
> As gushing stream to thirsty wayfarer.'

There is no more wonderful feeling in the world than
when you are feeling really rotten and unhappy and
ashamed and nervous, to feel a great strength and confidence
come over you, owing to someone having confidence in you
and loving you. Our love will always be the strongest thing
in the world, and when everything else is gone, when every
brick is fallen and every beam rotten, it will stand as strong
and as straight and as safe as it ever did. With such a force
to help me I can have no fear, no shame, no hesitating. Darling, I thank you with all my heart for the great and many
and good things which you have given me. My life has been
one long daydream of happiness, and you have made it so.
May God bless both you and Daddy and make me able to be
worthy of you both always.

During this summer our correspondence dealt largely with morals and religion, and once more I give the letters on both sides. The subject is opened by Antony, who wrote to me on June 3rd:

I have very little to write to you about this week, but I have been writing about the 'Natural Rights of Man' this evening and so have got into that vile habit of thinking. I think man is naturally good, but I cannot satisfy myself about religion.

To begin with, I cannot bring myself to believe in hell or damnation, or any of those awful pictures painted for one in one's childhood, but seeming to me wholly to lack conviction as one grows older. Now, if I don't believe in hell, where am I? Supposing I am as wicked as I can be in this life—licentious, idle, selfish, deceitful, immoral, what happens to me when I die? It is no good saying I shall by being wicked punish myself, because I have tried and far from being unhappy am blissfully happy. Then as to God, I have believed in God to this extent—The stars (they impress me so that I feel there must be a God) and prayer (which does give me much help when most I need it). I know that proof concerning God is both impossible and ridiculous, and one can only believe if one has faith. But logically faith is only a matter of ignorance, as history goes to show. A savage would have implicit faith in God if suddenly introduced to wireless. It is supernatural and a divine manifestation, and the savage has got something to go on. We have nothing to go on except our faith. Isn't our faith really ignorance? Another thing, of course, is life. Man has not an inkling of the secret of life, but is this only a question of time? Surely. He can explain the stars, and no doubt a psycho-analyst would explain the consolation and elevation of prayer. How can I believe? And yet in a way I do. But I am writing blasphemy. If there is a God, why am I not stopped? But I'm not. It is hard to believe in God when one really thinks. What do you feel about it? Have you just a blind but certain faith and knowledge that there is a God worth serving? If I do what I know to be good

in this world, I've no doubt I should be happy and therein
lies the proof of the existence of God. But if I do what I know
to be wrong always, I fancy I should be very happy too. You
see I am not by any means convinced, and whenever I argue,
or try to, on the subject I am quickly converted to atheism.
And yet always I have just enough faith to prevent my saying, 'I am an atheist, I do not believe'. I can't do it quite, but
I am not convinced. Is what little faith I have really only
ignorance? The arguments for atheism are so strong I can
hardly resist them, and yet I won't fall. I go on vaguely
saying, 'I don't know, but I believe', and in my bones I feel
that it is weakness and really only ignorance. . . .

To this I replied in two successive mails:

> You say 'I cannot bring myself to believe in hell or
damnation or any of those awful pictures painted for one in
one's childhood'. Pray, who painted for you these awful pictures?—certainly not your Father or your Mother. Don't be
silly—we never tried to frighten you into being good, and if
all you have lost at Oxford is a belief in hell and damnation,
you have nothing to complain of. You then go on to say, 'If
I don't believe in hell, where am I?' Why, just where you
always have been, my lad, since you never have believed in
hell or have ever been asked to, so far as I am aware. Yet
for all that, hell is pretty real and quite inevitable. It comes
not from the recollection of the good times you once had,
and which you would have avoided if you could have known
it would be so severely punished—'how sad and mad and
bad it was, but then how it was sweet'. Hell is not the belly-
ache after eating too many sweets—it is the realization that
in ignorance you have injured those you love. It would be
hell to me to realize that in my desire to do you good I had
ignorantly done you an injury. For human beings whose
love is very limited and whose knowledge is less, such a hell
as I have described is rarely experienced and only dimly conceivable. But when in the fulness of time we have attained
unto the love and the knowledge of God, then it must surely
be hell to learn how much mischief we have done without

knowing it. It is in that sense alone that we shall cry to a
God whose mercy is indeed infinite, 'O Lord, we didna ken!'
My advice to you is not to worry yourself because the conventional formulas of religion lose their sanction as you
grow older. . . . Exact from everything you cling to sincerity
and truth. Faith does not, I think, mean asserting what you
have found to be untrue, because someone has told you it is
true. It means rather sticking to something you have found
to be true, although someone has used arguments which
you cannot refute to prove it false.

The argument was continued a week later:

The best definition of faith I can think of is 'belief in
authority'. I may have faith in God, or faith in my friend, or
faith in my country, or faith in the Church, or faith in the
Government, etc., etc., and that means that I accept the
authority of these agencies and accept their word against all
comers. But faith to be strong must, I think, be based upon
experience. It cannot, as you say, be based upon argument,
it is an emotion not a reason, but it must have a foundation
in experience. If I say I have faith in the word of an Englishman, it means that in my experience I have found that
Englishmen speak the truth; it does not mean that no Englishman has ever told a lie, but merely that it is more characteristic of them to speak the truth than to speak falsehood.
Therefore, if a man says, 'I give you my word as an Englishman', my experience enables me to have faith in him even
though my reason may prompt me to disbelieve him. Faith
in God or faith in a future life are, of course, more difficult
matters, because there experience is necessarily more
limited. But here too I retain my faith in that which con-
forms to my experience and I reject that which is in conflict
with it. . . Christ himself said 'God is a Spirit, and they that
worship him must worship him in spirit and in truth'.
What then is a Spirit? Anyhow, not a man on a throne, not
a policeman with eyes all round his head, nor a judge from
whom no secrets can be hid. If you cannot conceive of a
Spirit, then it were better to give up thinking about God

and do without him, for the conception of the Judge on the throne, or the policeman with a big stick, is much more akin to the Devil than the sort of human dragon with a forked tail that is usually depicted.

But if you can conceive of a Spirit, then you must think of it as something which is not subject to time or space, something which can permeate the material world and become incarnate in the human body. I believe, then, that I am God incarnate and you are God incarnate, and that what we have to try and do is to recognize our own divinity and that of others, to interpose to it as few barriers as possible, to subordinate as far as possible the fleshly structure which is called me and you to the Spirit of God which inhabits us both. The difference between Christ and other men is that in His case the human was so completely dominated by and permeated with the divine that the barriers between the two were completely removed. He spoke with the voice of God, He saw with the eyes of God, He was inspired with the love of God, and He therefore exercised the power of God.

If, then, God is a Spirit, animating mankind with the law of love, what is the Devil? Some may tell you that he too is a Spirit—the spirit of evil. To my mind the Devil is a myth, because the words spirit and evil appear to me to be contradictory terms. I cannot conceive of a spiritual evil—I would say that the Devil is the name we have given to all false conceptions of God. The Devil is the god of the ignorant. Evil is not a spiritual force in opposition to good—evil is the misrepresentation, misdirection, perversion of good due to blindness, and ignorance caused by fear. Evil is God seen through the eyes of man—Good is man seen through the eyes of God....

The subject was continued in two further letters. Antony wrote from Gabas on July 19th:

. . . I think your ideas are awfully good and very helpful and really what I feel myself, but first of all you say the only standard of right and wrong is the individual conscience. Well, I feel this, too, really; except that some people have no conscience or very little. I'm sure that I might get to feel quite all right about things which I should now think wicked. For instance, when I was 14 I should have thought it wrong to get drunk—now, though I do think it wrong to be a drunkard, I have no qualms of conscience, no sense of having done wrong, when I get that way. Along the same lines I feel I might get into the way of doing very much worse things, and not feeling that I was doing wrong. I admit that I don't think it is right to get drunk, or that I should ever persuade myself that many of the conventional sins were *right*, but I might think them not wrong, and that negative quality is applicable to most of one's actions. There are few things I do which I feel are *right*; many that are not wrong. All this may be true, but it seems a pity to me that by being really vicious and beastly and killing most of your conscience you should be good. Don't tell me that it's not possible to get that way, because I know you can, and to me the drunken example is a good proof. This has always appeared to me the great difficulty of laying morals solely on the individual.

I replied on August 5th:

. . . You criticize my remark that the only standard of *moral* right or wrong is the conscience of the individual—that what a man does believing it to be right is right, no matter how other people may judge it, and that what a man does believing it to be wrong is wrong, no matter how successfully he may himself defend or excuse it. Your answer is that people's consciences are elastic and are easily lulled to sleep by being continually denied a hearing, and therefore this pliant judge cannot be a reliable arbiter. You think you have a conclusive argument against me by saying that at one time you thought it wrong to get drunk, and that now you don't. This, however, if true, is not really a refutation of my contention, but merely an illustration of it. If you really thought it morally wrong to get drunk when you were 15, and if you really think it not morally wrong to get drunk at 21, then I should say that if you had got drunk at 15 you would have done wrong, and that in getting drunk at 21 you have not done wrong. But, as you yourself admit, that is not the position. At 15 you had no experience, you accepted your standard of right and wrong on the authority of others, and because you had a moral sense you did what those whose opinion you valued told you was right, and you avoided what those same people told you was wrong. Now at 21 the opportunity occurs of testing the truth of what you have been told. In the company of your friends at Oxford you drink more than you have ever allowed yourself to do before, and you reach that state of semi-intoxication that you call 'blind' or 'tight' or 'blotto', etc. At the time the experience is pleasurable, the next morning the after effects are not so agreeable, but still not sufficiently distressing to obliterate the memory of the previous pleasure, and you ask yourself 'Have I done wrong?' You are not conscious of any lasting bad physical consequences, you have not lost the respect of your friends, you are not conscious of any moral delinquency, and so you say my advisers must have been wrong, and my own experience does not convince me that moderate intemperance is a sin. Now, all that this really means is that you have discovered for yourself that occasional drinking to excess is not an affair of morals at all, any more than making a mistake of grammar in a Latin composition, or bowling a wide at cricket. When we were young, many things were called 'naughty' which were not 'naughty' at all, but merely inexpedient, and as we grow up we learn that the 'sins' of the world are not as many or as great as we were led to believe, and ultimately I am convinced that when the secrets of all hearts are revealed and the judgement book is opened, it will be found that much of what we thought was on the debit side has been entered on the credit side of the ledger. You do not yourself argue that drinking to excess is morally right, you do not claim any virtue for it, you only say that you have found it to be not so evil as you once thought, and you argue from that that your conscience has become less scrupulous. I, on the other hand, maintain that it is a definite moral gain that in this matter you should have emancipated yourself from conventional standards and that you are now applying the test of your own conscience. But are you quite sure that your conscience has delivered a final verdict? Here are some considerations which I should like you to put to yourself and to answer them honestly after mature consideration.

You have said yourself in your letter to me that your conscience condemns a drunkard. Are you quite sure that you have sufficient control of yourself to prevent an occasional excess from growing into a habit that will become your master? Remember that habits grow by indulgence, and the day may come when you will look back to your first excess and wish that you had never indulged in it. Don't let a time come when your conscience may condemn you after your will power has been destroyed. Then too, to get 'tight' at a friend's house would be—if not a moral—at least a social offence. London society would condemn what Oxford undergraduate society may condone or even admire, and your conscience would condemn you if you disgraced your family or your friends by a social misdemeanour. Lastly, excessive drinking always impairs physical efficiency. While you are young you have such reserves of physical strength, and the injury caused by an occasional excess is so small, that you may not notice it. Every repetition, however, is an accumulation of the injury, and even if you check the habit before you lose control of yourself, you may impair your physical efficiency beyond repair, and your conscience may one day condemn the injury to your body, though your character may even have been improved by the experience.

To sum up—if your slight excesses at Oxford have merely made you independent of conventional standards and taught you to learn by your own experience what is the limit of wisdom, and the extent to which the pleasure of an hour must be subordinated to the happiness of a lifetime, then that experience will actually have been a moral gain, and your conscience will rightly exonerate you from any moral blame; but if you create a habit which becomes your master, be sure that your conscience will not absolve you from responsibility. . . .

The discussion closed with a letter from Antony written from Porlock on August 28th:

You are really rather a remarkable man. You sit up all night (Tuesday, August 5th) writing me the most wonderful letter on morality and ethics, you say that you won't have time to read it over, and there is not one single mistake in it—not one word written wrong, not one stop forgotten, not one syllable omitted! That's the stuff that makes the Swarajists look small—that's the stuff that sends the awful name of England ringing out into every quarter of the globe —that's the stuff that makes the Bengalee tremble, the Boer curse, the Chinaman lie, and the black African savage eat sand from the hands of the most disreputable, disowned, drunken debauchee that ever fled the night-clubs of Tottenham Court Road and the scandalised gossip of Mayfair society! That's what makes Mr. Kipling talk about the worth of the flag of England, Mr. Chesterton shout about the beer-drinking Anglo-Saxon of Wessex, Sir Henry Newbolt sing of the glorious traditions of the Navy, and Mr. Belloc dance as he breathes-in the thyme-scented air on the Sussex downs! That is a grain of dust off the old original brick that was re-sponsible for the veritable construction of what is commonly termed the British Empire! 'You deliver the goods', as the most inimitable of the great historians of the day—Mr. Wodehouse—might tersely remark!

Well, anyway, I was much impressed by your letter, but shan't answer it word for word, as correspondence on this subject spread over intervals of six weeks is not only be-coming redundant but is very difficult to remember. But one day we will have to have out the pleasure v. happiness argument. I am by no means convinced by your rather idealistic optimism. I still cling feebly to the schoolroom traditions of sin (in theory). I would not for a moment deny that a life spent continually in either ski-ing or dancing or riding or drinking would become monotonous. These are pleasures, aren't they? But unfortunately I can ski in the winter, ride in the spring, drink champagne in the autumn and dance in the summer. So that happiness to me is 99%

pleasure, and the odd 1% which relieves the ennui (i.e. work) comes so rarely that compared with the pleasure the happiness—true happiness—is a negligible quantity in my life. I am a miserable creature! But this argument is endless. One day we meet again—then let's talk. God, I long for the time.

Secondly, the drinking controversy is now becoming a joke here—no doubt it has long been one in India. Whenever the mail comes in I say cheerfully, 'Another letter from Mother, saying, Don't get drunk, darling, and one from Father explaining why', or if I forget to say this, someone asks, 'Haven't you had the usual warning?' In fact, I am getting sick to death of the everlasting subject! Let me finally assure you that I have no fear of my health being impaired by 'occasional excesses', and I am 'quite sure that I have sufficient control of myself to prevent an occasional excess from growing into a habit that will become my master'. *C'est fini.* . . .

Apart from this subject, Antony's letters during the summer term were all about parties, either in Oxford or London. They were merry and gay. By the end of June he got tired of dinners and dances and longed once more for a healthy out-of-doors life—for the sun and country air, so he went off to the Pyrenees with Edward Woodall. Before starting he wrote to me from Oxford, where he had gone to pack up:

I am feeling so happy and contented today, and as if I were entering on a new stage in my life—that of more serious and interesting things. I had dinner alone in my rooms last night, and nearly had a bottle of champagne to celebrate the new life. Then I thought that perhaps the champagne would be more in keeping with the old, and so I didn't open it, but drank beer instead!

They went to Gabas in the French province of Basses Pyrénées and stayed at a small inn among the hills. At first they were disappointed with the weather, the hills being wrapt in mist, but when the sun came out they were satisfied and enjoyed climbing, bathing and lying in the sun.

They only stayed abroad about a fortnight and were back in London by July 17th. Antony wrote me a long apology from there for his dissipated life, on which we had frequently commented in our letters:

I am always drunk (he wrote) not constantly but always. Sometimes it is with the sun, sometimes with excitement, sometimes with happiness, with an idea, sometimes with depression, and sometimes with what the prohibitionists call 'liquor'. When one says 'drunk' one imagines a man unconscious and ill in the street, obsessed by the approaching arm of the law in the form of a burly policeman. The picture is sickening. When I am drunk, I am as I am when doing the Männlichen on a sunny day. It is a more pleasant method, and quite inspiring. I should hate you to picture me pea-green, bloated and unwholesome. No, my darlings, don't think me a rotter, but I have a love of doing mad things, I have a love of people and dancing and female society, and all the sparkle of night-clubs, but it is inconceivable to me that it should become my life or mean anything serious to me. I like paddling, but I have no intention of drowning. . . . My real happiness lies in health and exercise, boxing, Scotland, Switzerland, etc.—those are the amusements that really appeal to me, but a little dissipation I also like at intervals. It is my nature.

To his mother he wrote on July 30th an amusing account of a ball given by Lord and Lady Curzon in Carlton House Terrace:

It was one of the best balls I have ever been to, everything perfect and all the right people. But I was amused by the way we were received for dinner. First Chips Channon received us with a few words of gentle badinage at the door. Then Hubert Duggan—who is now the rage of London and the *adoré* of the girls—shook us each warmly by the hand

and gave us a cocktail. Then we were announced, and received by Baba.* At this period I was getting a bit tired of shaking hands, but concluded that it must be Baba's party and that Grace† was not coming. However, when all the guests were assembled—and there were several hundreds—the doors were flung open, and George and Grace swept in arm in arm and solemnly proceeded to shake hands with everyone, saying to each as they did so, 'Oh, I hope I haven't shaken hands with you before; it is so confusing, you know'!

When his brother came home from Dartmouth at the end of July, Antony and he went to stay with Colonel O'Connor (who had been our host in Nepal) near Ilfracombe. He wrote from there to his mother on August 5th:

Darling Mother,
        The papers are full of 'ten years ago' and 'justice and liberty' and pictures of Belgian soldiers evacuating Louvain and the 'Blücher' sinking in the North Sea. What a funny feeling it gives even me, who was quite tiny at the time. It all seems so very wonderful and splendid, and makes the present day seem so cheap and shoddy and artificial. My goodness, the war must have brought things really down to bed-rock, and then afterwards the world spends its time in rebuilding all the artificialities which it took centuries to conceive, and which those years of war shattered into a thousand fragments. But I suppose peace without petty quarrels and conventional superstructures would be like a battleship after Jutland—no masts, funnels blown to pieces, deckhouse swept overboard—a lifeless floating hulk—at least not lifeless—still possessed of its sting and filled with a spirit and will to go on and on and conquer. But what is a battleship without its masts and turrets and funnels and wireless, and what is society without its general elections and its plays, its writers, its balls and its conventions and morals and scandal? These things only go when realities and war come along, and I suppose the finished, adorned and decorated article is

*Lady Alexandra Curzon.   †Lady Curzon.

a better permanent institution than the grim fighting hulk
shorn of all 'pomps and vanities' and even wounded as to
some of its most necessary possessions. But some things are
gone for ever, and the things that come back must be essen-
tials, so I suppose again one should be thankful for the peace
which has given the battleship back its masts, and society its
chaperones. But I can't help thinking this way when I look
at the *Daily Mirror* photographs of August 4th, 1914, and
see the wild enthusiasm in Paris, and the silent determination in London, which sent both countries wholeheartedly
into the most ghastly and, who knows, unnecessary of wars.

> 'It all seems now in the waste of life
> Such a very little thing.'

Meanwhile I sit in what outside is a charming little
Devonshire farm with white outhouses and a little courtyard at the back, like a Scotch shooting-box, and inside is a
cross between a boarding-house at Westgate and a drawing-
room at Osborne, in the days of the 'Great Queen'. And for
three days the rain has fallen without stopping, and I have
got fatter and fatter and eaten more and more and become
unhealthier and unhealthier. This is the place Colonel
O'Connor* has taken for August, and John and I are learning, I hope, what it is to be a really unselfish and perfectly
charming host; how always to give and make it appear that
you are receiving, and how to lay yourself out from morning
until evening to satisfy and amuse others. I have never met
a man who was so completely unselfish and charming and
kind as the Colonel. I think John is very happy, in spite of
the God-forsaken climate (Colonel O'C. lets him drive his
motor all day long, which he does very well)—but I am
rather missing the society which I spend my time trying to
ridicule, and above all Paris. I am going up to London at the
end of the week to see the Bloomfield v. Gibbons boxing-
match, which, I think, should be the best thing staged in
England for a long while. Then we all go to Porlock to one
house there until I go to Stanway (I may also go up to Anglesey,

*Sir Frederick O'Connor, Political Officer in Nepal.

as I have been asked to and want to awfully). I wish we
could all be at Knebs together again. I hate being miles
away from anywhere with nothing to do, unless it is with
you all, or with someone I simply love. . . .

Goodbye. I do love you. Try and not think too ill of me
for my love of pleasure. Satan's awfully strong, I'm afraid,
in this child.

Your very loving son,

ANTONY.

The holidays were a failure, as John got the mumps, so
Antony was obliged to cancel his projected visits. This bored
him considerably; he had little to occupy him at Porlock,
the climate did not suit him, and he wrote very irritably
about everything. His only consolation was a Morris-Cowley
motor-car, which I had given him for his twenty-first birthday. This was a great joy and a most treasured possession.

Of the letters written from Porlock, the following to his
mother is the best example:

PORLOCK, August 26th.

Well, darling, here I am still. All the ancestral doors
of England's most aristocratic houses have banged-to in my
face. None of those ladies whose tiaras make dazzling the
ballrooms of Mayfair feel that they can compete with a
mump-infected young man projected suddenly among their
anaemic children! So I stay at Porlock and pretend that I
quite understand their objections, and of course they
couldn't possibly have had me. But really all my broad-
mindedness and honesty have deserted me on this point. I
have become bitter, deceitful and sly. If the world won't
have me with its eyes open to the mumps, it shall damn well
have me with them shut and I hope it gets them! That's how
I feel. Sweet, isn't it?

But every now and then a spark of more tender understanding creeps into my brain, when I think of the unfortunate John lying in bed with his new riding-breeches beside him and the horses clattering by outside his window. Or

again, when I think of 'those anaemic children'—Fiona,
Ivor, Anne Charteris, and a whole mass of Pagets struck
down with large mumps behind their ears. It is hard to bear,
but how right everyone else is but me, and how much more
miserable John must be! . . .

I am becoming quite a melancholy bore. I write letters
but get no answers (except from the shops), I read books,
but get little satisfaction from them, and I drive my motor
but get no exercise out of it. In fact, I am entirely tiresome
and rather on my own nerves. I think that stag-hunting is
only a very moderate form of sport and not half as much fun
as it should be, but I have an inexpressible longing to play
polo. Shall I be able to in India? I think I have got such an
infantile mind that I only derive pleasure from games. I
believe that I should love polo as I never can hunting or
shooting. I have at last come to the conclusion that I have
nothing of the sportsman in me. The prospect of a day's
grouse-shooting leaves me quite cold, while a good game of
tennis has many anticipatory thrills. Hunting I like only
fairly, what I have done—there are many things I would
really rather do. I love riding, but I would rather ride some
wild horse than a lovely hunter, because of the fun and
difficulty, and I would rather ride with a few people I like
and do something crazy, than with a whole field out hunting.
But polo I think would embody all that I most enjoy. It is a
thrilling game, and I love games above everything, it means
riding and it is fast and furious. I think I should also be
rather good. They tell me I ride well, but why I don't know,
nor do I know in what riding well consists. I fall off on every
occasion and am beastly to the horse. But—I had meant
never to reveal my only half-hearted appreciation of *les
sports anglais*, but it has slipped out. The best thing about
them is the country I do them in. Gabas was supposed to be
a chamois-hunting centre, but I was happier chamois-less on
those hills than I should have been had I shot 4 a day. Can
you believe this? It's the idiotic things that please my child-
ish brain. Bathing in a pool in one of those streams is fifty
times better than a whole week of the best grouse-shooting

o

in Scotland. . . . There are only three things that I want. The first is you and Daddy and home again. The second is to play polo, and the third is to go to America. You may say they are inconsistent, but they would all give me immense pleasure.

But above all, darling, I long for you all again. It's no good screaming or sighing about, though, and besides it's just after breakfast. So I will express the sentiment which I feel so very deeply and pass on into this dammed up world of selfishness and callousness and money, and try and be even more indifferent to all that is humane and sympathetic and lovely than the rest of my fellow fiends on earth. Hell will soon open and swallow me up, I expect, which will be a pity, but I'd like to play polo first. God, what love I have for you, darling. I cannot describe the hole in my heart which there is for your absence. I long with my whole soul for you again. But who cares? No one but you and me. All the love that my beastly heart contains is yours. I send it you in this letter.

Your very loving son,

ANTONY.

Do you like this poem of mine?

THE GOLDEN CORD

I stood, one evening, on a little hill
And looked towards the setting sun,
Towards the restless sighing sea—
A thing which men have very often done!

That little hill was many aeons old,
Old was the sun-kissed western sea.
Youth knew them not, that aged pair,
But I was very young and youth knew me—

So youth allowed me, as I westward gazed,
To dream what thing for me was best—
To dream upon that little hill
The dreams that called Columbus to the West.

To me that happy little hill meant home;
The sea, the western sea, meant life—
Between the little hill and me
There stretched a golden cord. I held a knife.

'To be or not to be' thought Hamlet once.
'Which is the best for me?' I said,
And still I gazed towards the sea.
The sea just sighed and put the sun to bed.

I thought 'It was a sea of whispering dreams
That called Columbus' soul away,
But if I seek the setting sun
I know I'll only find the U.S.A.!'

And so I never cut the golden cord
That bound me to that little hill,
But turned and smiled and thought of home;
The cord became a chain and I'm here still.

He returned to Oxford on September 20th, in order to write a paper on Napoleon I, which he had undertaken to read to the Knebworth Literary and Debating Society on October 7th. The preparation of this paper gave him an intellectual interest which he had missed during the vacation. He wrote to his mother on September 23rd:

I am at present completely immersed in Napoleon. I came up here on Friday, and since Saturday morning until yesterday afternoon I have not moved out of my chair, but have lived in a world now 100 years in its grave. I have been transported to the side of Napoleon I, Napoleon II, and Napoleon III. Time and food have meant nothing to me, I have never been so absorbed in my life, and for these days I have been absolutely oblivious of the world. It was wonderful, and I have never been so happy.

I am going to read a paper to the Knebworth Literary and Debating Society on October 7th. I came here to write it, thinking that books and solitude would help. I have never regretted anything less. These last 3 days have been the

happiest of my life. I thought it would take me a week, but
once I had plunged *in medias res*, I never stopped but became absorbed. It was wonderful to watch the thing grow
and grow, always longing to get on to the next bit, which is
going to be so good! Now it is all over, and I find myself with
a headache, a pale face, dark lines under the eyes, no energy,
and a mass of closely-written pages of foolscap containing
the concentrated attention of my mind during fifty hours.

I think the paper is brilliant!!! I wonder if anyone else
will think so???

Oxford is empty and boring, but I never noticed it till last
night. I have cleaned out my whole room, been through my
drawers, and sorted my letters from India since 1922. So I
think I shall go to London today.

After completing his work at Oxford, he paid three country
house visits, and wrote us an entertaining comparison of the
three afterwards. In one of these occurs the following dramatic
account of an experience which might have ended in disaster:

I motored down to Lulworth to stay with Daphne Gladstone last Thursday. It is a most lovely country, with wonderful cliffs and hills and caves and bathing, and they are a
divine household. Daphne is very pretty and quite charming, clever and delicious, and her younger sister, Pam, is too
sweet—quite babyish, with tearing high spirits, the figure of
a nymph and a sweet little face. I was wildly happy there
and we laughed all day long, bathed and played bridge. It
hardly rained at all and one day was really hot.

The first day I got there we went up on top of the cliff, and
they said it was impossible either to climb up it or round the
bottom of it, so of course I had to slip away unseen and try
it. The bottom part was easy, great rock ledges with lots of
foothold and grip and all quite firm. I started to climb round,
but found I was held up in one place, so went back a little
way and climbed up. Then I got to a ledge and saw that
round the next corner I was only a yard from the top, and
the rest of the way there was grass and earth and it was easy.
But I could not get round the corner. Eventually I went up—

an awful piece of climbing in which I durst neither stop nor look nor think. I was hanging on by teeth and nails and the inside of my tummie, and slipping all the time. I was terrified, with 100 ft. sheer below me and still no sign of a firm foothold. But I couldn't turn back or stop, so I went on and eventually arrived in a cleft with my hands bleeding, trembling all over and sweating like a frightened hind. I climbed into the cleft, kissed it all over and lit a cigarette to calm my nerves. When I had recovered I tried to go on, but found what looked dirt easy was too difficult. There were several ways, but I was on mud now which lay on top of the rocks and did not feel firm. It might have borne my weight or it might have slipped—anyway there was nothing to hold on to as a safeguard, so with death as the alternative I didn't trouble to risk it! I appeared to be stuck, so I climbed back into the cleft and went to sleep, deciding that when my fingers and nerves were rested I would try and go down the way I had come up. When I woke up I saw a boat out at sea with Daph in it. She said it was 3.30 (I had started at 11.0) and I remarked that I was rather stuck and very hungry, and would they get a bit of string to pull me up with. This caused much joy among the coastguards, who never have anything to do. They got a boat and a rope and did lots of signalling. Eventually they threw me a piece of cord from the top, which I feared to put much weight on, but which gave me the necessary moral support to reach the top. I arrived on grass again with a happy heart, and the slope up to the top seemed like a meadow after the precipice (when I went to look at it next day I didn't dare walk down, it looked so steep and frightening, but at that moment it appeared flat). I felt such a fool at causing all that disturbance, when I had been specially warned. . . .

He then went to Knebworth to read his paper, which was a great success and brought him much praise.

He wrote to his mother from Oxford on October 15th:

Oxford again, and only eight weeks of 'daily round and common task' business before Switzerland. It's almost too

exciting, and already I am getting out my skis and playing
with my boots and looking at Daddy's rücksack with an expression of yearning! Photos fill me with a crazy excitement,
and I have hardly ever looked forward to anything more
than I do to this Christmas. . . .

Oxford is like the historians say France was after the wars
of the Empire—exhausted. There are many different faces
and many missing, while those which are here are elongated
by the weight of immense bills which their owners carry in
their pockets. I shall never be able to live down my last
term's extravagance. . . . But I have started right in on my
New Year resolutions by smoking gold flake, and I hope that
in the end I shall be able to leave the University without
dishonour. But still there is a very heavy atmosphere of
sobriety and good resolutions in the air, and everyone has
changed their rooms, so you never see them and imagine
they're working. . . .

Now you know what Oxford's like. It is a good atmosphere
for plunging into work, and I have plunged, in the silent
rapture of contemplating December 10th!

I think I have lost all my interest in games. I don't want
to play football; boxing has become a necessity rather than a
pleasure and I am happiest sitting in the little room reading
or writing. The result is that Oxford says I am becoming
aesthetic, and I am very flattered and shall go out and buy a
velvet coat and side whiskers! . . .

In this month occurred the political crisis over the Zino-
vief letter, and the Labour Government which had maintained a precarious existence for a year was defeated and
went to the country. Antony's views on the General Election
which followed were expressed in a letter to me of October
22nd. They are characteristically blunt and necessarily
immature, but are worth quoting to illustrate his state
of mind at the time:

The General Election (he wrote) leaves me rather cold.
Everyone seems so tiresomely factious and incompetent, and

there is not the faintest chance of any party getting a majority. The Conservatives are just boring, I think, and their blunder over Protection was almost unforgivable. I fancy much the most the Liberal ideas of Free Trade and no Imperial Preference. I don't see why England shouldn't be able to compete with the best producers in the markets of the world and hold her own. It is the only means of assuring fundamental and lasting prosperity. Why should Australian wines, for example, having obviously failed to compete with French wines, be supported by a Protectionist theory and preferential tariff? The one thing which infuriates me about England is that it will not work. It's quite understandable, because there is too high a demand for employment and consequently a low standard of workmanship. And yet the *Daily Mail* hollers that German goods will swamp the markets and destroy British trade. I think if they will and can, they ought to be allowed to. Everyone says the British workman is the finest in the world. My suggestion is that he should do a little work for a change, like the German. That, as I understand it, is the Liberal view. But of course they would get no votes if they said that. I also hate their leaders, Asquith is certainly a scholar, but he is so abusive and cheap. Lloyd George is cheaper still. I love old Winston, but like the rest of them he's got no constructive policy which he can bring forward, and mere abuse is just sickening.

I adore Ramsay MacDonald, but I neither understand nor trust the Labour party. They seem cheap to me too, and I don't know but what they are really after Communism, which is hell. I couldn't be a Socialist or a red flag Chief, and I hate the Bolshevists and Trade Unions and all such things. But I like the labour people, because

1. They couldn't do any better over strikes and things than anyone else.
2. Their German and Russian loan business will, I hope, make England do a job of work again.

Don't laugh at me and say 'What do you know about work?' I loathe it, as do most people, but I am quite certain it is the fundamental condition of success in any sort of business whatever.

That's what I feel about the election. None of the parties interest me, and I don't much care what happens, though I think my inclinations are Liberal. Everyone must pull their weight. The Conservatives want to make Labour row the hardest, and Labour wants to make the capitalist do the same. I don't know, but I hope and think the Liberals want to kick them both. They certainly want kicking themselves! Switzerland draws nearer (cries of 'plutocrat') oi—oi!

The letters we continued to receive from Oxford each week were all entertaining, but they were so long that space does not admit of more than a few quotations from them. The following anecdotes of our great friend Father Waggett are amusing:

One morning last week, the first this term, I forgot to get up. Eventually I made the supreme effort and struggled along to the bath. It was then too late to get breakfast in Hall, so I collected some eggs here, some butter there, bread somewhere else, and finally a pear from J. C. R.* Returning thus laden, and feeling very unshaven, to my room at about 10.15, I find seated in my chair Father Waggett! We fell upon each other's necks, the eggs fell upon the floor, sleep fell out of my eyes, and the cigarette fell out of his mouth. We talked all the morning about God knows what, and bit by bit my breakfast got cooked and eaten, and then I went with him to feed the birds in the Botanical Gardens, though he had first to assure me that it 'was done'. He was too delicious and in such good spirits, I do hope he'll come again.

Father Waggett took me up to London the other day to hear him speak. Really I took him up, but he made me come. I motored him. He wore twelve coats, four cloaks, eight scarves, nine hats, three handkerchiefs, twelve cassocks and two rugs over his knees, and he was (*a*) invisible and (*b*) unconscious from cold! He spoke at the —— Club.

*Junior Common Room.

It consists of a large gathering of women between the ages of twenty-five and sixty (or 70) possessing all those qualities which are most odious in men, women or child—

1. Talking ninety to the second.
2. Very knowledgeable about queer authors and things no one else has ever had cause to think of or about.
3. No sense of humour.
4. No intelligence or common sense.
5. Inestimably high opinion of self and complete failure to recognize the existence of others.
6. Religion—Intelligentsia. Just a queer kind of educational learning which is found only in this type. It is dogma with no breadth or charm; very little of it and mostly inaccurate.
7. All the wrong things exaggerated, all the good things left in the nursery.
8. Immense efficiency misplaced.
9. Complete ignorance of human nature. They have none, you see.
10. A profound disrespect for the rich and an immense personal income.
11. A love for the poor combined with no knowledge of them.
12. High standard of morals founded on an absence of sensuousness and an adoration for curates (no, Bishops, I think).
13. Huge powers of critical appreciation, but no ability to criticize or to appreciate.
14. A complete shallowness of intellect, nature, faith and understanding.
15. A devotion to tea.
16. Too many hairs on the upper lip!

Do you know the type of people I mean? After this description I daren't name an example! As a matter of fact I know no one who would quite fit into this description of the —— Club. There were about 80 there!

Father W. spoke of 'England 100 years ago' in theory and in practice—everything. He was quite brilliant, very amusing and very radical. No one dared criticize him at all. They gave us a good dinner, anyway, and I motored back in about an hour and $\frac{3}{4}$.

He's a perfectly heavenly man, I think, in every way, only I should like him to be stronger. I daresay he is really, and anyway you'll say his frailty is his charm. Perhaps, but to me it's rather ridiculous. What a brain, though. I don't know of any that I like better or think more perfect.

To his mother:

I had the most marvellous little glimpse of land this week-end (the metaphor is—here at Oxford, sea—one swims vaguely). Generally one sees only mere sea. When one sees land, it is good. Land must be very solid. Some places I love, for instance, are not land. They float, perhaps, but then so does oneself while swimming. A night in London is not land—just a new way of swimming. All these things float, you see, alongside of one, but one looks for land. Knebworth, good solid land—Auntie B., land. Anything that really stands on the very bottom of the sea and is immovable— doesn't float. Well, last week-end I was on dry land. It was wonderful, but it made me jealous for home at Knebs again. Never mind, good land.

I went to stay with the Meades from Friday to Monday for John's Confirmation. It was too wonderful to shake the water off one's back and come into a real delicious home with divine children and divine parents and all happy—

'Momma loves Poppa
Poppa loves Momma
Everything's dandy
Sweet as could be'.

Awful! I'm sorry, but it's rather sweet. Everything being dandy's what I like.

I adore Mrs. Meade, I think the Captain's superb and I'm going to marry their youngest daughter! We played every game and roared with laughter, and it was altogether a perfect bit. If only people stayed as attractive when they grow up as they are at 5 or 6, I should get married twice daily!

John was very well, rather silent except when giggling, but absolutely without qualms. The Mothers of two of his friends were down, so there were three of them who were friends all together, and it was great. We played 'bears' all over the house and I ran into the corner of a spiky thing backwards and haven't been able to sit down yet!

I have enthused enough about the Meades, and besides I have been boxing and feel all different now. How being hit brings one to earth again! No matter how ethereal, how romantic, how clever you feel—when your brain is working wonderfully, your pen running like a Rolls, and your ambitions and ideals materializing in the realms of your dreams, go and box! It's like falling into the river when you're drunk!

His last letter of the term contained a description of the effect produced on him by Hardy's *Tess of the D'Urbervilles*:

I have just finished *Tess* and I must write of it, though it will not catch the mail. But what does the mail matter? One feels that way after reading such a book.

I think it is almost too horrible. It leaves one with a great revulsion of feeling—a longing to take the whole thing and hurl it into the fire. One is worn out, tortured, enraged. Such brutality, such horror—what does anything stand for when the end is a black flag over Winchester gaol? The end to what? Perhaps only to life, but at any rate to all that one is concerned with about Tess, or indeed about anyone. And what a life—a life so tortured, so cruel, so really good and so strangled by misfortune. If with all the beauty of thought and intellect and intention in the world one is dragged into the commission of the worst crimes against society, either society is at fault or all beauty and sincerity and feeling count for nothing. Society can't be at fault—though, of course, it is—for on it rests the very existence of mankind. So what is the use of thinking great things, loving truly, if it means doing bad things? One can go on this way for ever —that book stands up too great and living and ghastly. It soars above criticism, ridicule would be profanity. I have never been so stirred by anything and at the same time un-moved. Perhaps I have got too old to cry over books, but probably it is the very ghastliness of it which baffles one's understanding, so that perceiving tragedy one is yet un-moved by it. One gasps, and by that very action one is made unable to cry aloud. My first feeling was one of wanton rage, so that I longed to break things and first and foremost utter-ly to destroy the book. To this succeeded a sort of hopeless helplessness. The whole world turns on a passion or a senti-ment. To be practical, law-abiding, unemotional, virtuous, is not possible. To everyone must come that passion which moves beyond all power of reason—that great feeling which rises so superior to reason and destroys it utterly. Logic is a great and fascinating study, and for a while man may live by it; but passions are life, and they are seldom regarded as a study. Didn't Browning see this?

'But priests
Should study passion; how else save the world
Which comes for help in passionate extremes?'

It is only by a great wave of emotion that events take place. There are no great men. Everything is personality—it is this which stirs and moves and inspires. Great deeds are not wrought through reason; great events do not take place owing to logic. How many men could go to their graves with the assertion that never had they been turned aside from the true, the just, the right course by the seductiveness of senti-ment or the fierce ardour of passion?

That is the way that book stirs me. It is a very great and moving one and it leaves me exhausted, full of hate and un-believing. What counts? What counts? Just this, I suppose, to be able to see the black flag go up over the prison and to turn away and go on. Go on always, where to or why God alone knows, but there must be some reason, some cause, something which makes it worth while. Go on, go on ruth-lessly and with determination over the bleeding corpse of every principle, every affection, every sentiment, every de-sire in life. That is what it means to be practical; set your

back to the wheel, your hand to the plough, and march ruth-
lessly onwards—to what? To Hell.

To be moved, crushed and humiliated, but never embit-
tered, never defeated, never exhausted. Never give up,
never fail, never submit to the tyranny of all that means
most to you. Great God, how ghastly a thought, and how
awful a character you would become. And yet such only can
rule the world. It is the party of the past and the party of
the future. The men who can never quite forget against the
men who forget while they remember. It is the men who
died for Charles because he was a King against the men who
let him die because they knew he wasn't.

And all this as a result of one—now old-fashioned—novel.
I wish to God there were some men today who could write
like that too. And yet I don't care about the book—I should
never say it was one of my favourites. It is just the great and
glorious and inexpressible essence of tragedy. I shall carry it
in me always, though I will never read it again. Poor Tess.

A.

Chapter VII

OXFORD: COMING OF AGE

1925

'It should be an occasion for a glad face and a strong heart.'

THE LONGED-FOR holidays came at last. On December 8th Antony set off for Switzerland with a few of his Oxford friends. The season was still so early that on arrival they found themselves like the first comers to a theatre, who watch the dust-sheets being removed from the stalls as they take their seats in the gallery.

Last year the trouble had been there was too much snow. This year there was not enough. The perfect conditions to satisfy the heart of the ski-runner are rarely attained for long.

To his father:

HOTEL BERNERHOF, WENGEN,
Dec. 13*th*, 1924.

Darling Father,

. . . There is hardly any snow at all and ski-ing is really very dangerous. . . . But what snow there is, is of a perfect quality—marvellous crystals—very fast and perfect for any kind of turn you wish to make. I have got a marvellous pair of Norwegian skis which John Carleton brought over from Norway for me this summer. They are long & very thin & very fast. . . .

I am frightfully well and strong & fit. Owing to the bad train service we do a tremendous amount of climbing & running about generally, and I can do almost anything in a day now! I have stopped drinking anything but water at meals

222

& hardly smoke!!! Immense energy & economy. The great joke is to cut down the 'extras'. Extras are beer, baths, tea, grog & gluvein (I wonder if you ever drank this in Switzerland. It is a marvellous hot red drink with cinnamon amongst other ingredients in it, & wonderful if you're tired). We talk about being 'a bath down' or 'a tea down', as the one manages to save the francs where the other succumbs to hunger, thirst or a desire for cleanliness. John* & I are streets ahead of the others in economy, but there's not much between us at present. He lost heavily yesterday because he had beer for lunch & *vin du pays* for dinner, but then I had tea. Today we both had gluvein when we came in, but otherwise no extras! I have never felt so strong or so well. I could easily climb the Jungfrau three times in one day!

John is quite wonderful on skis, second only to Mac & Amstutz. I have never seen anyone else as good & never anyone who was prettier to watch. I am ski-ing quite well on the whole. I have not really fallen down today—at least only once or twice, and am getting quite strong at my down-hill christies. Life is perfect beyond anything imaginable, and if only we have some snow now I have nothing more to wish for.

We found a marvellous little run today, half way up to Wengenalp, and sweated all the way up to do it again. Having done it again, we found there was no way out except to walk down a path to Lower Wengen. To *walk* down anything appeared sacrilege, so we climbed up again & ran home another way. So you see we are energetic! However, I won't go on with the wild joys of this place, or you will long too much to be here. It is great fun being a crowd of young, hearty & happy young men, and they arrive in fresh batches all next week. We shall have a fine team this year & with any luck should get the first 4 places against Cambridge. But as has happened every day so far, pride comes before a fall! ...

The room is full of people working, reading, writing, but all like me, I'm sure, filled with an immense happiness and energy & beginning to think of their beds (We have 10 hours every night!)

*Carleton.

Forgive this letter. I said at the start it would be bad, but one is sometimes too filled with Swiss air, laughter and energy to be able to write coherently or intelligently. I am that way. Great literary works are produced only in electric light, amidst broken decanters in a room reeking with smoke, by emaciated, seedy working men with great foreheads, who write feverishly. Here the bestial supersedes the intellectual, the forehead recedes, the smile widens, the air is pure, & strength of body wrests the soul from strength of mind.

I feel that way. My face is happy, my jaw large, my forehead negligible, & my hands too large to hold a pen.

Yr loving

A.

The chief ski-ing events this season were the Anglo-Swiss Universities race, the race between Oxford and Cambridge, and the Kandahar Cup race. Antony took part in all these events, and though he did not win any of them, he succeeded in competing creditably with the other runners, who were all of the first class.

As usual when he got back to Oxford, his letters were very depressed for a time, the dullness of school or College life after a Swiss holiday being almost unbearable.

To his mother he wrote:

At present I feel almost as if Oxford was the worst thing in life which could possibly happen to a chap. But why not? One has said goodbye to the best place in all the world and the best sport ever invented. Also to someone whom one adores, and one is faced by months of history work, a Thames Valley climate, a lot of boxing & the usual drab life of this University—when—it's—trying—to—be—economical!

On the other hand, you will be home very soon. What is a few months in a lifetime? . . . So I should not really be depressed. But good things come to an end, partings are unpleasant, and nothing seems nice at the beginning. Hence the pianissimo look which stares from the eyes. Tomorrow I start work.

I have at last seen Davina. I went to meet her when she
came up from staying with the Asquiths at Mells. . . . She
was divine beyond all imagination, and so strengthening to
be with. . . . I just felt as if nothing could go wrong, as if one
could have no doubts, apprehensions or misgivings, for

> 'By God's death the stars shall stand
> And the small apples grow.'

We simply adored Peter Pan, & then I put her in the
train & saw her off to Knebs. She has got the most beautiful
hands I have ever seen and the most delicious voice. Very
quiet & silent and understanding, & saying the best things
that ever dropped from the lips of man or woman. What an
angel she is. The afternoon was much, much too short, and
I felt like a sort of coarse ugly harsh jackdaw that has got
into the same cage as a nightingale. . . .

During this term Antony was working hard for his schools
and hating the work. He was restless, discontented, busy,
but none the less merry and entertaining at times.

To his father:

January 28, 1925.

I am deep in the correspondence of Warren Hastings
& find him a most odious man. That he was an able man and
a great man I have no doubt, but I can more than understand the antipathy felt for him by the brilliant & wild
politicians of 18th century England. He seems to have been
what Belloc calls 'a parvenoo'! His letters show no tact or
taste or sense of humour, an immense regard for himself,
and an extraordinary narrow outlook. All his opinions are
final & arbitrary, admitting of no criticism or doubt, and he
goes to great length to explain their brilliance & the great
debt which England & the Co. owe to *him*.

He writes frequently about the vindication of his honour,
the high standards of his morals, and the loftiness of his un-
impeachable character. His agents in England were no
better, and totally unable to appreciate the nature of parliamentary debates & proceedings. That Ld North or Fox or

P

Burke should venture to make a joke on the subject of India overwhelms with horror the Hastings cortège. They all seem to me dull, arrogant & insignificant little men with no breeding & a very good eye for business. I do not like them. I do not like Hastings, but I fancy that on charges of peculation, dishonesty, cowardice or neglect of duty he stands acquitted. . . .

To his mother:

MAGDALEN COLLEGE, OXFORD,
Feb. 4.

I have just been reading through examination papers & be assured now, so that you are not disappointed, that there is not a dog's chance of my getting a first. I know nothing, and feel that I shall be not unlucky if I don't get ploughed. They are impossibly difficult, & my ignorance so incredible that I gasp to think of what I have been doing all these years. . . . I feel I have learnt how to be stupid, idle, silly & extravagant—and if I don't know all that I should, I at any rate know most things that I shouldn't. It is an old-world principle of education—the system of 'don'ts', but I have learnt how to say 'don't' to myself & to know when to say it. The things that count stand out more than ever they did, and the deceptive things which allure but don't count have been tried & found out. That is learning, even if it is the learning of fools rather than of wise men. But what better brain is there than that of a fool who has been taught? Surely the wise men must retire into the solitude of their Universities & Colleges, there alone to find appreciation of the wisdom which they have learnt from the experience of others:

'For though I lie on the floor of the world—
With the seven sins for rods,
I would rather fall with Adam
Than rise with all your gods.

'What have the glad gods given,
Where have the strong gods led,
When Guthrum sits on a hero's throne
And asks if he is dead?'

At any rate, I have not fallen to that. I rejoice rather that I
am alive & happy & well, & have

> 'More heart again to lose
> Than you to win again.'

But I haven't entirely lost yet either, and perhaps the spirit
of the moment should be one less of despondency about a
probable future than of determination to avert that probability. God knows I'll try, but I wish it could be a sudden &
supreme effort instead of one spread out over months. Where
tonight I am brave and determined, tomorrow the spirit
may be weak. I felt this way once before, and felt that with
your help I should win through. But then I hadn't read the
Examination Papers!!

A few days later he wrote to a friend a description of a
night he had spent under the stars, when his car broke down
on the way back to Oxford from London:

I started back at 10. Just before Slough a man stopped me
and said he'd run out of petrol, so I gave him my spare tin,
and relieved him of 2/-, which I thought philanthropic! Six
miles short of Oxford at 11.35 the car stopped. No petrol!
I tried to play the trick the man had played on me with the
only two cars that passed, but they both ran me over! The
next village was a mile and a half on, the last $2\frac{1}{2}$ miles back.
So I walked the mile and a half, raised an irate pub-keeper
and said 'Oh pub-keeper, some petrol, please.' He replied, 'Go
to hell, you won't get any in this village.' I threw a brick at
him, then walked back to the mote. It then occurred to me
that it was the most lovely night God ever made—full moon,
not a cloud in the sky, and very warm. I became romantic
and sentimental instead of cross. . . . So I pushed the car into
a field and lay down in it and slept all night.

It was really wonderful. I don't believe there has ever been
such beauty in England as there was last night. No tropical
moon, or bright lights on Broadway, could compare with it.
I just gasped at the beauty of it all. . . . Even more wonderful
was the early morning. I woke at 6.30 to the most marvel-

lous lights and an absolutely inspiring early-morning air. Birds singing and cocks crowing. Next thought, 'With any luck I'll be sent down now'. So I walked the mile and a half again, discovered a cottage where they kept petrol, roused it and obtained half a gallon. Walked back, inserted same, wound car for 20 minutes, and found I'd forgotten to switch it on! Eventually returned to cottage and found it belonged to a man from my garage, who was full of consolation, said he'd see the car's absence was not reported, and produced a divine motherly wife with a cup of tea.

I had intended to take leave this year, and was looking forward to seeing Antony at Oxford and celebrating with him his coming of age at Knebworth. But these plans were upset at the last moment by Lord Reading's decision to go home for 4 months, and the fact that I was asked to officiate as Viceroy in his absence. So Antony's mother went alone for his coming-of-age, leaving Hermione with me.

Antony wrote to her at Aden before hearing of our change of plans:

MAGDALEN COLLEGE, OXFORD,
Feb. 18*th.*

I decided it was too idiotic to be in a state of morbid depression, and also had a long talk with an American whom I do not know very well, but from whose lips there seemed to drop pearls of wisdom. He told me I was unhappy because I was not interested in anything, which after due consideration seemed to be true. At least, my only interest seemed to be Antony. I don't really care as I should about my work, I don't care about boxing or really anything. You have always told me that same thing too—that I didn't really try—so it's not a startling discovery! It is a mental attitude which I have rather cultivated, having disliked people who cared, as I thought, too much about everything. Now I can't get out of it. I told him that it was all very well, but I wasn't responsible for not being interested in anything and that I couldn't make myself interested in things. This he said was untrue,

& that one *could* make oneself interested in things. How? By
giving up things to them. He had given up all his pleasures,
etc. to painting—not from necessity but from intention, &
he was very happy. This seemed to me true!

The other thing he said which impressed me was that one
should have oneself in control. One should not let one's
thoughts & sentiments & passions & desires run riot all over
one's life but should always be perfectly in control. Then,
the argument went, you have the world at your feet. This
also seemed to me a sound remark, but a great deal more
difficult to act upon than it appears. To be perfectly in control and have the world at one's feet one must be ruthless
and prepared to ride rough-shod over people. This I could
never do. But I do see and feel that the thing that counts is to
give things up to something, and consequently to love & be
interested in that thing. While I was in the depths of depression Father Waggett came in, cheerful and full of good
things, & that made me feel more than ever that here was
I, with everything in the world that I could want, sitting in a
chair moping, & there was he with nothing—but nevertheless happy—simply by sacrifice.

All of this is just irrelevant talk which will show you a
little bit my mental attitude and that I am happier....

As usual he found in boxing the best cure for depression
and boredom. He wrote to me on February 25th, saying
that he had begun training for the Inter-Varsity boxing and
had given up smoking and drinking—'not from any mis-
guided idea that it is good for me, but just to see if I can. One
should be able to make oneself do, think, act, as one likes....
I seem to have lost all interest in things—the little things
that used to be amusing, and I just go dreaming along very
much like the lotus-eaters in the Odyssey, or a dog after
luncheon in July sleeping on the lawn.'

The boxing match took place on 9th March, and Antony
was successful, winning for Oxford in his class, but he wrote
little about this, as his mind was full of other things. The

shadow of his approaching examination was upon him, and he was already thinking of what he was to do in life after leaving Oxford.

When the term was over, he had a few days with his mother in London and then went with her to Knebworth to prepare for the coming-of-age celebration, which had to take place before the end of the Easter vacation, and in time to allow his mother to return to India at the beginning of May.

On March 26th he wrote: 'My dear Viceroy! With Mother's return I have had quite a rise in the social scale! I lunch with Lady Cunard, dine with Margot, have breakfast with Lloyd George and tea with the Duke of Devonshire. On we go from strength to strength. . . . It's such a marvellous thing to have her here again that apart from 'talking with Kings' one's whole life seems to be revolutionized. It is only in such moments that one can realise how much one has lost by being away from you both so long. I seem to see things with different eyes and understand with a different understanding. Whatever was difficult becomes easy, what was uncertain becomes obvious, what was misery becomes happiness. I haven't felt so profoundly happy at the bottom of my heart as I do now for ever so long. It's the most wonderful metamorphosis imaginable, & it doesn't feel like me at all.'

KNEBWORTH, *April 6th*, 1925.

Darling Father,
          Here we are all established in the family mansion, and it seems impossible that you & Hermione should be so far away. I am writing at your table in the library, and the rain is coming down outside with that persistency which, until you have been to Bengal, you imagine is peculiar to Hertfordshire, the Thames valley, or whatever place you happen to be staying at! . . .
There is apparently another gold rush in Alaska, and I have been asked to go and dig by a tough friend of mine at Oxford, who has apparently pegged out a good claim! It's not

really a very serious plan, I imagine, but surely if there's really gold there it would be fun. I am obsessed you see by the desire, which I suppose is Oxford-born, not to do the ordinary conventional thing. I have a dread of becoming just one of many young men living miserably in London & working hopelessly in the city. Literature and youth have combined to make me feel that any alternative is preferable. It is a form of vanity—just not wanting to get lost in the humdrum monotony of every one else's existence. If it's money to be made, I want to lose myself for five or ten years & come back rich, and it seems that that is what is to be the aim of my life. But I suppose really the conventional life is the right one, or else it would not be the conventional one. Oxford, I think, makes one want to kick against the pricks all along the line, and so one cultivates that attitude of mind which the uninitiated call 'bolshy'. I hate the thought of Parliament, or of the city, or of London, or of anything, except something quite peculiar. I long to be like the hero in a novel, who has made money, but no one quite knows how! But I think I shall live that down in a little while, and Mother's return has already sobered me down a little and brought me back to a saner outlook on life. It's really a desire to do one better than all the other uninteresting young men whom one despises so, because though nice they are sensible. I have been too long at Oxford! 'There will be too much of me in the coming by & by!!'

So I expect you will see me a polished, dapper-like A.D.C. next winter, easily accommodating myself to the conventionalities of Government House. I wish I was an artist or a musician with a definite trade to pursue passionately, a definite excuse for shunning the conventional, and quite definitely no prospect of ever rising above the mere level of art for art's sake! How soon I should tire—but at the moment I feel just like Lewis in *The Constant Nymph*.

Don't bother to take any of this to heart. I'm sure it's all the Oxford manner. A little hard disciplinary training would do me a power of good. I often think of going into the Church just so as to preach against it!! How I dislike the school of Modern History! How little I get done! How little satisfaction I have in doing it! There is about as much chance of my getting a first as there is of my getting all the work done, and there is about as much chance of my getting all the work done as there is of my coming out to India on April 7th. I persistently cart wads of books about and occasionally dip into one or the other. But as before I can really get interested or start comparative work I have to read at least six books, and as it takes me a week at 8 hours a day to read one, I am not full of hope. . . . But it is divine to be at Knebs again and we are all so frightfully happy in our home that my outcry against everything (Antony v. the World) does not really ring very true or deep! . . .

Such love to you. It seems very near now that we must meet. Probably self as a budding young soldier. . . .

Yr loving

A.

To this letter I replied:

I don't think much of your idea of digging for gold in Alaska. I fear it may prove to be 'fairy gold' which will vanish at the touch. But then I have a silly prejudice against any short cuts to wealth.

Don't be afraid of your Bolshy tendencies. We have all got to make terms with our own Bolshevism, or it will play us some bad tricks. It is best to have it up and look it squarely in the face. If you suppress it, it will turn nasty and make you intolerant of the Bolshevism in others. Your dread of the conventional—the humdrum of life—is sound enough, but you are mistaken in thinking it is outward circumstances which make people conventional. If you are ordinary by nature, you will be conventional even in Mexico or Alaska, and if you have any originality you cannot be ordinary even in the House of Commons! There is plenty of romance and adventure to be got out of life, if you have them in yourself, and if you have not got them, you may chase them all round the world and never find them. You will find that out directly you come out here. You will then see whether India stirs in you hitherto unknown depths, or whether you feel as bored here as you do at Oxford. You will never be 'like everyone else', so don't worry about that.

The great event of his coming-of-age celebrations took place on April 24th, and Antony's next letters to me dealt with this.

On the 23rd he wrote: 'Tomorrow is the Tenants' luncheon for my coming-of-age, which we are dreading whole-heartedly, and I suppose I shall have to start thinking out a jolly little speech to deliver—the which I dread most of all. ... I wish you were going to be here.'

There is unfortunately no full account of the proceedings. The mail of one week left the day before the luncheon took place, and by the following mail day the news was regarded as stale. As the Press was not admitted to the luncheon there was no report of the speeches, and my letters from India were full of reproaches at the inadequacy of the information supplied to me!

Antony's own account of the ceremony is contained in the following letter:

KNEBWORTH, *April 26th*, 1925.
Darling,
      They have all gone to church and left me to pack up my things. I have done all my packing and feel I must write to you. For today I start upon the last course of my Oxford life, as yesterday & the day before I was welcomed upon the first course of manhood by Knebworth. I am acclaimed as being twenty-one, and immediately afterwards I have to start forth upon the last stage of the first effort in my life. It should be an occasion for a glad face and a strong heart, but somehow my heart is heavy and I can only keep on regret-ting the past. I wish that I had worked harder during this bit and that I had got more done, but the remedy is in the ensuing seven weeks. Then again I feel as if once again I was launching out on my own, when I have a perfect long-ing for the harbour. Mother goes back to you in a minute, I

go back to Oxford today and it feels very like the end of my childhood. When we meet again I shall have finished with Oxford and shall be a man, and all the glorious memories of the past which have surged around these few weeks at Knebworth will be one with Nineveh, Tyre & the first twenty-two years of this child's life. But it is not all gloom— for there is this—we can at last talk of meeting again, and I am at any rate going back to Oxford for the last time.

If life has been good to me so far I have nothing really to regret, for it has only just begun, and if there was ever anything to be done in the world, it is to be done in the future. It is only the men who during their lives realize that, glorious as has been the past, the future must be different, and who have striven unknowing of what that future may be to convert it not into the past but into a present as glorious as the past, whose names history holds illustrious. And how more than ever with so great a breach to fill up & with so stupendous a past to vindicate should one look upwards & on, on, on.

All of which is rather priggish, but when one has been told for two days that a great many people are very glad one has lived for twenty-two years, and what great traditions one has to rise up to & what stupendous things are expected of one, one has, if not a right to be, at any rate an excuse for being priggish! . . .

I have done enough lamenting the beauties of the past and bewailing the struggle of tomorrow. Give us to awake smiling, help us to play the man, and in a trice the last lap has been run; Oxford has been said goodbye to for ever, and away we go madly shouting & laughing together across your odious continent!!

But in the outburst of priggishness with which this letter began, I said much of 21 & the last two days. What can be the sinister meaning of the boy's words? you will be thinking. Ah, I will tell you. Last Friday we had a huge luncheon-party of the tenants. Mother is sending you the menu, I believe, so I need hardly tell you what we had to eat! . . . John will almost certainly tell you how he dislikes having to make conversation, so that part I will leave undescribed. What no one in all probability will dream of telling you is how extraordinarily charming all your tenants are. So that is the first thing which I must explain. I was most extraordinarily touched by the way in which they subscribed to my present and by the sweet way they all behaved & the sweet things they all said. Considering that half of them I have never even set eyes on, I thought it was very sweet of them. Lord Salisbury made the most beautiful speech, and said perfectly wonderful things about you. As a matter of fact, what I thought quite the strangest part of the whole proceeding was the awfully nice things everyone said about you!!! Everyone regretted your absence, every speech had some wonderful allusion to you, until by the end I could hardly believe that I was your son or that you were my father. My word, they do love you, Father.

Mummie's speech was the most wonderful thing I've ever heard, and it was only by inches that I didn't cry. How I managed not to I don't quite know, except that I buried my face in my hands—but I felt like a half-wit. She read your telegram out and it was wonderfully received. In fact I can't tell you how sweet they all were, how appreciative, or what extraordinarily nice men. I sat between Lady Salisbury and the Duchess of Rutland, and drank far too much to keep up my spirits! But it apparently reacted in the form of tears. They cheered me to the echo and sang 'For he's a jolly good fellow'. It is not good for one to have many occasions like that—one does not deserve it.

Then yesterday we had a tea-party for the village—all the old ladies and young ladies & children, and they all seemed to enjoy it so much. They again said such good & sweet things that I felt it was hard for me to be present. They had a walk in the garden & then a cinema. They showed the film of your arrival in Calcutta, which I hadn't seen before, and I was so excited that I nearly burst. I have seldom enjoyed anything so much or been in such a state of giggles & tears & excitement. . . .

Well, it was all very wonderful & on the whole moving,

though I feel very strongly that one does not give as much as one gets.

My presents have been too lovely. A magnificent suitcase & gold watch from the tenants. And oh, I forgot, best of all a clock & cigarette-lighter given me by the house, estate & village. They presented it in 'the room', at 10.0 on Friday morning. Mr. Vincent* gave it me and made a little speech. He nearly cried & made mention of you & Mother, whom he said he loved very much. It was too pathetic & sweet and really the best present of all, because so many had subscribed and it was entirely spontaneous. They asked if they might do it. Everyone you can think of gave something, according to their lights.

Now I must stop and pull out on the long trail—the trail that is always new. To Oxford and the last lap. Goodbye to Knebworth & Mother, but in a few months the best moment in my life.

Yr loving son,

A.

I got your lovely telegram on the morning. I do thank you. It nerved me to the operation considerably. Oh, if you could have been here!

From Oxford he wrote to his mother on April 27th:

Oxford's really rather quiet & calm & welcoming, and there is a very friendly atmosphere about it. In a way it's rather fun to get back to one's little room and belongings and the absolute disinterestedness which everyone shows all the time. But I don't feel that it is a very real place—nothing seems quite to ring true, and an atmosphere of scorn rather pervades it. This is perhaps because I have been living so near such very real things this last month. It has meant more to me than I can ever describe having this little bit with you at Knebworth. I feel as if my whole soul and mind had been dusted and tidied and cleaned up! I seem to myself such a completely different human being

*Our butler.

from having been in touch with you again. I am just incredibly happy with all the wonderful goodness of life.

Again, just before she sailed for India, the day after his twenty-second birthday, he wrote:

Life is so shining to me, and my soul so profoundly contented, that I can't realize any single pang at your going. For me it is only the first glorious step to better things. At last I have a definite object, near at hand, to grasp and rejoice in. I look forward to the whole of this year so passionately that your departure only heralds-in its wonderful prospects. Schools are so near that they are almost a pleasure. In a flash they will be of the past, a thing possibly to regret but I think not to be ashamed of. At any rate, the first rather important tangible thing I have come up against. I don't much mind how they work out. I feel that I have done something to tackle them. Then a glorious care-free summer in England with the best of the world to enjoy, and after that the crowning moment of all. How can I be unhappy? Time cannot go slowly, and I just live for this wonderful future.

His letter to me of May 6th is an amusing and characteristic example of how Antony could fill a letter with entertainment that had no relation to news:

MAGDALEN COLLEGE,
May 6th, 1925.

Darling Father,
         Having played a hard single at tennis for two hours and eaten an enormous dinner, before sitting down to work I will try & write to you. Unfortunately I am in a very limp condition, and it is just the hour at which the other inhabitants of my 'quad' wake to the joys of life.
I should like to write a very funny poem on the peculiar habits of my fellow tenants of St. Swithin's. I know few of them personally but as a quantity I can read their souls, so great is my intimacy. They don't come to life at all until

11.0, then they start with a burst of boyish enthusiasm to discuss their plans for the day under my window. Their days must be singularly lacking in organized energy, because they all talk at once and vary the polylogue (good word?) by occasional snatches of some popular tune. When I say some popular tune I mean many very popular tunes. This goes on for half an hour, & then apparently wearying of the hardness & excitement of life they go each to their separate rooms. Here they take up their stance in the window and recapitulate the arguments of the previous half-hour—only being farther away from each other, louder. This till lunch time.

Between 1.0 & 2.0—dead calm. Then at about 2.30 the real business of the day begins. I suppose there are about twenty or thirty of them. Well, they each have two gramophones; some of them have six friends, all of them have four. At lunch they meet their friends, and by half past two, the concourse being assembled, the gramophones are set in motion, and accompanied by the friends (out of unison) maintain a persistent serenade until 4.0. At 4.0 I go out, and this is apparently the signal for the daily siesta. Calm descends on St. Swithin's, and all is at peace until my return after dinner.

I imagine that somewhere between 4.0 & 8.0 they steal out, fetch more friends and have a good drink. Anyway, by 8.30 one's ears catch a sound not unlike what I imagine the Carmagnole sounded like from the windows of the Tuileries on August 10th! But there is no one for the inhabitants of St. Swithin's to put their Carmagnole into action on, and so their only alternative is to persevere with it. This is their real hour of triumph. Whatever their other qualities may be, perseverance will stand out as their predominant feature when Oxford is one with Nineveh & Tyre. They may all be Scotch or, untrue to Darwin, descended from bulldogs. I don't know, but the toughest soldier who ever stood in a square or even a bit of indestructible radium itself could learn a little in endurance by listening to them. They never draw breath, pause or modify the volume of

their song before 12.0 o'clock. At that hour some of the
friends have to go, and since talking is with them a forgotten art they say goodbye for a quarter of an hour or so,
as if they were trying to communicate vocally across the
Sahara.

After the friends have gone, on some nights the survivors
persevere for a bit with the old song. But more often they
just drift up to their rooms & play their gramophones until
they fall asleep and the gramophones run down. At any rate,
by about 1.30 it may be confidently asserted that youth
sleeps & that until 11.0 next morning one can hear the
clock ticking, so you see that I really do know them all quite
well. It is now just about time the fanfare started, though
my ears are now so trained that it all sounds like the merest
rippling of the merest brook. What more beautiful setting,
to let the thoughts wander in poetic & romantic contem-
plation?!

In your letters this week you both beg me to come to
India directly I leave this peaceful retreat. I wonder if I
shall. . . . It is getting quite terribly exciting, and I don't
reckon the goodbye to Mother next week as anything at all.
It only brings me nearer to *Der Tag*.

Nothing I can say will ever be able to describe what she
means to me or how entirely different-souled I become when
she is here. It is a subtle influence, but it is as strong as sunshine after rain. These few months have been indescribably
happy for me, and no power, heaven-sent or manufactured
in Birmingham (for what can be more powerful?) could ever
enable me to love her enough or to say how much I do love
her.

We had the most delicious day together here last Sunday.
Just sitting & talking & laughing & doing a good deal of
eating too! . . .

I must work now. How I long to see you and share your
gilded cage, as you call it, God alone knows. But it is very
soon now.

Yr loving son,

ANTONY.

His letters for the remainder of this term tell of the over-shadowing anxiety concerning his impending examination and his complete preoccupation with the work which it imposed upon him.

MAGDALEN COLLEGE, OXFORD,
May 18*th*, 1925.

As for my letters being depressed, I think that is really to be attributed to 'Schools', which honestly do hang over me awfully, the way thunder does in June before the rain starts. In your letter this week you say you have a prejudice for believing capital the reward of labour, and condemn my Alaskan scheme. I unfortunately have an exactly opposite prejudice & believe it entirely the reward of luck. But that is because, at present for certain, possibly for always, I do not thrive on work! See me now—a poor, depressed, emaciated little creature with hardly the strength to laugh, much less the will, bending feverishly over books with no other object than to offer myself a good excuse for enjoying the better half of an English summer when the schools are over! So that if my letters are short owing to a placid contentment, they are depressed owing to a nervous anticipation!

I dislike work so intensely that anything which appears to be connected with it, such as a theory, is damned. But I look forward to 'after the Schools' so intensely that possibly my voyage to India in Sept. may be the best way of quieting the scandals which will no doubt be associated with the fair name of Lytton by that date.

You have written me a delicious long letter all about my coming-of-age, amongst other things, and I feel that I told you nothing about it at the time. I can't tell you anything about it now. But there are three things which really appealed to my vanity, & which I shall remember when my great-grandson comes of age and I have forgotten when I last could bite! The first is Mother's speech, which went nearer to make me cry than anything has since I shook hands with you last at Dover. The second is Lady Salisbury's remark to me, when I sat down after making my first speech, which went nearer to making me scream than any thing has since I got my house colours. She said 'Brilliant'. The third was the most touching of all (was the second touching?) and rang so true at the moment that it gave me a lump in the throat. Mr. Wilson* rushed round after luncheon, seized me by the hand, and said 'God bless you, dear boy'. Perhaps also I shall remember Lord Salisbury's laugh at a moment in my speech when I hoped for laughter. It made it seem really as if it was funny. I was so pleased.

It was sweet of him to send you that very charming telegram, and I do think it was extraordinarily nice of him coming at all.

Well, I said I couldn't tell you any more about it, but these things will stick in my memory for ever, and when I am 'making good' somewhere in the Colonies I shall feel as Napoleon did at Acre—*J'ai manqué ma fortune.* . . .

MAGDALEN COLLEGE, OXFORD,
May 27, 1925.

. . . As I have told Mother, I have no time to write for my soul is in distant lands, in far-off times, and I am kept pretty busy, now hastily signing Magna Carta, now marching with Henry to Agincourt, hastily invading Silesia with Frederic & rushing back in time to see Charles' head cut off. Now cheering beside the tumbrils in the Place de la Révolution, now charging into the smoke at Assaye or amassing a huge fortune by robbing the Nabob of Arcot of his subjects' money. Back to France in a flash, to march into Madrid behind the Napoleonic eagles, & then back further to be present in the House of Commons to hear Mr. Burke support the great India Bill of 1783. Then for a moment I must be present at the death of Henry II, and away again over centuries & seas to see the Peshwa, a British agent, march into Poona on May 13th, 1801. I have not time to celebrate my birthday, but must sit for a moment beside Hobbes while he pens the *Leviathan,* and gaze with Rousseau across the Lake of Geneva, all unconscious of the havoc our imagination is

*Our agent.

Q

to bring upon history. I must see Cornwallis surrender at
Yorktown, & dictate terms to Tipu at Seringapatam; I must
see Wolsey, Henry & Thomas Cromwell, one with the earth
from which they came, I must sing psalms at Naseby & be
washed by the blood on the field of Culloden. From country
to country, from continent to continent, and from sea to sea,
I pursue the great & low, the rich & the poor. I have seen
Kings executed & battles lost, great ships sunk into the
ocean & whole columns slaughtered to a man. And all in a
few short weeks.

So you see it's rather a busy life and I don't really have an
awful lot of time to remember that it is 1925, that I am
Antony Knebworth, and that in India I have a Father, a
Mother, and a sister all waiting to hear some news of me!

What shall I say? My life is Schools, and I would give my
eyes to beat them into pulp. But I'm afraid that I go forth to
the battle so ill equipped in knowledge that I may even get
ploughed! Oh, but do pray a little for me and hope that by
some frightful chance of fortune I may possibly get a first.
If that happened I really believe I should go mad. But it
can't, & if it did—well, I daresay it's better that it can't, because I really might do something beyond words awful
which it would take me the rest of my life to live down. So
perhaps you'd better not pray—do the opposite & hope that
if I can't be clever it is better to be respectable!! . . .

Today is Derby day. Davina, I believe, has gone & people
are shouting in the streets about the result. But as you know
(or should have guessed by now) I am dreamily forgetting
that it is 1925 and wandering back once more through the
centuries to do brave things & laugh coarse jokes & ride out
to win my spurs over the sodden mud of Northern France.
Goodbye, Father, goodbye England, goodbye the 20th century. 'For Harry King of England!! . . .

MAGDALEN COLLEGE, OXFORD,
June 10th, 1925.

. . . I dined in All Souls the other night, and it was
much funnier and more exaggerated than any description

could make it. There was only one real old fellow there, but
I sat next to him. He could only talk Greek & occasionally
quote from Shakespeare's sonnets! I didn't understand a
word, but tried to be pleasant and good-humoured and smile
at the right moments. Eventually he was so exasperated
with my stupidity that he said 'What pleasant weather we
are having'. I collapsed. What a chance for Bateman—the
man who talked about the weather in All Souls! But even
then he had to quote Horace to prove the sun had been
hotter in B.C. 40! I said that I was not alive then and would
consequently have to take his word, but that though I did
not doubt his veracity, I thought he was a liar! He coughed
into his beard & turned to his other neighbour. They discussed Greek mathematics until the port came and someone
lit a cigarette. Then he was sick & left the room. I felt that
the *aspera* had been a little too much for me and that I had
failed to reach, although I had seen from afar, the *astra*!

Schools tomorrow. It seems so very funny, as I have really
forgotten all about them these last 3 days. ...

I am happy—very happy, and before my merriment
everything seems to pale and grow unimportant.

What can man want more than a happy mind, a sunny
day and joy in life? I have them all and if I was struck by
lightning tomorrow I should not regret having missed the
Schools!

We meet, it seems so soon, for I have come to the end at
last.

Your unintellectual son,

A.

After his Schools were over and the strain removed, he
went to London and stayed with the Lutyens, at 13 Mans-
field Street. From there he wrote many gay letters describing his London frivolities, and one gloomy one announcing
that he had taken a second.

He returned to Oxford to take his degree, and in the late
summer paid some visits in Scotland before sailing for India.

Antony felt none of the sentimental regrets on leaving

Oxford that he had expressed on leaving Eton. His three
years there had been a time of great mental growth, and in
particular the desire to write had become insistent. In one
of his letters he sent me a poem on his second, and said 'I
apologise for so doing, but it is gradually becoming the very
marrow of my bones to write. I can hardly stop. I seem per-
petually bursting into verse, and at any moment I am going
to start to write a book. I am sorry, for literary men are
weakly creatures with physical disabilities. But I am not
really a literary man. I only know & feel that I must write;
that is what I want to do, and whether I turn out trash or
classics there is stuff like a cancer inside me, growing and
growing, which must be turned out. When I sit down with
hours alone to myself I itch sometimes for a book, but always
for a pen and a blank sheet of foolscap—so that is just that.'

Oxford gave him much for which he was grateful, but she
never bound him in her service for life as Eton had done.

The President of Magdalen wrote to him appreciatively:

You will know, I am sure, that it was with genuine interest that I saw your Class in the History School. It was
what, as I told you, I expected. In itself a Second Class in
History is a real distinction, and for someone like you quite
a good class to go through life with. It demonstrates that
there is a certain good level of diligence, information and
command of expression below which you do not fall, and
which will sustain solidly any more brilliant superstructure
you may later and in other ways build upon it. Of course, I
should have liked for you the very best and something
brilliant (not showy), but I am well content with this for the
present, as I feel assured that you will go on to be and do
something really worth while for yourself and others in life
and in the world. . . .

Taking it all round, I think you have not done amiss with
your Oxford career, and I am very glad to have had you at
Magdalen. I believe I may feel that I have added another

young friend to my list, whose career I may watch as long as my own day lasts, & dream of, dreaming of the years which will come after. . . .

The cloud of a family separation which had overshadowed these last three years was now passing away, and on the threshold of manhood Antony left his schooling behind him and sailed at the end of September with his sister Davina to join us in India, full of high hopes and joyous expectation.

Chapter VIII

INDIA

1925-1927

'I feel as if India had added many years to my understanding.'

THE GREAT meeting to which I had been looking forward for 3½ years came on October 12th at Darjeeling. It was one of those perfect days which come in India at this season, when one wants to sing a hymn of thankfulness for the passing away of the rains and the return of the sun to valley and hill-top; when the shy snows on the high mountains unveil their full beauty, and all the world seems aglow with new life.

We drove some way down the hill to meet the travellers. The whole world seemed to have been washed clean, and the atmosphere was marvellously clear and transparent. Hills and valleys that we had not seen for months stood out with startling clearness. Usually so far away and inaccessible, to-day they seemed to come near and to be joining in our welcome. Little red roofs and brown 'Busties'* smiled on us as we passed, and everything seemed to be dancing and singing in the sunshine.

We stopped at a wide part of the road, from which a superb panorama of the distant plains below was visible, and almost immediately we saw their car coming round the next corner. In another minute they were with us. It was a wonderful moment, and we could not have had a more lovely spot for our meeting.

*Villages.

When I had parted from Antony he was a boy at Eton. He was now a man who had finished with Oxford. Yet he hardly seemed to have changed at all. He was just his radiant self. With beaming smiles and whoops of delight he ran up and down the Khud and turned somersaults like a child.

The first few days after his arrival were spent in showing Antony our favourite walks and rides, and introducing him to our friends. He was in no way affected by the height at Darjeeling, and outwalked us all. When our walks led down to the tea gardens, through bits of forest, he invented a new game. He would climb up the young saplings, and leaning outwards bend them over until they deposited him again on the path. Sometimes this manoeuvre was completely successful, but more often the tree either snapped in the middle or came up by the roots!

I am fortunately able to record Antony's impressions of India in his own words, by the courtesy of two of his friends who have allowed me to reproduce some of his letters to them. The first is Edward Woodall, the Eton and Oxford contemporary who had accompanied him to Gabas in Spain in the summer of 1924. The second is Mrs. Philipson (*née* Daphne Gladstone), the most intimate of his girl friends during his Oxford days, for whom he always retained a very special affection. His letters to these two friends reveal his changing moods during the eighteen months he spent with us in India. To Edward Woodall he wrote three days after his arrival:

Government House, Darjeeling,
Oct. 15, 1925.

Dear Edward,
  I had always imagined that perfect living was to be found only in P. G. Wodehouse's books, and experienced by the very rich in America. I felt that the essential thing about

the existence *sans reproche* was Jeeves; that without a flat in
London, a range of American expletives, a good cocktail-
shaker, a pair of check spats and the inimitable 'man', one
might as well be contented with an ordinary humdrum
existence. I was entirely wrong. The perfect life, the only
absolute luxury, is to be found amongst the poor inexplicably
raised to the dignity of a Governor in India. Had I the pen
of Macaulay, the genius of Michael Angelo, and the imagination of Ethel M. Dell, I should be but ill-equipped to describe this thing. But I have none of these things & so will
describe it admirably!

I have a divine bearer (*valet de chambre* or 'man') black,
& with a heavy moustache. He wears a little round black
hat, a blue serge frock coat, different-coloured trousers every
day, no shoes or socks, and he bears somewhat magnificently
the name of Lal Bahadur. He is supposed to know English,
but his knowledge consists in repeating everything I say,
answering every question in the affirmative, lying like a
trooper, and doing exactly the opposite of everything he's
told. In England one might feel this to be detrimental to the
character of the perfect servant; here it is oddly enough the
essence of it! He knows everything, and whatever he does is
perfect. He has nothing else to do except to look after me,
and he sits outside my room all day. I have also a private
man who washes my clothes and another who irons them.
Lal Bahadur dresses me as carefully & perfectly as Molyneux
one of his mannequins. My clothes are kept, washed,
brushed, ironed, packed with a religious devotion worthy of
the followers of the Prophet. My bedroom is the size of an
ordinary drawing-room, and I have a private bath-room. A
man shaves me in bed in the morning before I wake up, so
that when I'm called I am quite clean & washed!

This house is like the most perfect English country-house
you can imagine. Huge rooms perfectly furnished, with log
fires smelling gloriously. At the front door there are always
eight men dressed in red and gold with black beards and
turbans, who salute whenever you pass and always make
me jump. At meals there is one huge man in a turban & red

and gold behind each chair, and they all salaam with both hands every time that Daddy comes into the room. You are allowed to do nothing for yourself. Changing trains on the way up I got out carrying two books which I was reading. They were taken away from me at once and given one to each of two coolies, who carried them for me lest the '*chota* Lord Sahib' should get heart failure (*chota* means little, it's the only Hindustanee I know).

Buttonholes just happen on your dressing-table, cocktails appear; at tennis there is one head man and fourteen little boys to pick up the balls! There are horses to ride by saying the word. There is roller skating, and the country is more beautiful than anything you have ever imagined.

One goes about in a rickshaw—at least I don't, because I don't like it, it's so humiliating being pulled by men. Yesterday I ordered two pairs of shorts from a new tailor, who didn't realize his customer was from Government House and charged only 5 rupees each. In the evening I received a present of a silver stick-handle with 'Lord Knebworth' written on it from another tailor. This morning he visited me, informed me he was the official tailor, that he had heard I had ordered some shorts from another, that it was unpardonable, that I must cancel the order, that it was his job. I was much embarrassed, thanked him for the present, and in the words of Harry Graham:

> 'Told the Bhong
> To run along
> And play.'

My God, it's a good life and so very funny. I adore being spoilt and looked after as if I were rare china.

Best thing of all—there is a guard of soldiers at the gate, and whenever Daddy walks in or out they turn out, salute and blow a bugle! One soon becomes Anglo-Indian.

Yrs,

ANTONY.

On October 19th we started on a fortnight's trip into Northern Sikkim. We were a large party, consisting of our five selves with Major and Mrs. Bailey, our A.D.C. Captain Blois, and Sirdar Bahadur Laden La, our Tibetan police officer and most efficient guide and interpreter. Accompanied by our little Tibetan terriers, we travelled slowly, making about fourteen miles a day and sleeping each night at a new bungalow.

This expedition proved both adventurous and strenuous. At times our route was rendered difficult and even dangerous, owing to broken bridges or avalanches of mud and stones caused by the recent heavy rains. On one occasion our party was separated, and Antony and Hermione, who were with the Baileys, had a rather narrow escape from a landslide. A great moraine of stones and mud and fallen treetrunks, about 400 yards in width, lay across our path. Those of us who formed the advance party got safely across it, but when the others reached the spot, the native guide who accompanied them was very nervous and advised them not to attempt the crossing. As, however, the alternative route was several miles longer and involved a steep climb, they decided to take the risk, going across one at a time. Antony and Hermione were the first to cross, and when they were about two-thirds of the way over the guide shouted and pointed upwards, where an avalanche of stones was starting. Fortunately Antony heard the noise and ran back in time to avoid the falling stones. The guide wept and wailed 'I told you this would happen, I warned you it was dangerous'! and later we heard that he had made a sensational story about the great luck of the young Lord Sahib—how a huge boulder had bounded a few inches from his head and struck sparks of fire at his feet as it passed!

Apart from this adventure the expedition was uneventful and entirely enjoyable, except for three very strenuous days which Major Bailey, Antony and I spent among the high mountains when we had separated from the ladies of the party.

Antony wrote of this expedition to each of his friends. To Mrs. Philipson:

GOVERNOR'S CAMP, BENGAL,
November 4, 1925.

My dearest Daphne,
    We are up 11,000 ft in the Himalayas and it has been snowing wet snow. The result is intense Swiss sickness. It's just the same—snow light on the ceilings, a delicious smell of snow, no dressing-table, but a table with an ordinary cloth covered with everything, *and* we sit indoors all day and play bridge.

We ski-ed this morning, but the snow was slush and the number of rocks legion, so that it was not really fun—only awfully sentimental and longing-for-the-real-things-making. We've been up to 18,000 ft which was foul. We crossed right over the main range & got out on to the Plateau of Tibet. It was all red brown like a desert, and the Himalayan glaciers shot suddenly out of it at your feet on one side.

We lived in tents, and it was quite incredibly cold at night and even unbearably cold (in spite of the sun) in the day time. You feel foully ill at that height; if you move or eat you can't breathe for an hour and are generally sick, and you have a cracking head all the time. We loathed it, but it was supposed to be pleasure. We had meant to shoot something called an Ovis Ammon, but decided that if it was fool enough to live there we had no inclination to disturb its vegetable life.

We rode about on Yaks—divine animals who subsist on snow and rocks, a diet, I need hardly explain, calculated to prove indigestible to less hardy animals! . . .

I long for news of the plays and the books and the good old conventional London things. I feel terribly homesick but do love the inestimable luxury of life in this country. . . . Now I am going to have dinner. Oh, for the gay places of Switzerland and London, & oh for just one more mad Oxford party!

Give my love to lots of people—keep heaps for yourself.

Yr loving

A.

To Edward Woodall from Gangtok on November 12th:

After a casual glance at this address you will know exactly where I am & what I am doing, you will grasp in a moment the vital importance of the N.E. frontier problem, you will perceive the threats of Buddhist invasion from Mongolia, you will congratulate me on my valuable information to the Foreign Office!

I've been having the most marvellous time in the mountains, & have crossed right through the Himalayas into Tibet and back over a pass 18,000 ft high, feeling dead ill, eating bovril, sleeping in a tent in 14 sweaters & riding a yak in the day time. Thus it is that we men win through. . . . Believe me, the plains of Tibet are horrid. They are all like a desert to look at; only the yak, who lives on rocks & sand & snow (poor sweet) can subsist there—they're so high you can't breathe, eat, or move without being sick, & you have headache all the time. I tried to shoot wild geese with a rifle & the effort very nearly killed me. . . .

So far I have only done the most interesting part of India (i.e. Sikkim & travelling). It has been quite divine, & so far from tropical extremely cold. . . . The Governmental idea of camp life & roughing it is rather exceptional. You have 50 servants, a laundry, a horse each, two hot baths a day, a bungalow to live in, 190 coolies, exquisite food, bridge, & a private post office! This is abandoned when you get up high. There it is exciting. I didn't undress for 4 days & one night —slept very coldly in 2 pairs of trousers, stockings & socks, thick vest & pants, a flannel shirt, a jumper (high necked *à la* Noel Coward) a sweater, a Jaeger coat & an overcoat (blankets excluded). N.B. This is quite true.

Do write to me. You can't imagine how I wish I was still at Oxford. I never imagined I should regret that place, but I would give my eyes to be there again—rich, indolent & in debt.

I shall return soon to England & accept a minor position in the City!

To the same friend he wrote again on November 23rd, after his arrival at Calcutta.

The enclosed poem* was inspired by the beauty of your address and its pun-able qualities (which were however not made use of!) It is a sad life, this life of exile in a foreign land, & the burden is made harder by the people being so much *plus Anglais que les Anglais.* You remind me, God forgive you for the impertinence, that East of Suez there are still, or should be, Ten Commandments. Why, there are nothing else. They're written in letters of fire all over the Orient. Before I came out here I never understood the allusion under discussion. I will now explain it to you in the sense that it was written, so that you may shout the news to all England and warn her sons, who, in the words of Burke, are about 'to drink the intoxicating draught of authority & dominion before their heads are able to bear it.' He also had never been to India.

Listen:

'Ship me somewhere East o' Suez'.

Alright—nothing to explain there, except that 'o" instead of 'of ' quite erroneously suggests a kind of devil-may-care bravado wholly foreign to those who seek fortune in the East.

'Where the best is like the worst'.

This line no one ever bothers to ponder on. Ponder on it. Imagine 'the best'—all the best things of the East, or, for that matter, of the world. What are they? No better than

---

*'MAYBANK'
(with apologies to Rupert Brooke)

How passionately I long to be
At Maybank, Longfleet Rd, Poole, E!
To feel the water icy cool
Down near Poole, down near Poole;
To watch the fleet come up the Roads,
To see old fashioned Maybank 'modes'—
But I sit here in Indian heat
Miles from Maybank, Poole, Longfleet
And England where
Mechanics ply their happy trade
Westward—to westward of Port Said—
Oh, God, that I were there!'

'the worst'! This line is a warning, much too frequently overlooked or misconstrued.

'Where there ain't no ten Commandments'.

Comment is hardly necessary. The simple synonym for 'ain't no' is 'are'. It is a universally accepted fact that Mr. Kipling too often twists his sense to suit his rhythm & rhyme. Forget the latter and seek out the true sense of the line. You will find that he considers it necessary in describing what lies East of Suez to state specifically that there are Ten Commandments.

'And a man can raise a thirst.'

Once again Mr. Kipling sacrifices his sense to his poetical instinct. That a man can raise a thirst in a country where the temperature is 120° in the summer, & throughout the winter the sun is so hot at midday as practically to preclude the possibility of strenuous exertion, it did not require the genius of Mr. Kipling to expound to us. Drink is necessary to the European in the East—cf. the greater wisdom of Mr. Belloc. . . .

> 'Stern indomitable men
> Have told me time & time again,
> The nuisance of the tropics is
> The sheer necessity of fiz.'

In short, Mr. Kipling, in order to get a rhyme to the word 'worst' has been compelled to take refuge in a most platitudinous truism. But here again, what is the moral of this execrable line? It serves only further to whitewash the East. Those who drink at home in an English climate of damp mists, fogs & rain, drink only for the love of drinking. To the East of Suez men drink because they must.

It would appear that no four lines in English verse have been more misconstrued than the lines alluded to. It is the habit of those, who in their smug English parlours, peruse the 'Road to Mandalay', to conceive of countries stretching 'neath a tropical sun and populated by a race of Europeans, cut off from the moral standards of their forefathers, forget-

ful of the sacred laws of Moses, drinking & swashbuckling
across arid deserts and sandy plains, at the beck & call of
some heathen god, with a whisky bottle in their hand &
profanity upon their lips. No conception could be more
erroneous.

We are of the opinion that Mr. Kipling's lines should have
been written as follows:

'Send me back to the East of Suez
　　Where the best is as bad as the worst
　　But where men still stand by the laws of Moses
　　And only drink to quench their thirst.'

In England only are the thirsty, blood-sucking creatures
of Mr. Kipling's verse to be found. East of the Canal are no
arid deserts, no care-free vagrants, no idol-loving subalterns.
The land is rich and green and plentiful. The European
population cherishes the customs of its forebears to the extent of drinking nightly to the King Emperor & not lighting
their cigarettes until this ceremony is duly performed. So
far from being forgotten, the ten Commandments are en-
shrined in the homes of the missionaries who form 30% of
the population from Lahore to Cape Comorin. They are
cherished in the bungalows of every middle-class Anglo-
Indian, who forms the backbone of the Imperial bureau-
cracy. They are made illustrious in every antimacassar, in
every silver photo-frame, in every palm tree, and in every
red plush settee which decorates the rococo houses of Mr.
Kipling's 'forgotten of God' householders. Wherever the
word mountain is pronounced 'maowntain', it is to the glory
of God. In no country, with the possible exception of the
Middle West States of America, are the inhabitants so English. In no country are the best things of England so quickly
forgotten and the worst so readily placed upon a pedestal of
worship to be the 'Lares' of every home.

It has been said that God loves the middle classes. His
devotion to the European population of the Indian Empire
cannot be doubted, & since that population has a reputation
(well founded) for generous hospitality, its affection for Him
must equally be accepted. It is a land of Churchmen, hard-

headed business men, keen soldiers and poor diligent officials. It is a land where the conventions are still maintained
to the extent of leaving cards on your friends. It is a land
where the Totalisator is an accepted & legal method of betting, unfeared by the public, uncondemned by the Government. It is a land of purity & sincerity, of chastity and good
living. It is a land where men are greatly tempted & where
they bravely do.

Well, now, I think I have sufficiently described to you
what India is really like, but of course I have not yet had
Kipling's experience. From sheer necessity, however, I am
sinking into the atmosphere of the land. One cannot live
amongst people & not join with them. If one is superior one
is bored & boring, and eventually begins to doubt one's
superiority! I always say 'Cheerio' before drinking, I refer
to horses as 'skins', and I enjoy myself! As you know, my
knowledge of horses is nil. I shouldn't even recognise my
own in a crowd. But it is the only amusing thing out here.
. . . the things to concentrate on are obviously the things
horses can give—polo—pig-sticking, racing, steeple-chasing,
etc. So I'm trying very hard. I occasionally get lent bad
ponies & I play all there are in Govt. H. stables, regardless
of their age, characteristics or qualities as polo ponies. Polo
is the only game in the world, and I have never been so
thrilled about anything before. It's bloody difficult & I never
know where to go or what to do. I never hit the ball, I never
ride anyone off, but I enjoy it hugely—only I never know
which pony I am riding or which pony I have ridden!

It is such a different atmosphere here, such a pleasant one,
but such a difficult, responsible, uncomfortable one. I long
like hell for Oxford, but I fear home means work, and so I
will stay here for always.

To Mrs. Philipson:

GOVERNMENT HOUSE, CALCUTTA,
December 15, 1925.

Dearest Daph,

Just between you and me and anyone else you may
happen to meet, I find Calcutta a trifle uninteresting! Per-

haps it is that there is a certain absence of adorable female society, perhaps it is that I find being the Prince of Wales a trifle heavy, perhaps it is that I am homesick. Anyway it is. . . .

I have been trying terribly hard to be a strong silent man and profit by the unrivalled possibilities for sport and horses, but as you know that's not really me. I thought I was a strong silent man, but I believe really I'm a giddy garrulous little boy with no real grip of life at all! . . . At first the English mail was my sole existence. But since I came here I have had no letters at all. Just one from Grannie! This so soured me that for two weeks I haven't written a line. But since then we have been in the Hills, and that has brought back to me everything that I love most in the world. Oh, the air! It was tremendously Swiss; and the sun was divine.

Darjeeling is the most lovely place I have ever seen, and it managed to remind me at odd moments of all the places I have ever loved; of the terraced hills of Italy, of Switzerland, of a summer's evening at home, of red sun, etc. Then when I got back here I found a good mail waiting, and now I feel at peace with the world and eager to write to everyone.

I have read *Cat's Cradle*. There is something about that man's books which absolutely transports me from existence into another world—into his world.

I long to be a Roman Catholic, I long to lead a miserable life, always unhappy, and eventually to die of a broken heart. I long to have a hopeless and shattering love-affair which is doomed from the beginning to be useless. . . . Maurice lugs me away with him into the world of his Cs and his Blanches and his brilliance and his stupidity and his great tragedy. I feel that his books are silly because they are so tragic. But that doesn't stop me from adoring them. As a critic, I should say the book overdid the Catholic-Protestant question. You *can* nowadays meet someone without saying as you shake hands 'Are you a Catholic'? and when they say 'No' feeling miles away. It is on Maurice's mind and he can't shake it off, and God knows I think he's the best propagandist I shall ever meet. But the sort of Catholic atmosphere is really

R

rather absurd. The Catholic parties, the Catholic Xmases, the Catholic scenes, etc.

Then again, if Blanche really loved that Bernard, what easier than to say 'I don't want to see so much of Horace Crane and the other man, because they are both in love with me and make me feel uncomfortable.' I can't see when you have married the man you love that you should make a tragedy and a secret sorrow of everyone else who falls in love with you. If you hate your husband it's different. But I can't understand the absolute absence of intimacy and love in the Bernard household. They never seem to have had one moment of affection together, and Blanche never seems to have told him anything or helped him in the least. Perhaps that's part of Roman Catholicism—that you tell your troubles to the Church and treat them as a direct punishment from God for having previously married someone you loathed and been faithful to him! I don't really understand it, but I feel it is so real in the book and so likely that I want to cry instead of getting angry. My God, what a writer. His is surely the most perfect English that was ever written and I think too the most perfect art. Really I like C. better, because it all seems nearer to me than the other. But they are both incomparable to anything else I have ever read. . . .

To Edward Woodall:

GOVERNMENT HOUSE, CALCUTTA,
Dec. 21, 1925.

I gather from your letter, which is rather sad, that working from different directions we have both reached the same conclusion. We have lost that sweetness which we never can regain. I feel like Marie Antoinette in Belloc's book, when she realised she had reached that stage in life beyond which everything is loss without replacement until she too stood face to face with the cold marble of the tomb! They say that life gets better & better as you grow older. I accept the dogma sceptically, and do not believe it in the least. But you, oh blessed one, have visited Oxford—'Ben

was in great form, full of airy & cosmopolitan brilliance.' It
makes me cry. Never again can one realise the brilliance of
Oxford. How clever we were; how we laughed; how we
talked! how bored we were by it all, and, by God, how happy.
It seems so far away from me, in this odious existence,
that I want to cry. And you write sadly of one day marrying Janet, while I moan, with all the luxuries of the
richest country in the world laid at my feet. To me it seems
real & profound tragedy. How I want to be brilliant again!
Can one only be brilliant at Oxford? I'm afraid so. For only
at Oxford can one know everything. Only at Oxford can one
feel that one has lived all life and found it boring. Now that
all that is gone & behind one, it seems painfully true that
one has lived no life and that one doesn't want to. At Oxford
one was negatively ambitious—not so much to do as to be in
the state of having done. Now one definitely wants neither.
Everything seems quite indefinitely awful, but then for the
first time I am suffering the odium of real boredom—not
just youth's bored affectation. You, on the other hand, are
suffering the odium of the opposite. *Plus ça change*—as we
used to say in those glad old days!

I seem, like Louis Napoleon, to stare vaguely down the
long avenue of coming years. And I have no plan, no scheme,
no idea of how to live them. I want only to be done with it
all. To live just for one month the old gay life of brilliant,
inexpressible youth, and then pass quietly into—well, just
to pass quietly. But that is because I am living in a world of
men; real men, hard-working, hard-headed, commonplace,
boring men. God, how I hate them, and yet they & all their
kind are LIFE.

Your letter has filled me with an unquenchable yearning
for the past and absolute horror of the future. Even in this
glowing Capital life looks drab. Well, it's time I started a
plain, ordinary, dull, underpaid job like everyone else &
gave up the vague illusions, ideals & ambitions of rebellious
youth. . . .

On December 29th I had my usual Eton dinner at Calcutta, and was pleased to have with me this year an Etonian

son, an Etonian A.D.C. (Captain Cripps, who had been with
Antony at West Downs) and an Etonian guest (Alfred Beit).
We mustered 38, and the company included 5 men of
Antony's year.

The first two months of 1926 were occupied with the
usual routine of a Calcutta season. Antony during this time
found his chief enjoyment in playing polo, which he loved,
and in pig-sticking, which he now considered the best of all
sports.

In February we went to Agra and Delhi, and also paid a
visit to the Maharaja of Alwar. Antony wrote to Edward
Woodall on February 14th:

At last I have learnt to appreciate India & will no
longer write to you about loving & losing at Oxford! I have
just got a lovely letter from you & have paid it & you the
compliment of reading it under the shadow of the Taj! I
believe one is not academically allowed to include the Taj
among the Seven Wonders of the World. And that, as
Browning would say, is right. How right! It is most assured-
ly the one and only Wonder of the World. One has seen so
many pictures, one has heard so much, one has read so much,
one expects so much. The Taj is so hackneyed; it has become
part of one's life. To say it is beautiful is to say the Bible is
well written. In these days of American authors one may
not describe it or write about it. One must concentrate on
life—real life, on society, the drama, civilisation. One may
not talk of the Taj & Hadrian's Villa, one may not think of
the Parthenon or ancient Rome; one must look for salvation
in the words of Michael Arlen & Noel Coward. But, Edward,
even I, the modern, the affected hater of affectation, the man
who found Monna Lisa plain, bowed down & worshipped
before the tomb of Mumtaz Mahal. It is a thing—perhaps
I should say the only thing in the world—in which it is not
possible to be disappointed. It could never be hackneyed,
common or overrated. You may know it as well as Rockefeller & talk of it as often as Paris, but it will give you the

lie, as the Georgians said, and always stand out, when you see it, as something of the same architecture as God designed heaven. As a building it is like its pictures & its models. . . . But the lines in it and the architecture are unbelievable. I have not your knowledge about architecture & I have not the artist's eye, but even to me the perspective is the most extraordinary thing on earth. Although it is domes & arches, it is also straight lines, and lines so perfect that to look at them they are not real but drawn. . . . Its point is its light & shade, its colour, which in the evening or the dawn are never the same. Its beauty is living, not dead; warm, not cold. But there you are—'See Naples Bay & die' may be all very well. I shall never see anything which, even to my unsophisticated & prosaic mind, can compare with the Taj.

We have been doing two days sight-seeing at Agra, and I have thought much of you. I hate sight-seeing & yet I would not have missed an instant. I think you would have gone mad with joy. It is perhaps not admirable—this Indian taste —but it's stupendous & it 'gets you'. Fatipur Sikri, the one-time Palace of Akbar, is better than Pompeii. It is alive & absolutely thrilling. . . .

I have become reconciled to India, & it is not because of the Taj. . . . At Oxford I got into the state of 'being intellectual' & playing games, taking exercise, as a necessity. I came out to India interested in books, people, plays & ideas, with a vague idea that health demanded exercise. I found a personnel of second-rate people devoted to doing first-rate things (Father's epigram, not mine) and I was unhappy. I had lost my intellectual brain and found myself with nothing to do. Now I am in it again. It is Eton. Play, sport, games, are the thing; work the odious duty, the side-show! I was unhappy because I could indulge in the former, but had not the latter. How dull would Eton have been with all 'after twelve', all field games & no early school! I have realised it at last, and I am still learning, learning hard, that all the world is the same. As you so brilliantly put it, *'Plus c'est la meme chose, plus ça change.'* . . .

In March we had a fishing camp at Jainti in Northern
Bengal, and while we were there we improvised a family
tiger-shoot. This was an exciting and entirely successful
achievement, thanks to the skilful management of Mr
Nelson, the District Magistrate, who organized it. We only
had two howdah elephants. Antony and Hermione were
placed in one of them, our Military Secretary and an A.D.C.
in the other. A tiger had been located in a clump of high
grass with a stream running through it. The howdah elephants were stationed at one end of this clump, Antony's
being on the bank of the stream up the bed of which we
expected the tiger to go. The rest of the party on three small
pad elephants (Pamela and Davina on one, Mr. Nelson and
I on the second, and two Jamadar shikharis on the third)
then entered the other end, and shouting loudly to make up
for our small numbers, advanced towards the guns.

We could see nothing, as the grass was above the heads of
our elephants, and we could only go very slowly, each elephant clearing its own path. The beat was a short one, and
we had not gone more than half way when we heard a
single shot. We paused and listened, but there were no more
shots and no shouts of triumph. So we moved on again,
feeling nervous and excited at the thought that there was
probably a wounded tiger ahead of us.

When I came in sight of Antony's howdah I saw him
pointing at the feet of my elephant, and looking down I saw
the tiger lying dead in the grass. It had gone up the stream
as we had planned, and shown itself for a moment. Antony's
shot had penetrated its eye, but as it had fallen without a
sound or a movement no one knew what had happened. In
a moment we were all crowding round the spot shouting our
congratulations. An army of professional beaters with 50
elephants could not have driven Antony's first tiger to him
more successfully than his own family had done!

The rest of our days in this camp were spent fishing for
mahseer. Later in the month we all went to a camp in
Cooch Behar, as the guests of the Maharani. Though we all
enjoyed ourselves enormously and had excellent sport, this
camp proved a disastrous experience for Antony and Hermione, who got bitten by mosquitos and sickened with
malaria a few weeks later, when they had reached Darjeeling. We had a very anxious time, as they were both very ill
with high temperatures.

Easter this year was on April 4th, and it was very different
from what we had hoped for and planned. In public matters,
as well as in our private life, it was a time of terrible anxieties. Hermione by this time was beginning to recover, but
Antony was still very ill, with high temperatures. Meanwhile serious communal riots had broken out in Calcutta,
and the situation there was very grave. I sent my Political
Member to take charge of the measures for restoring order,
and remained in daily communication with him, ready to go
to Calcutta at a moment's notice if he thought it desirable.

In a few days Antony was also convalescent and was quite
himself again. By April 11th he was sufficiently recovered to
write a long letter to Edward Woodall, in which he tells
how he has been captivated by India, and makes no mention
of his recent illness:

Here the world has moved back to the old public
school philosophy of despising brains & yet possessing them,
instead of idealizing them & having none. How strangely
different the world seems to one's Oxford conception of it, &
how very utterly removed from it this Indian world! When
I first came here how I missed my Michael Arlen! My gay,
clever, meaningless conversations, my Shelmerdines & sup-
pers at the Berkeley, my *crème de menthe*, my old brandy,
my music, my beauty! How I missed those delicious empty
kisses, good plays, taxis, and bromo-seltzer in the morning!
. . . How I hated India & its middle-class smugness! And now

—How I love it all!! I have lost my heart to India, I have got the call of the East heavy on my shoulders; I have forgotten art & literature, I have seen no good plays, I have read no good books, my literary ambitions have crumbled into a heap of dry papers, I have forgotten the lights of London & the long lazy Oxford mornings.

I adore horses & polo & pig-sticking; I love the atmosphere of the bungalow and the dull talk of dogs & tigers & horses, the lies about shooting and the whispered word of a new polo team come down from the north. I don't want to go home at all. . . .

The next day he wrote to Mrs. Philipson:

Thank you for your sweet though depressing letter. I must have written to you in a sad moment, talking of the 'early pleasures of home—that sweetness which one never can regain' & lamenting a dreary future wedged in the rut of conventionality. One ages rapidly on the road from Marseilles to the East, as Philip Guedalla would say, but I'm not really an old man yet & quite certainly not a wise one! I suppose one must accept life a little more than one did at Oxford, where one was scarcely alive unless one found that the world was mad & wrong, the Church dissolute & useless, God a doubtful existence, all public men dishonest, & most women wicked & clever (though not so clever as an undergraduate) and the world just made as a playground for young men with critical minds and a profound disrespect for any established order! Later on one wonders if this is so, & so one gets desperate and talks of falling into the rut & doing the same as everyone else is doing and has always done. But just think what an enormous rut it is & what very amusing things a great many people are doing & a great many more have done! No, Daph, I'm not really in that complacent frame of mind which sends man with bag daily to catch the 8.37 yet, thank God.

You say that I seem to get more out of life than a great many people. At present I have got a real good tummy pain which brandy & His Excellency's dispensary seem equally unable to check!!! If you can't get anything better out of life than that, I recommend the humdrum existence of George Smith, Esq., his bag, his office and his morning paper, not to mention the little woman who keeps the home warm for him, puts his slippers in front of the fire, and boils his egg for breakfast at 8 a.m. sharp. But I have got more—I have got a good dose of malaria, which has kept me raving in bed with 105° temperature & left me now like a wet umbrella in a snowstorm—inadequate. But it is great joy. In the years to come I look forward intensely to producing a bottle of quinine, shivering all over & shirking to my bed (when I have promised to dine with Lady Bloomfity to hear Mangolaro play the piano) murmuring 'Ah, just a touch of the old fever again'.

One should not, I feel, return empty-handed from India, and I like to feel myself part of the great Imperial tradition which Mr. Kipling has built up round the villas of Cheltenham!

Well, Daph, my dearest, you also ask me what I am doing. And I am afraid the awful truth is that I have felt the East a callin' & fallen in love with this God-forsaken country. I may now never leave it. I have become a man who wears Jodpores & carries half a polo-stick & talks only in terms which Mr. Woodhouse Adams (of 'Mayfair' Prologue Lord great friend of ——) & Mr. Woodhouse Adams alone would appreciate.

Then I have found romance amidst the elephant grass & under the tropical moon where incense burns & the black pearls in her ears glow faintly in the half light! In short I am conquered—conquered by another 'rut' & in another land by the spirit of the East which sends men home to die miserably in middle age, in the most despised villas of England.

Mother goes home next week & my thoughts go with her. Father goes home in June & my thoughts go with him, but it will not be for another year that England welcomes this slang-bitten, sun-dried, middle-class relic of what was once an intelligent English gentleman! At least that's the way things look at present. Because though sometimes I am very

homesick for London & a few nice faces, & for Switzerland
& a pair of skis, I say to myself 'These things Antony are to
be your life—if there's anything you enjoy in India enjoy it
now or forever hold your peace.' So I am off with my
romance & my horses to enjoy a summer in India hunting
& playing polo & worshipping strange men in turbans. And
perhaps when I come home everyone will have forgotten me
& married husbands & be very busy knitting knickers for
their babies. But I shall hope that Daph will say I did know
how to get the best out of life!

This letter seems to be all about myself & rather dull.
How are you, my dear, & is life a brighter thing altogether,
& is there after all fun to be found apart from that ghastly
aftermath which people call contentment & which means
the end for us all? The stage when one writes to one's
friends that it is very beautiful & peaceful here & the
flowers are simply more lovely than you can imagine. And
little Johnnie has grown into such a fine big boy, & there
was a new calf born on the farm last Monday. You must
come and see us, it is very beautiful, though there is nothing
much to do, but I think you would love the garden & the
roses quite remind me of Vienna.

That is a stage in life which older & better & wiser
people will tell you is real happiness & what life truly means.
It is the atmosphere which novelists choose as the perfection
of everything, & it is in a garden of roses that they love to
leave their creations, sleeping peacefully now that life's
fitful fever is done.

In the meanwhile, Daph, join me in a humble prayer
that the Lord for many years will deliver us from all gardens
& all roses & all peace & contentment!!

I must stop because I think I'm mad.

Be happy,

Yr loving,

A.

No sooner had Antony recovered from his attack of
malaria than a new trouble occurred. His Irish terrier

sickened and died, and was found to have had dumb rabies. As a precautionary measure Antony was required to undergo a course of Pasteur treatment with very painful injections, and a new anxiety was created for us all. I was reminded of the Chinese proverb, 'Ills never come singly, so when you arrive home and find your house on fire, be sure and count the change you have received from the cabman!'

At the end of April I went down to Calcutta with the two girls and their mother and saw them off to England. It had been arranged that they should go home this spring before the hot weather began, and that Antony and I should follow them in June, when I had been granted the four months leave which I was unable to take the year before. It was the last of the many partings which were the worst part of our Indian life; but the bitterness of this one was diminished by the knowledge that I should follow them myself so soon, and that in a year's time we should all come home for good.

Antony met me on my return to Darjeeling, with the good news that he had completely recovered and was now quite well again. He had been for a long ride and felt none the worse.

We only had a few happy peaceful days together at Darjeeling, for almost immediately fresh riots broke out at Calcutta, and I had to go there to help restore confidence. A few days later, on May 3rd, Antony fell ill with an attack of dysentery. I had to leave him in a nursing-home and go to Simla, in order to give the Viceroy a report of the situation in Calcutta. On my return I found him once more convalescent. He tells of this illness in the following letters:

To his mother:

This is far the worst kind of illness I have ever imagined existed. I have been exactly a week now without food, and except for the first day have not felt the tiniest bit ill. Everyone says I'm lucky to have it so slightly & to have nipped it in the bud. But I feel the most wretched thing alive. They have started, thank God, to feed me on milk, so that I feel stronger and at times almost jubilant, but for the most part my mind is in a continued state of unrest. I feel like a trapped animal, & can concentrate on books & writing for only little bits at a time. Mostly, I lie and dream of food, the future, & being out of this home again. The cruel part is that the moment I am out all will seem ordinary and the agony be forgotten. Now it seems that to be told 'You may go; you're well' would be a greater joy than entering the gates of Paradise itself—much stronger than that, because that sounds so ordinary. Then again, imagine being a week without food. I feel as if my first meal—proper meal, absolute Berkeley - Ritz - Rue-Royale - G.H. Calcutta - Firpo meal —would send me off my head with sheer delirious ecstasy. But I suppose actually I shall be worked up to it so gradually that I shan't notice it!

However, I think I shall have learnt the great thankfulness one should feel simply for being alive & free & well, with good food to eat, good air to breathe & good things to do.

I have really suffered a good deal this week—not physically, because I have been pretty well—but mentally, because I am imaginative & could make the things I wanted so near that they seemed within my grasp, and then—they weren't there! It has been very hard—but even the milk & sugar & brandy which they have fed me with today has so strengthened me that I feel the end is near and I shall soon be clear of this & well again.

How strange life is. A week's bed in good health should have given me time to write volumes & read libraries, but I have done nothing but dream & rave & hate. I have not been able to do anything else, & now when life starts again it will be the same life, though I feel as if it would be altogether heavenly & blissful & different. Perhaps it will— perhaps I shall have learnt a great lesson. Perhaps that's why I got ill. Who knows?

What of England & the strikes? Quiet reigns in this city
again, and only because Father said 'You are to do this & I
shall see that it is done'. Then, not the quiet of a people
sullenly bullied against their will into doing what they don't
want—not a sulky inevitable quiet—but a gay happy peace,
the peace of a subservient people accustomed to obeying
orders—at last having been given orders again after a terrible era of freedom! Oh, India, India! . . .

Father is at Simla now, but I shall see him again before
the mail goes, & who knows—add a line to you to say all is
well. . . .But I look forward to our last weeks at Darjeeling
together, when we both grow strong & well & can talk the
sun out of the sky. Who knows what fate has in hiding to
mar them? This letter ends—

Your A.

To Edward Woodall:

May 11, 1926.
SOME HOSPITAL IN CALCUTTA.

My dear Edward,
    In the last month I have had malaria, hydrophobia
& dysentery, which I think does justice to the tropics. I am
in bed with the latter now, but fortunately only very slight.
But I've had no food for a week and I am nearly half-witted.
Malaria makes you dog-ill, with terrific pain and temperature
& then—is gone. Hydrophobia is most depressing. A needle
a day, no exercise & no drink. They stopped my treatment
when I had got 14 out of a possible 28 holes in my tummy!

So much for the medical treatment of India. You will
observe that I have not been blessed with good health. The
weather? It's 99° in the shade here, & sticky. I came down
with Father—he to stop a riot & self to see it. He stopped it
and went to Simla, I never saw it & got dysentery! One up
for Dad, as they would say on the halls!

And yet this land has me still under its spell. I am absolutely caught, and whenever I shake clear & think of home,
suddenly something pulls me back. A flat-roofed house
standing amongst trees in the twilight—the great open
peace of the countryside from the train—the sunset falling

on something or other & making it a wonderful pinky colour
—a divine memory of the great coloured splendour of the
Taj—the dust, the whiteness, the smells—oh, a hundred
things. In another year these will be part of me, and then I
shall be longing for the hedges & the comfort of home.

I have been helpless mentally & physically for a week—
unable to write or read; just lying thinking & cursing. But
I see a great literary future ahead of me! The minute I get
home I shall start and I shall turn out the most wonderful
stuff. My head is seething with ideas which only need a
little harness & time to shape themselves, and then there'll
be great books.

I have read *The Constant Nymph* again and come to the
conclusion that it is one of the best novels of this century, if
not of always. It binds me by its brilliance and its understanding, and a sordidness which is not sordid really. I love
the Jews!

I may be imaginative, Edward, but there is still more
romance in the world than anyone dreams of, and there's
most of it lying about here. For all the dirty smug middle-
class militarism of India, which is what one sees at first, the
place is a veritable home of Doris Keanes! It's crawling in
romance, & I have got that way now, so that I see it in every
bamboo-clump in the countryside.

I'm bored & this is a silly letter & they're going to wash
me, so goodbye.   Yrs,

ANTONY.

I arrived in Calcutta from Simla on the morning of May
13th—Antony's twenty-third birthday—and finding him
well enough to go to the hills I left with him the same night
for Darjeeling. Unfortunately I could not stay with him, as
I had to be in Calcutta while the Legislative Council was
considering an Emergency Security Bill, so I returned the
next day. This business was successfully accomplished in a
week, and I was able to rejoin Antony at Darjeeling on May
19th.

He had written to me on the 15th:

GOVERNMENT HOUSE, DARJEELING,
May 15, 1926.

Darling of the sultry Calcutta heat; how I hope you are not melted or broken with fatigue! The literary frame of mind in which you left me this morning has been developing quite alarmingly. I have in the course of the day smoked about 10 pipes and a hundred cigarettes, written 20 sheets of foolscap & about thirty letters, drunk a bottle of Burgundy and read Keats & your grandfather's life and most of your Indian diary. Moreover, my hair has fallen lower and lower over my eyes and my coat got more & more full of holes. This terrific burst of literary neurasthenia (hyper-thyroid) has fortunately burst with a loud bang about a quarter of an hour ago, due to three causes. First of all your diary about Sikkim, which as a literary work is supreme, but as a stimulant to health, energy & a longing for fresh air, far surpasses Eno's or Kruschen. . . . Secondly, the sudden realisation that I was wholly incapable, as well as unfit, to pursue the career of Oscar Wilde, Browning or Maurice Baring. And thirdly, that venturing to put my nose outside the garden door at about six fifteen, I quite distinctly smelt snow in the air! That was altogether too much for me, and though my body still feels like a kitten playing the part of Atlas, my mind reacted suddenly from Bishop Blougram's fireside to the fierce mountain hills! The whole Natu La range was visible tonight above the clouds, stormy-looking and angry with dark blue hills, a sullen sky, and snows colder & more cruel than the Arctic itself. None of the big range were to be seen. . . .

I have, as they say of horses, completed the first part of my training & put on fat; I must now get to work with the munch, and I hope to greet you on Wednesday very nearly 'beautiful, bold & browned'!

I hope the heat won't be too horrid, & that your speeches will echo down to posterity, & that the Council will vote your Bill, and that you will soon come back to your loving son,

A.

We had three weeks together and made several delightful expeditions, both to the high hills and to the tea-gardens in the valleys; but the rains began early this year, and Antony found the mist & the cold of Darjeeling very depressing. This helped to reconcile him to coming home with me. His letters to Edward Woodall show how much India had taken hold of him, and all through this spring, in spite of his illness, he had stuck firmly to his determination to spend the summer in Kashmir and Ootacamund while we were in England. Having been separated from Antony for the last three years while he was at Oxford, the idea of going to England and leaving him in India was quite intolerable to me, and I had many talks with him on the subject, hoping that I might one day find an argument that would induce him to abandon this odious plan. During these last weeks in Darjeeling he finally and very reluctantly decided to fall in with my wishes, and his letters to his mother and sister were full of this subject. Fortunately in this as in all other matters, he was able to pour out his feelings without restraint, and by doing so got the better of them.

To Hermione he wrote on May 25th:

GOVERNMENT HOUSE, DARJEELING,
May 25th.

I have been feeling rather as you were when you wrote to Daddy from the Mediterranean—bowed down by the weight of family love! Only not so nicely as you. You were miserable because Mother would insist on serving you instead of allowing you to serve her! I am merely regretting that I have been brought up to love, admire and understand my parents instead of obeying them!

I've got to give up my plans—if only it was a command, an injunction, a threat, how happy I should be! I should then rebel. But of course it's not. It's a reasonable request reasonably explained, & leaving me with no alternative.

When you have such nice parents it is impossible to be angry
with them—to disobey them, deliberately to hurt them. If
only they were a bit less nice, how much easier life would
be! And so I am groaning under the tyranny of love and
nursing a secret grievance because I can't—I simply couldn't
—do what I want. It only makes it worse to feel that I am
not entirely an aggrieved party, and that I am even looking
forward to England & London again! It was always a wrench
and a difficult thing to balance—whether I wanted to stay
or go. I decided for the former only because I felt that I
would not have that particular chance again, & all new experience in life is good. But I released the other alternative
sadly and with misgiving. I am disappointed that Ooty is off,
but I am glad to be coming home. I can't say the tyranny
has been cruel. I am not miserable, but I am furious. I don't
so much mind not going to Ooty & coming home instead,
but I am absolutely bubbling with indignation that I *can't* go
and stay there & that I *must* come home!

In less than three weeks we shall be gone, and India may
be over for me for ever. I have been very happy really. I
have learnt a great deal which no one knows about me &
perhaps no one ever will, and I felt a romantic spell which
I should not have believed existed anywhere—much less in
Babu-land! So I think I shall come back. But now for home
and the old games & the old folly, and a little beauty but no
romance! I feel sad, glad and mad. And now to ride Birdine
and see the hills & Darjeeling.

Just think of London! What's it like? Who's what? What's
what? What's the rage? What's happening? Who's lovely?
Who's sensational?!!!

I long for Polly, my silly girls, a theatre, Caroline, grand
houses and lunch at the Berkeley!

To his mother he wrote in the same strain, adding:

And now in less than three weeks we shall have turned
our backs on this strange country, with its commonplace
English and its gloriously old history. It has cast a very
strange spell over me which lies deeper than horses and polo

s

& Tajs & Viceregal Lodges—deeper even than pig-sticking.
I don't know quite what it is, whether it will last, or if in
time I shall forget all about it, as I seem to forget everything. . . .

It will be fun, and sometimes I scream with excitement
to think of London things again. A ballroom with pretty
faces! Restaurants, Duchesses, and the dark streets when
they are watering them just before dawn! All so mad & so
gay. And John Revelstoke; and the Gaiety Theatre! There's
lots of change and variation and life! . . .

I don't know. Anyway I'm coming home, & the hedges in
the fields will be fun again. Since the change came about I
have rather gone mad here, am living too fast & too hard &
caring too little. But yesterday I played good polo. Two new
coats for hunting at Ooty are pretty but rather wasted.
Skating, riding, tennis & great walks across the hills. All the
Darjeeling things and more besides, and my brain which
has been so active just killed & told to sleep & keep quiet
and not worry. . . .

I can't argue with Father because I know he's right and
he would always win, but I am not great enough to be in
sympathy with him, and I'm not even great enough to try &
be in sympathy with him. I feel vaguely 'I wish it could
seem like that to me.' He is so nearly perfect that his views
on things will convince & work & hold water. I am so far
from that, I need a little more of human remedies—discipline, hard work and suffering. Then I might grow wiser,
but I am not going to seek these things because it is not in
my nature to look for that kind of trouble! I have nothing of
the martyr about me! Too much of the Sybarite.

And so we meet again in a minute in our own land &
amidst our own people, and it will be very happy. We'll have
sole—not mackerel—in the Ritz grill, and we'll forget the
pilau & the khitmagars. . . .

In the few days that remained Antony played polo, and
went for long walks with me. Finally we made a last expedition to our favourite place in the high hills.

He wrote to Hermione from there on May 30th:

We're at Sandakphu in a thick mist, and I am oddly
enough feeling neither healthy, wealthy nor well. I'm afraid
the old fever has got me with a vengeance! I only seem to be
really well in fits and starts nowadays, and the moment is
neither a fit nor a start! Now that it is definitely England
for me, I am dying to be off and terribly excited to see all my
friends. . . . I have so loved my horse fun out here, though
there hasn't been nearly enough of it. Even polo at Le Bong
has become my chief joy since the mists descended on Darjeeling, and I have joined the ranks of the Colonel and his
friends who hate the place!

But it's not much fun walking in the clouds, and alas I
can't regain my Sikkim health! I think it is as well I am for
England, though I am still not entirely reconciled. Mummie
wrote that I was old in understanding but young in mood.
I don't know about the former, but the latter, I feel, is, oh,
so true. I am still a perpetual mood, now mad with joy &
health & now in the depths of depression & not too well.
Loving now one thing and now another. Quite quite uncon-
trolled but always really happy. . . . My friends have told me
almost in the same words that they loved me, because more
than anyone they had met before I seemed to get so much
and the best out of life. I wonder if it was true—if it is, &
anyway what it means. What a conceited letter and all
about me, but I am terribly fond of myself and think I'm
awfully nice! Father would probably say that subconsciously
I hate myself, because the comfort of one's subconscious as
far as I can see is that it is always the opposite to what the
conscious is. Thus if you are an awful swine, subconsciously
you're an angel, & that's alright. If you are, on the other
hand, an angel, it doesn't matter what the subconscious is!

A.

We sailed for home on June 9th, and returned to India at
the end of September. Our last season in Calcutta was a very
happy time, and we had a large party for Christmas. Antony
did some work for me as an assistant private secretary, and a

lot of riding in the paper-chases at Jodhpur, and in the Horse Show at Tollygunge. He played polo and had some pig-sticking expeditions. As we were all living together at this time I have no letters from him, but one of his best letters was written to Edward Woodall on the eve of his departure from India:

GOVERNMENT HOUSE, CALCUTTA,
March 24, 1927.

Dear Edward,

     I didn't mean to answer your letter, because as I am just coming home it seems foolish to pay any attention to 'mail day'. But as it was probably the best letter that has ever been written in any language—the professional 18th century letter-writers in no way excepted—some tribute must be paid, I feel. I've never read anything more lovely or more beautifully expressed, and I cannot but feel that neither Bournemouth gas nor the bar can have the least idea of what they are dealing with.

But it's a sad day when we chaps become serious and begin to realize that life isn't just one howling joke. I feel like Danton and those poor Revolution people, who grew years older in the course of a single day. And, alas, I have begun to realize what people mean when they say school is the happiest time in life, and also what they mean when they say that each year of life is better than the last. One can never recapture the laughter & the contentment and the finality of school, but who would be at school again? Every day almost I realize some new & infinitely fine shade of thought or emotion in life which I could not even have understood then. And if one thinks more & suffers more, and grows daily more perplexed, at any rate one has those flashes & glimpses of a thing infinitely beautiful & remote, which make the mild pleasure of a game of football very small indeed. All the school things were good, because they were simple & happy & life was easy. And all the grown-up things are better because they are intricate & spasmodically sublime & difficult. After all, when you drink wine, you have first the pleasure of its taste, the delight in its quality, and that in itself can be a man's life-work to understand. Then you have the question of its reaction on you and its reaction on those with whom you drink it. And then if you drink too much of it you have your condition the following morning to consider, your relation to the coming day and to the previous night, and your general attitude to life and to wine.

But when you drink water, you drink it because you are thirsty, you drink as much as you need & no more, you enjoy drinking it because you were thirsty, and when you have drunk it is at once finished & forgotten & its effect is but to satisfy a momentary need. And so God turned water into wine, and so we cease to be children & become men, and so life spreads out before our eyes—a thing difficult and full of interest to be met with and overcome, and so in the full flood of my sermon I suddenly find that I am laughing at myself and stop. And I thank God that I haven't altogether lost His gift of humour!

I am afraid that just now I have got the mind of a woman who is going to have a baby, which the clever modern men describe as being full of complexes. The simile for some reason or other society has condemned as improper, but for all that I am profoundly conscious of my baby and permanently marvelling at it. But how it will turn out I don't know.

I'm coming home next week, and arrive in England the Saturday before Easter. I have no plans & no money & lots of ambition in a mild negative way. It's hell and bliss to leave India, for it is a country infinitely sad, but as full of profound wisdom as the ages. It's like finding all the beautiful pictures in a house, the fruits of a collector's life, hung on the nursery walls and the children on whom they look down unconscious of their beauty. And yet, since children know, they grow up beautiful themselves, and since grown ups don't know, they never remember why & are never thankful. India's rather like that, but I don't quite know how! And when I come home I shall only remember that I played polo and stuck pigs and enjoyed both, that I shot tigers and lay by the side of sparkling rivers in the sunshine and saw the blue line of the Himalayas in the distance. And if I want to tell anyone

about these things, they will say 'Yes, how lovely. Have you
seen the new revue at the Adelphi?' And in six months time
I shall have forgotten too, but there will be a piece of me
that won't, and it will have to try & be satisfied with 'Mandalay'! (on the road to . . .)

But you see the crux of the whole thing is not to be able
to laugh, and I am beginning to understand why Indians
have mostly sad faces, or only laugh like Germans when
you break your neck. The sun goes right through you. It's 96°
everywhere now and the humidity something terrific and
everyone looks liverish. Gosh, what a land!

I spend my time writing affectionate letters of farewell
and thanks to every sort and kind of person, and the tears
stream & roll down my crocodile face without ceasing! For
I have already begun to smell English smells & to see
English trees and green grass, to feel the cool quiet of a summer's evening when the shadows are long. And it makes me
long for Piccadilly!!!

Lots of love,

Yrs,

ANTONY.

We left India on March 28th and travelled home in an
Italian ship to Genoa; going from there to Baveno on Lake
Maggiore, where we spent Easter. Antony did not accom-
pany us, but followed in a P. & O. liner to Marseilles. From
this ship he wrote long letters to us all, some passages in
which are of general interest.

To his mother he wrote:

To India I am determined to return, because it means
so much to me—even the queer degraded poverty of it,
which has touched something in me. I never thought to love
dust but I do, and that's the difference between people who
love India and those who have only liked certain things
there. I have taken the whole land to my heart. But what
does it matter? It is not my life, it is not my home, it is not
for me—just an experience, a good one, sacred and now to

be forgotten; and so immeasurably I thank God for the P. &
O., its inertia and its deadening atmosphere. . . .

Ahead of me you sail gaily homewards, happy, full of
faith in the future and having few regrets. I hope it has
been good and that your Commandante is kind. We shall
meet again soon, and after then, God knows what—but
there will be something of virtue, of happiness, and of
striving, I hope. I don't ask for much more now I have been
so happy, and feel that to make up for that I should suffer a
little—but here, no it's not suffering on this boat, thank God
—it's death.—And the strange thing is that I know I could
write a great book, that I could make my living with my pen,
that I could be really great in that line, and then I should be
happy. But I know too that I never shall. I don't suppose I
shall ever write what is in me, let alone publish it. Well,
never mind. Perhaps I could be a second Henry Ford and
make millions and be rich and odious, and pull the stucco off
Knebworth, and own newspapers, and be feared, and have
achieved something. But what? Or perhaps I shall be Viceroy
and always in debt, and everyone will say 'the third in his
family' and we shan't get much forrarder. Or perhaps I
shall stay Antony and no one will know why, and nothing
will ever happen at all, and life will be a permanent P. & O.,
but I'll have a few friends—anyway it doesn't much matter.
My 23 years have been very full and happy, and I am thankful. I suppose the others will be happy too—but who would
be happy as a Boxwalla or Henry Ford is happy? When all
the world turns round to the tune of rupees and dollars,
where is Kanchinjunga in the dawn? . . .

I feel confident we were right when we said that for India
—soldiers. We deceive ourselves in thinking we aren't a
military nation. As a nation we are just one solid Army,
pure, pure soldiers. Don't you agree with me about this? It
seems to me that we are essentially a nation of soldiers—not
militarists.—As a people the English seem to have all the
qualities of a good soldier, and that is why we have a small
Army and a dislike of militarism, & yet when there is fighting to be done we suddenly become rather fine. There is the

grit which makes good soldiers; there is the love of order and the hatred of discipline, there is a sense of fairness & justice, efficient, rather ruthless, but inevitable; there is a tremendous corporate spirit, a comparative carelessness about death, and when it comes to fighting a nice light-heartedness. There are certain qualities I feel in the English which make them born soldiers, and consequently no sort of good at soldiering as an art. They win because the possibility of losing doesn't seem to exist. There is something in the make-up which eliminates the exertion of running away. That's not good soldiering, but it's amazing good at making soldiers. Napoleon made war an art and his armies were amazing good at soldiering. They won so easily, but when they didn't win they ran away. That's the art—like chess or any other game at all—you win, or if you don't win, you lose. And that's what makes military nations, and that's why we pretend we don't like militarism. We don't indulge in that art because we're such good soldiers. The Germans & the French and the Romans of old were all much better at soldiering than we shall ever be, but they weren't nearly such good soldiers. Knowing the game, they considered the chances of losing & took peculiar pains to win. We, not knowing the game, have never considered the possibility of losing, and so —as people who have fought us have said—we don't play fair because when we're beaten we don't realize it. I don't think a British army has ever run away except perhaps once or twice in the 18th century, and then there was a vague idea in the land, brought in from Germany, that we knew something about soldiering! . . .

His letter to Hermione so completely sums up his feelings about India that it may fittingly close this chapter:

P. & O. S. N. Co.,
S.S.

There *are* no places, dates, times or names on this ship.

I have become quite clear in my own mind about India & England, the only thing I don't understand is how

one can change so easily and with so little mental effort
from the one to the other. I think perhaps only I can do so,
because my mind is so extraordinarily supple and easily influenced. But the difference is exactly—more than I thought
even—the difference between Eton and Oxford. India is
Eton. The admiration for strength, a healthy out-door life,
the love of games, the noisy fun. A need for work—a little
work to make a grievance, like early school. But the thing—
polo, pig-sticking, riding, shooting, instead of football, cricket,
boxing. That was life & the real people were those to whom
that life belongs. That is why the soldiers show up in India &
one loves them. They are men physically, & that was all one
cared for at Eton. The criterion there was the much-criticised
criterion of games, and people who couldn't show up in that
aspect were tiresome. . . . The clever ones hadn't got enough
spunk to be loved at Eton. They loved Eton, I've no doubt,
and found in it what I could never have found—the dawn of
intellectualism in themselves. But the only thing there was
manliness as embodied in games. In a way India is the same.
The thing there is the men. Somehow intellectual, clever
people, with ideas & thoughts & hobbies and interesting
minds, didn't fit. . . . My gods in India were the soldiers. . . .
I don't know why this should be so, but with me it was
so. . . .

Then Europe is like Oxford. A world of books and people
& art & literature & learning & clever talk & humbug &
genius. . . . And my mind, in a vague attempt to keep pace
& fit in, turns from polo & hunting & pig-sticking to think
of books & plays & people and a gay brilliant world. And
similarly the soldier goes down & seems to become the dull,
stupid creature who went to Sandhurst because he couldn't
get into the University, who hasn't an idea beyond horses
and the drab talk of the mess, who is in short unbearable.
And up come the brilliant, soft, cultivated intellectuals, who
make you forget in the wit & charm of their after-dinner
conversation, that if you hit them once in the tummy they
would die. I can't quite reconcile the two things ever. But I
am double enough to be able to live on books & plays in

England & horses & sport in India. And I don't feel, when in England I say the soldier is a dull, narrow sort of man with few ideas, and in India that the intellectual is an effeminate, odious parasite, that I am betraying either. Because I am betraying myself. Both things belong to me, and while I abuse only myself it doesn't matter.

In India I should be really happy in an Indian Cavalry Regiment, married, with ponies for my life's interest, and with a certain dullish regular work to live for. In England I am happy unmarried, trying to write, an occasional game of tennis, drifting, friends, talk, wine, etc. I could never write a book in India, I could never join the Army in England. I want to be married & settled down all the time in India, I want to drift and laugh & flirt in England, I want to live out of doors with horses & exercise in India, I want my writing-table, my books & my plays in England. Of course the two things are not quite as divisible as all that, because at some points they must necessarily cross & interlace as they both lie inside the same individual. But I think that the line between East & West is a line drawn pretty clearly between Antony and Antony, and is simply personified between Eton & Oxford. I don't feel this is quite the same for anyone else, but you may understand it. The only thing that amazes me is the ease with which that line is crossed. . . .

What a long dull letter. I get that way on a ship. But for the first time I am not groping after a lost and ungraspable philosophy. I have found something which to me is clear as daylight, and all I want to do is to explain it.

It was sweet of you to write as you did. I know that we shall always understand each other perhaps more than anyone else. Only as we grow older & our lives of a necessity become more separated, there will be a growing shyness about some things between us. Perhaps we shall now and then be able to break down that barrier, & once it has been broken we shall find what we were looking for—sympathy, understanding, love. But the barrier must exist and I'm afraid grow, because although we are brother & sister we are also man & woman. Every day of my life it seems to me that the difference between man & woman is more distinct. Mentally, physically & emotionally they are so far apart. Often they can meet over some thing or other & perhaps feel that they have met over all things. That is the great mistake. There is nothing I dislike more than a certain modern attitude which tries to make them the same. Their souls even are so different I feel that understanding between the two is almost impossible. But when you fall in love, that barrier mysteriously goes, and not understanding you can yet understand. That is to me the most wonderful thing about marriage, the strange way in which it becomes possible for them to become the same. A man can never really understand what goes on inside a woman, nor can a woman understand some things in a man—though that way is easier. But when you are in love you do understand—you both understand, although it is impossible. Love & sympathy provide that understanding when the intellect & the emotions break down. . . .

I daresay you will not have the faintest idea what I am talking about. But the point of it is that I see a very real & curious difference between man & woman which all the clever modernists cannot destroy. And that, darling, is all that lies between you & me. It is a barrier that makes us sometimes shy, but when it can be done away with, then we are as we were when we were children, hand in hand and entirely intimate.

And now, as you say, we have got a future, but if you come to think of it we shall always have that. The great thing in the 20th century is not to have a past! And talking of pasts, I think we already have passed you! I don't know. Perhaps we shall meet at Port Said.

I am having quite fun on this boat, but just when I think it most fun I suddenly realise that it isn't & that I can't be bothered. And then just when I want to give up altogether & sulk, I find it's quite fun after all! And so we struggle along through this icy cold, rough Red Sea, & as far as I can see we might as well be heading for Spitzbergen!

As we get older we get wiser, & as we get wiser we laugh less until in the end we become stupid again & die with a happy grin—though a bit toothless. Fortunately I'm still very stupid and so can laugh now & then—generally on Wednesdays!

Such love

from

ANTONY.

Chapter IX

SEEKING A PROFESSION

1927-1931

*'The young mood will die, and the old thought prevail,
and who knows, I may yet be an engine-driver or a Rear-
Admiral, a bus conductor or a Cabinet Minister. I shall be
Antony anyway——'*

ON OUR return from India in the spring of 1927,
Antony's chief preoccupation was to find employment
which would, if possible, be remunerative and either a preparation for or compatible with his ultimate career. As some
of his letters have shown, the question of his career had
frequently been discussed between us both in conversation
and by correspondence.

In the family discussions Antony's own mind was very
undecided. He recognized the need for making money, but
he had no taste for the kind of life which money-making
seemed to necessitate. His tastes were all for an active out-
of-door life, with as much adventure in it as possible. He
repeatedly insisted that he had no capacity for business, and
no ambition to make money. But it was characteristic of him
that when later the opportunity unexpectedly came his way
he threw himself into business with the same conscientious
thoroughness and zeal that he applied to politics and to
sport, and found in the development of the business, and the
human relationships which it involved, all the interest
which mere money-making could never have aroused in
him.

His first venture was not a success and was of short duration.

Through the influence of a friend, he was offered an opening with a firm of Stockbrokers in the City. He started work there in May, but found the nature of the business entirely uncongenial. There was little to do during the office-hours, except answer the telephone and follow the news of the buying and selling transactions in which other members of the firm were engaged. It was not paid work, and his only hope of making money for himself was to secure clients, and earn a commission on the orders they might give him. Success in this could only be achieved out of office, and he found that he was expected to make use of his social engagements in the evenings and at country-house parties to obtain orders from his friends. This was distasteful to him, and he never became a successful stockbroker. He stuck to the work with ever-growing impatience through the summer months, and abandoned it for work of another kind in August. Excusing himself, he wrote to his mother:

You say I have no ambition. At least as you mean it—the ambition of achievement, the ambition to be in the future—I have not. But I have an ambition which is different—not Wolsey's ambition, nor yours. Mine is the ambition to be *now*, not the ambition of achievement, but the ambition of life. You would have me make my life for the future. I would make my future out of my life. My ambition leads nowhere, has no backbone, but is happy. Yours makes Prime Ministers, successful business men, etc., but I doubt whether it makes happiness. . . .

His next venture was of a different kind, and gave him some experience of the machinery of political organization. In September he started work in the Education Department of the Central Conservative office. Here he had no expectation of making money, but he received a small salary and had regular office hours with definite work to do. With the object of interesting the rising generation in Conservative politics, he visited the Universities, and travelled about the country in the winter months.

During September I was attending the Assembly of the League of Nations at Geneva, as the leader of the Indian Delegation, and Antony wrote to me there on September 8th:

I have a palatial office here—worthy of Rockefeller at least, enthusiastic Conservative men to work under, no data, no knowledge, no ideas and a more or less completely open field to work in. I am hampered by the one & only existing report on political activity in the Universities (1925) telling of an almost universal apathy towards politics. My sympathy being altogether with the apathetic undergraduates, I am startling the Central office by suggesting that they are better got at through beer and football than by Conservative Associations. My theories are as usual clear & definite, my constructive policy, as usual, nil!

From next week I am a permanency nowhere, but must wander over the face of the land seeking to persuade young men to do things they don't want to, and that I don't particularly want them to do.

I horrified my Chief's Private Secretary by saying the day of my arrival that the University apathy to politics seemed to me a really healthy sign! He said that he knew he was a fanatic, but he believed that every individual in England should think about & care for nothing else. I told him he needed a long holiday! On the whole I'm afraid that I haven't started too well.

From Leeds he wrote to his mother on September 27th:

The more I see of this political business, the more convinced I become that it *is* a class war. Some may follow us a little while yet, probably because they like us. But it only takes a bad generation & the thing is gone & gone for ever.

The Labour people are bound to win, as the French won, and as the Russians won, but our tradition will be maintained, & it will be a bloodless revolution. How much they will do or undo I don't know, probably less than we believe, but it has got to happen and in my lifetime, & there will be great changes, and an aristocracy destroyed. After all, we are the last aristocracy surviving in all the world, and it doesn't much matter whether we give way to wealth or Socialism. What will come after I don't know. A gradual sorting and sifting, I imagine, & in the end a new aristocracy like the American one which will be all money. But I think our day is done, because though we are trying hard now to build on logic there is too much logic the other way. . . . We may be nice a little longer, and loved here & there a little longer individually, but the ice we walk on is cracking. There are great holes, & where a hole opens up the ice never closes over it again.

We are trying to make a political issue out of a class one. Perhaps we are right, and I have no doubt that we have wisdom on our side. But we have nothing else. . . .

I put no faith in the creeds, the politics, the business issues at stake. I put it only in the personnel, but when that begins to fail—and surely it is failing fast & with education will fail faster—we are doomed. . . .

Directly after Christmas we went to Switzerland together. His achievements this year in the principal races were not up to his previous standard. In all sports when one gets near the top it is constant practice alone which brings success. The loss of two years while he had been in India meant that he could not defeat men who during that time had not only maintained but improved their standards of two years ago.

He wrote to me after his return to his office, when he was feeling the usual irksomeness of work after play:

January 24th.

I'm afraid that politics seem to matter most excessively little, and it is with even less enthusiasm that I set out to tell the youth of Britain to be Conservative. On the other hand, it seems a quite ordinary & natural thing to do. . . .

It is hard to find *the* thing in life—the one that counts most, that makes you happiest, that seems best worth while. But Switzerland is near it, and one day I always feel it may alter the whole course of my life.

However, as I say, one is adaptable, and now I'm rather looking out for the next amusement. One must after all have something to look forward to besides Easter eggs! . . .

When I returned from Switzerland I suggested to Antony that he might now stand for Parliament, as if he was going to make politics his profession I thought the sooner he got into the House of Commons the better. I asked him what he thought about it. We had many talks about this, and he wrote to me on February 2nd:

I feel not sure about it yet, and so want to leave it until after the next Election. It would mean £50 a year less than I get now, but the point is that I want to write. I am going to start trying as soon as I am settled in London, and I don't want definitely to associate myself with any party until I know more.

If I wrote under my own name as a Conservative M.P., I should have to write the kind of stuff I would be supposed to believe in. I am not sure about it yet, and don't want to link up irrevocably with the party until I see how the writing goes.

I admit the virtue of starting a profession young, but I don't admit the virtue of labelling yourself as any particular thing young. I'm not crazy about politics either.

I'm quite happy at this job, which isn't too dull, is quite well paid, and I think a good political training-ground. I want to do it for a year, try my hand at writing, and if that is a success, plank for it altogether, as it is what amuses me. If it is a failure, well, I am no worse off, and anyway I should have to chuck this job if I was going to stand. I think it sweet of you to say you would pay my expenses, but yet I am not all-together enough for it.

T

Another subject which we often discussed with him this year was whether or not he should join the Hertfordshire Territorials, and on this subject he wrote to me on March 16th:

About the Territorials. If I must, I must, but I loathe the idea of infantry, and walking and walking. If I have got to be a Territorial soldier, I had rather be a man with a horse. However, the real point is this—Will they give me extra leave from here as a Territorial for camp? From some offices they will, from others they won't. I don't intend to use my rather scanty leave serving my county (not country) on foot and in camp! I will find out about this, and then be able to consider and discuss the question on its merits. If they do let me have leave, I am not sure that then I wouldn't rather spend it on a battleship in the Mediterranean as an R.N.V.R.

Antony settled this question for himself two years later by joining the Auxiliary Air Force. He thus found the means of serving his country without the tedium of 'walking, walking', and in the air he found all the thrills for which his adventurous nature craved.

His chief interest this spring was in the search for a flat in London. We were living at Knebworth at this time, and Antony felt that both his work and his tastes required that he should have an establishment of his own in London. The difficulty was to find something sufficiently small and inexpensive to suit his requirements. Finally he selected a small flat, in the rather unconventional locality of Bond Street. He took great pleasure in furnishing these rooms with an assortment of spare furniture from Knebworth, and moved into them in May. He wrote happily from there on May 30th to his mother, after a brief holiday at Knebworth:

My darling,
This is just a line to say goodnight—like it always used to be from school on the first night back. It was a grand

holiday, with sun and no clothes and a great wave of returned health. I loved it as much as anything ever. If I was
ever sulky, if I am ever sulky, I don't mean to be. It's because I'm twenty-five, and one doesn't always see things as
clear as daylight then. I was so very happy and I am so very
happy.

And now I am back in this new exciting home, and tomorrow the daily round starts again, but with a refreshed &
renewed spirit. It starts as it has always started since that
January long ago in 1913, when I was nine years old, and as
it will go on starting, I suppose, until some January in 2002
when I am ninety-nine. But things get easier & happier &
the little things less real & important until the daily round
becomes life, and the sun & the water & the green trees, the
running bare-foot & the old clothes & the fresh air just its
background.

For the present there is virtue in the daily round, just because it is the daily round, and it is always a mystery to me
why I should be paid for it! I never used to be, and it seems
all that I do now is less pointful, less worth while than anything I have ever done. But there is virtue, as I have said,
and there is, incomprehensibly, money. One is a spoke in
the wheel, though to what purpose it is hard to say. But
there, I am twenty-five.

And so now a great thankfulness for the other things, for
you, for my home, for all those years of happiness, for the
sun and for laughter. And with that thankfulness the daily
round is gone & vanished and becomes just a new glimpse
of life, a new joy, a new excitement. Good old 108, New
Bond St.!!

> Yr very loving son,
>
> ANTONY.

He worked at the Conservative Office during the summer, and as usual found it impossible to reconcile himself
to an office chair while the sun was shining outside. At
school and College it had always been in the summer
months that he was most restless and discontented. This

mood is reflected in a letter he wrote to his mother on July
25th:

> . . . I have just read your divine & not in the least
> 'soppy' letter. I should work perhaps, but I must answer it
> now. And in that sentence is the whole embodiment of
> *me*. . . .
>
> What I suffer from is a too sensitive barometer inside me.
> It is heart, soul & body—everything, mind, brain, etc.,
> rolled into one, & I can only call it a barometer. . . .
>
> What I mean is this—I have not got a consistency, a line
> of thought, an ambition, an object. It is coming more &
> more, I think, and will be there in the end—a definite
> guiding light. At the moment I am a martyr to, or a slave
> of, the last book I have read, the last cinema seen, the last
> person loved, the last idea thought of, the last conversation
> held—whatever it may be.
>
> I think that way one cannot be entirely, fundamentally
> happy. But I would rather it were this way. I feel that this
> must inevitably be the hardest moment in a young man's
> life. Those who get the best of it are those who drift happily
> —who have not got the sensitive barometer. They don't
> think or worry; they don't care about overdrafts, women,
> health, ambition; they don't have ideas & complexes; they
> just live & they are happy. . . . Or else they are the type
> with a definite object who know without a shadow of doubt
> what they *mean* to do. . . .
>
> I was like that at school, & no one loved life more. No one
> does more, for that matter, & I would rather have that baro-
> meter, & know the heights of happiness & the depths of
> despair, than be content. It so happens that at the moment I
> am going perhaps through rather deep waters. Good—I
> must & shall win out.
>
> To some life is a drift of material nonsense, mine is a
> mental drift. You can't be fundamentally happy on cocktails,
> gambling, night-clubs & talk. You can't be fundamentally
> happy on complexes, ideas, ambitions, hopes & doubts. . . .
>
> You said once I was old in thought but young in mood. . . .
> I feel that you were tremendously right.

That is me. I am not really unhappy. . . . Sometimes I have felt that I am essentially a physical being—my mind depending so much on my health & my happiness on my body. A week or so ago I was sure that in London I should never be happy. I decided to emigrate; to live a healthy life in a new & healthy land. The joy of the body & the happiness of the agrarian mind. But I know deep down that the one thing would please no more than the other. If I learnt agriculture & estate management & settled on Knebworth as a profession—was in the air all day, well, interested, content, etc—if I did—it would be the same. Then I should feel that was not enough—not satisfying. It didn't lead anywhere; it did not make for achievement; it did not exercise the mind; it was not great enough.

If I am unhappy in London it is because I want the sun, the country, the air; to ride, walk, swim & laugh in the life God made man to live. It is all the same, you see. Just that barometer.

Boiled down, it comes to this—I am inevitably a reed much blown by every breeze, but I think with the root planted solid enough. The winds will drop and my contentment come when something absorbs me. It may be a wife; it may be some work; it may be ambition. It will come though, I know—that fine day when the reed doesn't have to wave all the time.

Work here doesn't happen to be interesting at the moment. Now & then it is, & then I am absorbed, thrilled, happy. Boys & girls don't happen to amuse me at the moment; now & then one of the latter does, & then I am absorbed, thrilled, happy. My future on the whole is still obscure, undefined, vague. Now & then I see it as a ray of sun through the mist, & then I am absorbed, thrilled, happy.

That is the way with me. I am not unhappy really, but I would not have it otherwise for all the wealth, all the wisdom, all the content in the world.

I may never be a very happy man, probably never a very great one, but I shall die, I think, with all the shades of life, joy, happiness, sorrow, despair, wisdom & ignorance, sympathy & understanding at my command. The young mood will die & the old thought prevail, & who knows, I may even yet be an engine driver, or a Rear-Admiral, a bus conductor, or a Cabinet Minister.

I shall be Antony anyway. . . .

I loved your letter, and my answer has far exceeded it in length, but I hope it will help you a little to understand. I thank God that we can talk like this, and I shall love you always—perhaps too much. But if there are deep waters to swim, or mysterious battles to fight, I feel I must do the swimming & wield the sword (better still a right hook to the jaw). Life is too good, darling, and I love it.

And now that breeze has blown itself out & the reed must, for the moment, remember the solidity of its roots.

I must stop writing to you & get on with my work.

In September we went to Geneva again for the Assembly of the League of Nations, and Antony wrote to his mother there from Plas Newydd:

How are the French and the League and the lake and the brilliant Continental Statesmen and the ancient traditions of Calvin? The Presbyterian peace engineered by a horde of swashbuckling War Ministers in a dozen different languages? It's like the Tower of Babel gone the other way round. As the Eton Master said, when someone proposed to build a great tower as a War memorial, 'Why not dig a great hole'? It's all rather inconsequent and incoherent this, isn't it? But I wonder how you are liking it all and whether you are carried away by the oratory and the Locarno spirit, or just prefer Diana?* . . . C — I love with all my heart. . . . She is as sweet as the whole calendar of saints, and I am unfortunately as sour and cynical as the weak fallen ones. . . . but things all mellow down, and really we are the same.

M. A. has all the wit and all the sweetness and all the talent there is.

I shall go and swim in a cold grey sea, I think, for the

*Lady Diana Cooper, whose husband was a British delegate.

good of my body and in the hope that it may be for the good
of my soul too. I have talked too much with crowds and lost
my virtue, and you will have walked with Kings and lost
the common touch. We should meet on fair ground again
when you come back with the peace of the world heavy on
your shoulders. . . .

A few days later he wrote joyfully from his flat in Bond
Street:

I am ecstatically happy. Have not been so happy for ever
such a long time. The *vivre caché* business is heaven to me.
There is work to do in the daytime—not too interesting,
perhaps, but definitely to be done. No longer a tentative
business of waiting and wondering. I am boxing again, as I
have two fights in October. I cook my own dinner, which is
fun, and eat it, which is better. I write a little, read a little,
and go to bed gloriously exhausted, and wake doliciously
refreshed. I have two engagements on Saturday afternoon
for the Central Office, and two speeches for them in the near
future. Lots of things at Knebworth to be done too. In fact,
I have become grown up and pompous and a Cockney, and
I love it all. Life's smile is bewitching, and a few months of
this life, which is at any rate economic, should cheer the
heart of our Bank Manager, I think. The simple life and a
good deal of work seems to be altogether my thing, and I am
literally basking in the sunshine of happiness.

His work at the Conservative Office terminated at the end
of this year, as the receipt of a generous legacy enabled the
Conservative party to acquire the property which came to
be known as the Bonar Law College at Ashridge, and this
College superseded the Education Department of the Central
Office, in which Antony had been working.

In November he accepted an invitation to contest the
borough of Shoreditch. This was a Labour stronghold, and
he had no chance in the then conditions of political opinion
of winning it from the sitting Member, Mr. Thurtle; but it
afforded him an opportunity of winning his political spurs,

and gaining at first hand some experience of the conditions of life in a poor district of London.

'On Monday I dine with Curzon,'* he wrote to his mother on November 23rd, 'and he is to take me down to the constituency. I suppose they want to vet me before they settle on buying me definitely. If I am passed as sound, I imagine there will be a certain amount of work to be done in the next month or so, and now that it looks so near I funk it!'

He was formally adopted as the Conservative candidate, and for the remainder of the year was busily engaged in making himself known in the constituency.

He went to Switzerland immediately after Christmas, and I joined him there on January 3rd. His strong wish for a long winter holiday in which he might recover his form in ski-ing could not be realised, as with the prospect of a General Election early in the New Year he felt that he ought not to be absent for long. Pleasure had to be subordinated to duty, and he returned early in January to nurse his constituency.

The first four months of 1929 were devoted to Shoreditch. Antony lived in his Bond Street flat and visited his constituency daily. He made such good progress, and won so many friends, that we even began to think he might secure a large turn-over of votes. But the tide was running strongly against the Conservative Government all over the country, and although Antony was very popular with all classes he made little impression on their political opinions. The experience, however, was of the utmost value to him. He learnt to know something of the suffering, the patience and the courage of those whose life is a perpetual struggle with poverty and unemployment. His heart was wholly with these people in their difficulties and anxieties, and his long talks with them in the public-houses, in the Clubs, and in

*Now Earl Howe.

their homes enabled him to understand the bitterness of their class hatreds. His own manliness, sympathy and sincerity did much to soften this bitterness in all who got to know him. His brief connection with these people was a mutual education. His own political opinions were broadened and enriched by contact with those so much less fortunately situated than himself, and he left behind him in the constituency memories of a bright and generous personality which will be long remembered, even by his political opponents.

The Election took place on the 30th of May and resulted in the return of Mr. Thurtle. It was a three-cornered contest, with a Liberal as well as a Labour candidate, and Antony was at the bottom of the poll. Although feeling ran high at the time, the Election was conducted without any unpleasant incidents. After the result of the poll had been declared it was Antony, not Mr. Thurtle, who was carried out of the Town Hall on the shoulders of those who had voted against him!

Immediately after the election Antony wrote his impressions of it to Mr. Ronald Cartland, with whom he had worked in the Conservative office:

> KNEBWORTH HOUSE, KNEBWORTH,
> *May*—No, *June* 2, 1929.

Dear C,
    Here is a fine P.S. to your great political novel. I can give you a lot of 'copy', if you want it. . . .

I have learnt more about the Labour party and about the working of the Labour party than I ever dreamed of, and also of the Conservative party. I am clinched for ever now in my fidelity to the latter. I have also learnt that none of this knowledge is of any avail if you want to guess the outcome of an election.

Nothing will ever get right in this country until there has been a strong Labour government, and then it will probably take 12 years as in Queensland.

I have seen first-hand the thing we are fighting against, and haven't been able to see it even though I did.

I was more cheered and better received everywhere in Shoreditch, even than Thurtle. But the Xs were not put against my name. It is forces without any doubt that win or lose elections and not people. Forces can be calculated in offices, whereas on the spot people eclipse them. At the same time, & this is what offices don't know, people create forces though they take 20, 30, 50 years to do so.

It may amuse you that one of our Imps Committee was working outside the polling-booth for the Liberals!

And thank you, by the way, for your telegram.

The only thing in which I have done right for the past two years was in advising you not to risk all and stand at this election. No one had a chance, because we were fighting not Ramsay but John Burns, not Ll. G. but *Laissez faire*, not for Baldwin but for Ld Liverpool!

Yrs, and thank you for helping with the Imps such a lot.

K.

To the same:

June 4, 1929.

. . . Thanks for your letter. I must see you some time & tell you all about it. I know all about the political situation, have incidentally gone raving mad, but believe that the hour for 'Young England' is very nearly ripe. (Hours dont get 'ripe', I know!)

Things move quicker in this century. It took the 18th century Tories nearly a century to get straight, and Dizzy about 50 years. It will only take 15-20 this time.

The signs are significant, as you say. The best men out, and only the country die-hards in. It was always that way— but it doesn't signify. . . . The Conservative party is smashed for eight years at least. The time is ripe for organization. If only we had a paper! If only we had a leader! Out of the chaos the latter may arise, but I doubt the former. The press people are bound to die hard because of their vested interests.

I think the key to the situation is Lord Cecil, but if I said so all would agree that I am mad.

We must have Conservative men & Liberal measures. The League of Nations, peace policy and the conquest of the industrial seats again.

Education yes, but it is difficult & not really what the people want themselves. The best education is experience, and the thing that we fight not so much ignorance as class. An intelligent electorate would equally have known that Baldwin was wrong. They will only know who is right when they have tasted Labour Government and been given a good alternative. At present there is none but the die-hard Toryism of the country.

But enough,   K.

To the same:

June 11*th*, 1929.

. . . I must confess that I am not a little guilty of all the things which you so rightly complain of. My difficulty is first of all that I have hated and disapproved for so long of the Conservative Government that I cannot but be glad in some ways at its fall. Secondly, I have made such friends with the Shoreditch Labour people, whom I believe to be worth twice the Shoreditch Conservatives, that I cannot but be glad that they have got their chance. Thurtle fascinates me. He has all the charm of the great demagogue. A second Danton, and I have never met a man who had the same kind of charm for me. But that is beside the point, and anyway he does not really count in the grand political issue. The other Labour people down there who are pleasant will, of course, come in when the new Conservatism is on its feet and the Labour party has failed. These are only personal prejudices like the charm of lovely ladies who, in the course of things, have to be trodden under foot!

Broadly, the political situation bears such a perfect comparison to that of a hundred years ago that as an historian, or one who founds all his beliefs on history, I am positively delighted. I expected it? Yes, though candidly not this time. I thought it would take one more election. But things move more quickly nowadays and it is all to the good. We shall get our chance and the country its the sooner. That's all. The late Government had to fall, and fall badly, sooner or later. It has done so sooner. It had no imagination, no policy, no ability even. But it did the spade work which always has to be done, first of all after a war, and then before the Government which is to count can find its feet. I dont mean the Labour Government. That will do no harm, but will do no good either, because it will not have imagination and because it is hedged around with prejudices. If it calls on the imagination which exists within its ranks and makes use of that, then it will commit suicide. Because it is WRONG. . . .

This is my prophecy. Two years of this Parliament, then another election and an increased Labour majority. After that our chance, though not yet, I think, our achievement. Labour has been built up over many years. The people have put their money and their work into the movement. The issue in the country today is not a political one but a class one. We shall not start to win important seats again until this prejudice has been broken down. There are two ways of breaking it down and bringing the issue back on to political grounds, I. Education—a slow process. II. A few years of Labour Govt—a much more rapid form of I. Much will have happened by then. . . .

For myself, I am still hesitating between doing the right thing in a small way and staying at Shoreditch to win the election after next and hold it thereafter, or doing the right thing in a big way and getting into Parliament by hook or by crook, even at the expense of marrying an American wife and thereby ruining the chances of there being a fifth intelligent Lytton! But in the cause of his country a man must, I think, sacrifice even the strongest family ties, and I fear that the days of an intelligent aristocracy are very nearly over. Perhaps a commercial Lytton would not be a bad thing after all.

However, I shall sit tight, wear the badge of party, say the right things, write some books, seem a little disinterested, know what goes on and wait until the moment arrives. But that cannot be for eight years at least. *En politique il est peut-être sage de peu parler.*

Now you know all about it, and if you want something to do which is well worth while, go and see the Guitrys in the best thing which has been put on the London stage in my lifetime.

The country air is very pleasant, and my study of the earlier prize-fights extremely absorbing. . . .

These letters afford an illustration of the rashness of political prophecies. They were written by a very inexperienced young man immediately after the General Election of 1929, and are interesting because they express the opinions of the writer at the moment; but Antony's opinions, like his moods, were continually changing, and the chief value of his letters lies in the fact that they are a faithful record of all the developments through which he passed. Not even an old and experienced politician could probably have foreseen at that date the economic crisis which developed two years later, and led to the formation of the National Government of 1931.

The last sentence of his letter of June 14th refers to a book on Boxing which he had been commissioned to write for the Lonsdale Library of Sport. He also contributed to the same series a chapter on Ski-ing, in the volume devoted to Winter Sports. These two books occupied him for the remainder of this year.

At the end of the summer he went for a round of visits in Wales and Scotland, and wrote happily of the open-air life which he loved. The following letter from Vaynol, where he was staying with Sir Michael Duff, contains an amusing description of an accident which occurred to one of the party:

Aug. 12.

We have just been bathing at Plas Newydd, where I regret to say Pauley * fell off the ring (that goes into the bath-

*Lord Sudley.

ing pool. Remember?) As there was no water when he fell, it was rather unpleasant, and the sole of his foot turned round and looked at him. We thought the leg broken, but his ankle was put out & is now well, I hope. It was a 'scene', and various people's reactions to it were amusing. Marjorie,* who alone permanently visualizes such things, had a doctor present in $\frac{3}{4}$ second and was as calm as a cucumber. Wissie † forgot she was a Scientist, fainted, and then threw a fit, banging her head against a table. Bill‡ was the best, competent, calm & efficient, with ideas for 'taking Pauley's mind' off his leg—a difficult thing to do when you are suffering the tortures of the damned, and able for the first time in your life to study the configuration of the sole of your right foot.

The children thought it the best party ever. All the horrors on which they had been brought up, & the existence of which they must, by now, have begun to doubt, actually being real happenings before their eyes.

Michael excelled himself. I said 'Hold his leg up, Mike'. 'W-w-wwwhich leg?' 'The bad one'. 'This one?' seizing the good one. 'No'. He then caught the bad leg in the grip of a vice and twisted it. To which Pauley objected. 'S-Sorry'—and let it drop with a thud on the floor.

'Hold it up, Mike'.

He then caught Pauley round the neck, and talking at the top of his voice proceeded to walk round & round him.

Marcella§ went for a walk—alone. Diana Cavendish had tea, and Dorothy Ashley-Cooper went back to examine the scene of the accident and settle exactly where which part of Pauley hit what. The butler was on the doorstep with brandy. Charlie‖ was away, and Bendigo¶ said, 'This kind of thing provides no fun for a chap at all' and went to sleep.

Pauley, I may say, was heroic, and in spite of all the help we gave, may yet recover. His mind leapt immediately into the future, and he could only envisage an old age with only

*Lady Anglesey.   †Hon. Phyllis Astor.
‡Hon. W. Astor.   §Mrs. Edward Rice.
‖Lord Anglesey.   ¶His dog.

one leg. On which prospect he made the only possible comment, 'Damn', and then spoke no more.

We have left him at P.N. on a sofa with a surgeon, a doctor and an anaesthetist, and Michael being host but hating
the sight of blood, needles, broken legs, pain and the doctor.

I must dress for dinner now. . . .

In a letter to Hermione from Plas Newydd on August
28th, he wrote:

Anglesey I find is eventually stimulating. The laziness,
the finality, the inertia of it, win for three blissful days and
then provide such an incentive to thought and work as the
stake provided to early Christianity. . . .

I find curiously enough that each stage in life is perfect in
retrospect, and each a little better than the last. At the
moment the petty troubles predominate, but afterwards
that same moment is pure gold. And yet I would never go
back. I have made, and I expect you have too, great mistakes. But I don't regret.

'Could we, by a wish,
Have what we will and see the future now,
Would we wish ought done, undone in the past?'

Each time it seems to me that a new thing begins which is a
little better than the last.

From Wales he proceeded to Scotland, where he enjoyed
with his friends, Sir Iain Colquhoun and Michael Tennant,
the joys of camp life and stalking on the hills. From there he
wrote to Lady Gage:

ROSSDHU, LUSS, DUMBARTONSHIRE, N.B.,
Sept. 14th.

Dearest Mog,

I am neither in the City, Wales or New Mexico, but,
as you will see from the above address, at a well known
French Spa!

I have been camping with Michael in the Island of Skye,
which is the bonniest, wildest place you have ever seen (or

not seen) in your life. For the rest I have been roaming over
Ben Vorlich. On really misty days when you can't see a yard
I shoot a stag. On days such as yesterday, when the sun
shines, I don't. Yesterday the hill-side was rather like Piccadilly Tube. The place simply thick with deer, & all in such a
tremendous hurry that not one would even pause to eat a
bit of butterscotch. They rushed hither and thither over the
hills, Royals, hinds, hummels, calves, switches, ten-pointers
& even foxes. We just sat in the sun & ate our lunch and
roared with laughter. Once we tried an elaborate stalk—
which consisted in walking 3 abreast over an open bit of
country for half a mile. Then the deer sat in the sun and ate
their lunch and laughed until at last we reached some cover.
They then disappeared at full gallop in all directions.

Your Broad life sounds good, though I don't fancy bathing
on the Dogger Bank. It's all fishy, isn't it? Might as well
bathe in the Aquarium at the Zoo.

I go back to lessons next week.

Bless you all and lots of love.

ANTONY.

The same day he wrote to his mother:

This is Black Monday, although it happens to be the
Sabbath. Iain, Dinah, Fiona, and the boys have just driven
off to Glasgow, London and school. . . . The house is empty
and sad as any forsaken home could be, and tonight I wish
that I were anywhere else in the world. Will the 'going back
to school' feeling haunt one all one's life, I wonder? And yet
I was not so bad at it, was I? Or do you think that when one
marries it all disappears? Ask Father. I don't suppose you
could answer the question. To me it appears eternal, with
this addition—that as one grows older it occurs more frequently and matters more!

There is nothing like Bendigo. Undoubtedly a dog is
superior in every quality and characteristic to any human,
and I fail altogether to agree with the wise people who say
'Who would be a dog?' I can see no good in what we call
civilization. It brings, as far as I can see, nothing but unhappiness, distress and suffering—an endless round of use-

less obligations and a perpetual struggle after an altogether
imperceptible end. Being a wise woman you should know
about this. What do you think? Man made the greatest mistake ever when he came out of the woods. Perhaps that is
why, long since conscious of the fact, he has laid the blame
upon woman, and hallowed the explanation with a thin
veneer of religion. 'The woman gave it me.' Well, we can
always fall back on that. But scientifically I can see nothing
to boast of in the development of the back of the head at the
expense of the jaw, and the transition from woodland content to slummy misery. But it is a fact, and that for the
simple should suffice. Meanwhile we must wait 'God's
instant, men call years'.

This is all rather pointless. But the pen runs on, barely
keeping pace with the thoughts. It is me, and you made it.
'The woman gave it me!'

On his return to London in September, Antony started
work on a new enterprise which gave him a substantial income and introduced him to the world of business, in conditions which were entirely congenial and called forth all
his best qualities. Lord Ebury, the Chairman of the Army
& Navy Stores, offered him a seat on the Board of that
Company. He himself had devoted many years of his life to
bringing this great establishment up-to-date and making it
a success. Under his unremitting labours the building had
been largely reconstructed, and the business had acquired a
high reputation for excellence of workmanship and moderate prices. He wished in the years that remained to him to
have a young man at his side whom he could train in the
business, who would become familiar with all the depart-
ments and qualify one day for executive duties. The policy,
to which his co-directors assented, was a wise one, and had
God so willed it would have borne good fruit, but fate
decided otherwise, and within four years death had deprived
this great commercial undertaking both of its beloved

U

Chairman and of the young apprentice, who by his industry
and talents had already begun to justify the confidence that
had been placed in him.

In the spring of 1929, while we were waiting for admis-
sion to the Peers' Gallery to hear the Debate on the Budget,
Lord Ebury had unfolded to me his project and asked me
whether Antony would accept the post. I was naturally delighted, as it seemed to offer the very opportunity I had so
much desired for Antony of a business occupation at which
he could work with his whole heart, and yet be free to indulge his tastes in literature and politics. I had written to
him from India, urging him to think rather of what he
wanted to do than of what he wanted to be, and assuring
him that opportunities would come to him in ways that
could not be foreseen. Now such an opportunity had come
to him unsought, and it contained all the elements that
made it welcome. The offer was gratefully accepted. It had
come at an opportune moment. It softened the disappointment of the Shoreditch election, and the loss of employment
in the Conservative Office. Here at last was the chance of
regular and remunerative employment in a business that
was full of human interest, with prospects of the most attractive kind.

Antony began his work at the Army & Navy Stores at the
end of September.

Although in a letter to his friend Cartland in October
Antony spoke of abandoning politics for business, this was
not in fact his intention. On the contrary, he felt that with a
settled occupation and an assured income he was now for the
first time in a position to enter Parliament, always provided
that his constituency was within easy reach of London. In
the autumn of this year an opportunity presented itself of
realizing his ambition. Mr. Guy Kindersley, the Member
for North Herts, announced his intention of retiring at the

next Election, and the local Conservative Association set about the selection of a new candidate. As this was our home constituency and we had many friends on the local Committee, we were very confident that Antony would be selected. As, however, there were still a few ex-Ministers and experienced Members of Parliament who had been unseated at the last Election and had not yet found a seat, the Selection Committee thought they would best serve the interests of the Party if they offered the seat to one of these men, and their choice eventually fell upon Mr. Harold Macmillan.

This was naturally a great disappointment to Antony, but he accepted the fact with the same philosophic resignation with which he had accepted his first failure in getting elected to Pop in the summer of 1921.

Among the letters of sympathy we received at this time was the following charming one from Mr. Baldwin, the leader of the Party:

7 XII, 1929.
HATFIELD HOUSE, HATFIELD, HERTS.

Dear Lady Lytton,

When you returned that little book of Priestley's you kindly wrote me a letter in which you told me of your hopes for Antony. I have but lately learned that those hopes have been frustrated.

I have hesitated whether to write; but I do know your devotion to him, and I think of you chained to your bed with so much time in which to think of your disappointment, and I want to hold out a hand.

You have no cause to worry about the boy. He is a sportsman to the core. He may for a moment curse the umpire who says 'Out', but he will accept the verdict with a smile and cheer the other fellow when he goes to the wicket.

I was turned down, long years ago, and my dominant feeling became pity for the asses who preferred some one else!

But don't let yourself be too deeply wounded by it. It seems to me one can so easily exaggerate both the causes for and the results of such an event.

Be thankful you have a boy like Antony, and have faith that all will be well with him.

Very sincerely yours,
STANLEY BALDWIN.

The words 'chained to your bed' in this letter refer to the fact that Antony's mother had fallen and broken her hip when staying at Belvoir Castle in October, and she was therefore in bed at Knebworth for the whole of this winter.

In December I went to Switzerland with Antony, first to the Engadine (St. Moritz and Maloja) and later to Mürren. We spent Christmas night in a small inn at Davos on our way to do the Parsenn run the next day.

Antony wrote to his mother from Zurich on December 27th:

> We spent the night before last in a very good little pub at Davos, and there was a Xmas tree in the dining room and we had a *diner de Noel* and went to bed early. A good way of spending Xmas, I think. Asti,* ski-ing clothes and a sort of holiday camping atmosphere.
>
> Yesterday we did the Parsenn in a snow-storm, but, despite that, it was a magnificent run and I adored it.
>
> I have torn all the muscles of my right knee and leg, so that I can only ski like a guide—solidly and carefully and slowly. I did it the first day I was in St. Moritz, got it practically right again at Maloja and then did it again (agony) the first day I got back to St. Moritz. It's a bore because I was going to ski rather well this year. Now I shall have to hold flags and carry rücksacks and cheer the others on and generally behave as if I remembered the first run down the Nursery slopes in 1873!
>
> I agree with Davina that the Corviglia is a nice run. But I go no further. St. Moritz I think is the world's end. It's far

*Asti Spumante—a sparkling wine.

more Biarritz, Deauville, Brighton, Blackpool, Southend, than I imagined, and the combination of all these set down in the midst of snow mountains is a blasphemy and a sacrilege which hurts me. But I am awfully glad that I have been to the Engadine. I understand it better now, and I learnt a lot. Above all, I acquired a taste for the Oberland. The thought of Mürren is like home to me! Ecstatic. . . .

Father is better than I have known him for years. As strong on the ski as a lion and quite unwearied by the utmost discomforts of our travel. He is like an undergraduate, happy to sit with wet clothes in a foreign third-class carriage with no prospect of arriving anywhere ever. I call that marvellous for him, don't you? Also he is ski-ing superbly. . . .

Antony was able to give himself a good long holiday this year, and he remained in Switzerland till the end of January. But the only success that he achieved in racing was to win the Scaramanga Cup—a race between roped pairs—with Miss Sale Barker. 'Wendy and I won the roped race yesterday', he wrote. 'I have never been so frightened in my life, it was like being harnessed to an express train. She dragged me through the winning-post while I screamed "Stop, stop" in vain!'

The chief family event of this year was Hermione's engagement to Mr. Cameron Cobbold and her marriage in April. They became engaged during the Xmas holidays and came out to stay with us at Mürren. Antony wrote about this:

Hermione is so radiant, the stars so bright in her eyes, that I feel we must all be little unimportant futile things beside her great joy. . . . It is God's loveliest moment, His greatest gift.

I feel so strongly glad for her, and for her real happiness, and I rejoice so much that she has chosen a man whom we can all love and whom I know to be the best. . . .

She is radiantly happy, and we who love her must feel the great strength of her happiness, and rejoice too. I feel it even here, and all the snow mountains feel it and look kinder, and wear their loveliest clothes and nod to the moon that there is a big wonder of joy in the world.

The wedding took place at Knebworth on April 3rd. The ceremony was, unfortunately, marred by a pitiless downpour of rain at the critical moment, but in spite of this it was made lovely by the affection of the Knebworth people and the spirit of radiant happiness which shone through the rain. After the honeymoon Hermione settled at Milan with her husband. In the summer we all went to visit them at different times at their country villa above Lake Como.

Antony spent the spring and summer in his flat in London working at the Army & Navy Stores. In June he wrote to Ronald Cartland: 'It is time I saw you again, for I am drifting more and more away from politics. I regard myself as a brilliant young man whom the party does not think it worth while to cultivate! So I am going my own way and pleasing only myself. . . . I have heard much talk and many views. . . . There are so many aspects. I thought that figures were definite things and that mathematicians saw clearly in terms of black and white. I thought accountants were mathematicians. But the other day I was discussing an Income Tax problem with our Chief Accountant. I said "Well, yes. But what is the real truth?" He smiled. His smile said "You are young and green and innocent." He said "There is no truth"... Perhaps Pilate had it over us after all!'

To his sister Hermione:

KNEBWORTH HOUSE, KNEBWORTH,
June 2nd.

. . . From now on I expect England to be at its best and loveliest, and the countryside at its most inviting. There will be good summer scents, the hum of bees and the noise of the mowing-machine. Everything will grow so big that it seems strange and mysterious, and a little field will become

a forest, and every green lane an adventure. Then later on
there will be the smell of hay everywhere in the air, and
there will be lots of strawberries and cherries and peaches.
And all the time the sun will beat down remorselessly.

But it won't matter. 'Cos you'll all be in Italy and I shall
be in London. But that's the way of things.

It is a pity that you aren't still here. But I have a strong
feeling that everything is moving on and moving fast. It
is not long now and there won't be a 'here' at all. I feel everything has changed and is changing and I don't like it, but I
think I always expected it. . . .

All this year Antony was making a serious study of accountancy and book-keeping, in order to qualify himself for
his new work. He had always protested that he had neither
the temperament nor the training for business, but now that
he was in business he realized that this attitude was not
possible. So he took up the work seriously and applied himself to it with the conscientious thoroughness which was
characteristic of him. The result was that he soon became
quite efficient even in those matters which he had hitherto
regarded as beyond his reach.

He also worked on his Boxing book, and wrote to his
mother at the end of July saying that he hoped to finish this
when he was staying with Hermione in Italy. He added: 'I
am tired of London and just sighing for the country smells
and the country air and rough clothes again, and I shall be
off to get them in a minute.' His first visit to Hermione's
new home was a very happy event, and he wrote to her on
his return on August 21st:

I came home in the train with an Empire-builder
who has been growing cotton for two years in the Soudan,
twenty miles from the next white inhabitants. He was keen
on rugger, cricket & education, and he drank a bottle of
Bass on the boat because there is only Lager in the Soudan,
and he is engaged to a girl in Cairo & he likes Cairo where

the girl lives, better than Kingston where he used to live. He was divine, and an awful die-hard. He said what was the use of teaching people anything when, after all, they had all got to go on being poor. Because someone had to be poor, and the Soudanese, who didn't know anything, were better at it than the English, who did. And he said it was bloody having to walk along to the Restaurant & get a drink instead of pushing a bell for a boy. And he looked out of the window and rubbed his hands & said he hadn't seen a cloud for two years.

This is a funny way of saying thank you for a lovely stay in the Casa. I did so love it all, your home, your life, your servants, your food, your company, your sun and your happiness. I feel I was a bore, but I do hope not, because to me it was all perfect and divine being away from where you have to fuss about nothing all day.

Evidently it is a good plan to be married, because you both seem to like it and because you are both fairly wise. Only Kim rather frightens me, because he is too clever without trying, and that's not fair! . . .

It was angelic of you to have me. Honestly I can't tell you how happy I was or how good it makes one feel to be surrounded with such happiness and such a great cloud of alright-ness. . . . You couldn't have found a better place or a better way of starting your new life, and I don't grudge you your happiness, as I did once, because it doesn't take but gives.

What fun it all is—this life—what with St. Moritz and birth control and Socialism and the sunny hills and Empire-building and the Manor House and Bendigo and Sporting.* And how difficult it is sometimes and how easy it is at others. And how incongruous today & well synchronised tomorrow.

Bless you a hundred times, darling, and thank you so much more for letting me share your life & your home and happiness and for being so sweet to me. You are a wise girl and I love you.

Your profligate brother,
ANTONY.

*Hermione's dog.

When he did get away, first to Scotland and then to Wales, and stretched his legs on the hills, and filled his lungs with pure air, he wrote happily to his mother from Plas Newydd on September 6th:

Grey skies and the good west wind with its little, sad, exhausted drizzle, but a great happiness and much laughter, and self as fit as a young horse. I feel it is good to be alive, and the sheer taste of fresh air is a grand thing in itself. Do you know that feeling? When everything is kind and glorious and wonderful and real from the green grass to Gibbon's *Decline and Fall of the Roman Empire*!

My Rossdhu visit was divine. Camping right up in the wildest hills, living in a kilt and on what we killed, trout, deer, rabbits. Bathing in an ice-cold loch, and the smell of one's own wood fire, the peat and the hills.

I have read Buchan's *Montrose* and a new novel of his, and am now on a book about the early colonization of America, so you can gauge my mood. The fresh air and health and strength and great ideals, which were not really ideals at all but the natural coursing of warm healthy blood through strong young veins. . . .

All this from the books and the Loch Sloy hills and the deer forest I have brought with me here, where it is complemented by the laughter and shouting of Marjorie's children and the real-ness of Caroline.

It doesn't really seem to go with towns, and knowledge, and cleverness, and civilisation, and houses, and politics, and rates and taxes, and the press, and motor-cars, and arterial roads, and slums, because it belongs to the rain, and the wind, and the heather, and something fundamental inside one. But these things just help one to appreciate the others, as a week's work makes Saturday afternoon sublime. Only it's more than Saturday afternoon. It's eternal. . . .

I love you all and I am nearly full of a hundred unsatisfied yearnings and indefinable creeds. Who would be young?

We all went to Switzerland again in the winter and spent Christmas at Maloja. Antony wrote to his mother from Melton Mowbray on December 22nd:

We had a good hunt on Saturday. My horse knew all the fences and all the hounds by heart, and all the people by sight. He told me to whom I should take off my hat, and whom it would be well to cut. He avoided the wrong horses, and walked chattily beside the important ones, so I left it all to him!

My train leaves at 4 p.m. on Xmas day. I have pretty well finished off the Book, and hope to let the publisher have it on Tuesday. Then I can come out and join you with a clear field behind me.

I am longing to be off. Ski-ing is I think a better sport than hunting. I only wish we had snow in England and it wasn't of necessity a continental recreation. . . . I am simply full of excitement about it now, and just longing for the feel of ski and the smell of the snow!

He joined us at Maloja, and after a few days of ski-ing *en famille* went on to Mürren for more serious competitions. Here for the first time since his return from India he succeeded in recapturing his true form at ski-ing, and he did really well in his races.

On 4th January he wrote to me from Mürren:

It is a long time since I have won a race here, but in the last two days I have excelled myself. Yesterday I won the Bernese Oberland Straight Race, equal with Bracken, and beating Mac and the rest. Today I did the best time in the Anglo-Swiss Slalom. I didn't win because my first time down was bad, but in the 2nd time down I did the best time of all. In the afternoon I won the Straight Race against both the Swiss and the English, including Mac. So I am awfully pleased with myself and feel like a schoolboy who has played football well—the best feeling I have ever known or shall know. They say here that my performances are the best advertisement for the Eagle Ski Club that it has ever had. Pull their legs about that! And tell them too that I have been strongly upholding the cause of touring against racing. . . . I am glad to have ski-ed at last in a race as I always felt I could if I really wanted to. Ever since I came back from India I have felt that I could do better than I have done. Now I have done it, and feel that I can give up racing and ski for pleasure with a good grace. But I wish I were with you. I was having such fun, and as pleased as anything by Davina's marvellous form. I am such a baby that in Switzerland I still have the exaggerated ski-snobbery, and Davina was a treat to watch.

Later in the season, after I had returned to England, Antony joined Davina at Klosters, and again wrote to me in praise of her skill. It was a year of such excessive snow-fall and unsettled weather that some of the later events had to be abandoned:

January 27th.

We were over the Parsenn on Sunday and again today. On Sunday the snow was bad and the light too. Today the snow was perfect, but it was snowing all the way down. I hope that one day I shall actually see the run!

Davina ran up to the hut in 1 hr 12 min. 25 secs. We spent 35 mins. over lunch and another 26 getting up to the Furka. A little over an hour coming down. Davina's ski-ing was superb. She never had a fall until after Schwendi. I am determined to make her go in for the Derby. The first time down she was waiting all the time for me and the man who 'was showing me a good line'. Today she was never more than 20 yds behind. She is strong as a lion and happy & brown & well. You never saw a better sight. It is grand to see how she loves it & how amazingly good she has got. She would quite soon give the Mürren aces something to think about.

In a letter to Hermione at the end of this holiday, he wrote:

Life is too good a thing to niggle over and spoil and cherish. You want to get hold of it in both hands, and simply

pour it over yourself like a bucket of spring water. And perhaps I am a bit too fond of doing this, and rather apt to
splash other people!

Two important events in Antony's life occurred this year.

Harold Macmillan decided to retire from the candidature
of the Hitchin Division, and to stand once more for his
former constituency, Stockton. Antony was invited to take
his place, and was adopted as the Conservative candidate for
Hitchin. Thus the hopes which had been disappointed two
years before were realized, and we had the satisfaction of
working for Antony's return to Parliament as the Member
for his home constituency.

In the summer he joined the Auxiliary Air Force and
started to train as an Air Pilot with the 601 Squadron at
Hendon. The friendship which he had formed with Dick
Waghorn over ski-ing had much to do with this decision.
This new occupation completely satisfied Antony's adventurous spirit, and flying became the absorbing passion of his
life. He spent the middle of each week working at the Army
& Navy Stores, or becoming acquainted with his new constituency, but every Sunday he devoted to his training at
Hendon. He soon made himself proficient, and was very
proud when he received his Pilot's certificate and became a
fully qualified Pilot Officer.

To his mother, who was naturally anxious about the
dangers of flying, Antony wrote:

You mustn't really mind my doing this for two reasons—
(a) Because it will take an edge off my delight and (b) because
you wouldn't really have it otherwise, for if you only bred
sons who stayed at home and gardened you wouldn't like that.

Incidentally, it isn't any more dangerous than boxing and
is good fun and excellent training, and supplies the two missing things in my life—a recreation which I enjoy and a kind
of society which I love! . . .

Another interest which he took up this year was the organization of a holiday camp for the boys from the poorer districts of London. From the days at West Downs, when his friend Captain Philipps had commended the East-End boys to his special care, Antony had always wanted to help these boys to enjoy some of the delights of games and athletics which had played so large a part in his own life. The chance had come while he was working in the Central Conservative Office, when one of his fellow workers had persuaded him to help in the establishment of a holiday camp at Ingham in Norfolk, between the Broads and the sea. He threw himself into this with great zeal, and eventually became the Chairman of the Association which was formed to run the camp.

This year Antony's second sister, Davina, was married to Lord Erne, but as we were all living together there are no letters on the subject. They became engaged in the spring, and by the courtesy of the Dean were privileged to be married at Westminster Abbey on St. Swithin's Day—July 15th. The defiant challenge to the weather implied in the choice of this date was not rewarded, and Davina's wedding was nearly as wet as Hermione's had been the year before! Lord and Lady Salisbury kindly lent their house in Arlington Street for the reception, and in spite of the rain the ceremony was in every way perfect and memorable. Antony had charge of the arrangements, and was proud of the success with which they were carried out. They spent their honeymoon in Spain, and then retired to Crom Castle on Loch Erne, which henceforth became a new family home.

In the late summer of this year occurred the economic crisis which led to the break up of the Labour Government and the formation of a National Government of all parties. In September I attended the tenth Assembly of the League of Nations at Geneva, as one of the British Delegates.

Antony, like many others at this time, found himself bewildered by the complexities of the political situation, and his mood is reflected in a letter which he wrote to me on 14th September:

> I am much distressed to hear of your filthy Geneva weather. . . . It is perhaps not so very curious how much more important the sun is than politics, and the hills than the consolidated banking interests of Central Europe. Donn Byrne well remarked that he had no use for politicians since none had made the apples redder or the corn more golden. But some have certainly succeeded in making both the corn and the apples worthless.
>
> I am utterly desolate about politics, because I am confused, bewildered and hopeless. My small knowledge of economics reveals absolutely no sign of dawn in a very black night, and my smaller knowledge of sociology can discern nothing but disillusionment and sorrow ahead. Being young I hate to feel like this, as youth should be optimistic, vital and constructive. I am profoundly conscious of the ancient shibboleths and standards, and feel uncomfortable, though sometimes admiring, in the presence of the old school. I seem to react like an elastic band to the follies and insupportable ideas of my own wearying world. I find the company of my own class (little Lord Fauntleroy!) too often repulsive, and its tone of life too often rotten and self-satisfied, and I am generally happier in what I believe to be the more sincere and simple atmosphere of my social inferiors (big Lord Fauntleroy!). At the same time, the only things which are more repulsive to me than the West-end and its philosophy, are the cheap vulgar modern substitutes for the old days. The wireless, the geniality of the *Daily Express*, the religion of science, the crowded south coast, dieting, education, bonhomie, cheap luxuries, Lansbury's Lido, and *vox populi vox Dei*, are worse than the economy of millionaires, the clubman's Toryism, the Christian religion and Tariff Reform. . . .
>
> God help us! We have made machines, we can produce thousands of miles of cotton fabric in 24 hours, we can talk

across the globe, we can fly at 400 miles per hour, we can measure the stars, we produce so much and so fast and so well that nobody wants our products, and where the hell are we?

I believe there will be a great collapse and a great disillusionment, and it will all come back to the only fundamental truths—the colour of the apples, the ripeness of the corn, and 'in the sweat of thy face shalt thou eat bread'.

Personally I am absolutely lost, so I have given it up and spent the day in the fields with a gun. They are black with birds, like the Maidan on a race-meeting afternoon, only the birds are more lovely and harder to hit than the babus! . . .

I firmly believe that the next twenty years are going to see the most stupendous upheaval in the history of the world, and that it will, as like as not, come down to physical strength. Hence I thank God and you that I am not made with a club foot, and myself that I am learning to fly!

Meanwhile the chaos in the western world was being watched with the closest interest in the Far East. During this month of September Geneva was startled by three sensational announcements which came in rapid succession.

The first was that Great Britain had gone off the gold standard. As the National Government had been formed for the express purpose of saving the pound sterling, it only added to the general bewilderment to learn that one of the earliest acts of that Government was to abandon the gold standard. The talk of Geneva was that Britain's credit was gone.

The second was the news of a mutiny in the British Navy. A local crisis caused by a protest against cuts in naval pay was quickly settled by the exhibition of wisdom and common sense, and in England the incident was soon forgotten. But the news was flashed all over the world, and announced with large headlines in the foreign press. For the moment it looked as if the very foundations of western civilisation were crumbling. Could we no longer rely either upon the Bank of England or the British Navy?

The third announcement, which was probably not un-connected with the other two, was that in consequence of an alleged act of sabotage by Chinese soldiers on the South Manchuria railway, Japanese troops had forcibly occupied the town of Mukden.

While I was sitting in the Glass Hall at Geneva, listening to the first discussion by the Council of the League of the situation which had been created in the Far East, one of the Chinese delegates asked me what was the meaning of Great Britain's departure from the gold standard. 'It means', I replied, 'that Britain's credit now rests upon the character of the British people alone.' Different and irreconcilable accounts were being given by the Japanese and Chinese delegates of what had happened and was happening in the Far East, and as if to put a touch of irony upon the whole proceedings, the speeches were accompanied by the ceaseless hammering of workmen who were busily engaged in erecting near-by the new great hall for the accommodation of the world Disarmament Conference, which was to meet in a few months' time!

I little knew then how much these events were going to concern me personally, but before the end of the year I received and accepted an invitation to become a member of the Commission of Enquiry which the League eventually decided to send to the Far East to investigate the dispute.

About the financial crisis, Antony wrote to Hermione on September 25th:

You shall have a little gossip on the crisis, since gossip from the uninformed is always interesting. As far as I can make out the informed know nothing because all is uncertain and of course depends on the degree of devaluation. Robert Kindersley's view is reported to be that the £ will drop to about 13/- and probably stabilise then.

The rest of us are in rather an amusing situation. A

month ago when the £ was saved we all rushed about explaining what would have happened if it had gone, talking about the mark, painting gloomy pictures of starvation, pitching into the Socialists, holding up our hands in horror until people trembled in their bedroom slippers and reviled the name of Henderson.

On Monday came the news that we were off gold. The papers have ever since contained such headlines as 'First great constructive step towards restoration of British prosperity'. There has been a boom on the Stock Exchange. Cotton mills are opening. Wholesale houses have placed all their stocks. The price has risen against foreign wheat. Unemployment figures have already fallen, and we are looking rather silly politicians. At least that is the way I see it, though of course one can take another view and put a better face on it.

But there seems not the least doubt that it will help our trade, and if people do begin to feel the pinch in the matter of prices I would be rather pleased, as it would wake them up a bit. From a trade point of view it is the hell of a nuisance. One has to buy a certain amount in foreign currencies, and now we shall have to revise many of our prices.

There is going to be an election in about three weeks, Ramsay is going to appeal as leader of a Nationalist party, and the election will be fought Nationalists v. Socialists. That, to my mind, is admirable. The thing one has dreamed of. There will be a big Nationalist majority and five years of useless, idle, stable, futile Govt. But there will be tariffs and a trade revival, and we shall be in a better position at the end to meet the inevitable ensuing chain of Socialist administration!

In October Parliament was dissolved, and the National Government appealed to the country. In the General Election which followed the Government secured an overwhelming majority. They were supported by the Liberals, and a few individual Labour men followed Mr. Ramsay Macdonald. But, as a Party, Labour opposed the Govern-

x

ment candidates, and as a Party they were almost extinguished. In the new Parliament the Government supporters numbered 556. The Labour Opposition numbered only 59, and had to accept the leadership of Mr. Lansbury, as every ex-Cabinet Minister in their Party had been defeated. Antony was returned for Hitchin as a National Conservative with a majority of 17,000.

He found himself in a House of Commons largely composed of young men, many of whom, like himself, were there for the first time, and some of whom had stood without the slightest expectation of being elected. The conditions were such as to make it impossible for a newcomer to shine, and easy enough for him to be completely submerged. There was nothing to be done at first but to sit and listen, become familiar with the procedure, make the acquaintance of as many members as possible, and wait for an opportunity to speak. Mr. Duff Cooper, who held the office of Under-Secretary at the War Office, made Antony his Parliamentary Private Secretary. This gave him a seat immediately behind the Treasury Bench and a definite status in the House, which is helpful to a young man. He was now definitely and successfully launched on a political career.

Chapter X

LAST YEARS

1932-1933

'Let us grasp what we can, be thankful for what was good, hope for the future, love, laugh and praise, and one day perhaps we shall know.'

A SWISS HOLIDAY was out of the question this year owing to the financial crisis. All the foreign exchanges were upset; no one knew how far the pound sterling would become depreciated, and even if anyone were rich enough, or courageous enough, to face these uncertainties, it was considered unpatriotic to spend money outside this country. The Duke of Connaught set the example to others by forgoing his usual visit to the South of France, and remained in England for the winter.

We spent a family Christmas together at Crom Castle— Davina's new Irish home—and at the end of January I started on my journey to Manchuria, and was away for eight months.

On January 25th Antony wrote to Mrs. Hughes, a dear and valued friend he had met in India:

> . . . I joined the Auxiliary Air Force in August, & now that Switzerland is not allowed because the world has gone mad, flying is my only recreation. It is fun. Having got into Parliament, I am bored with politics, and now that business is difficult and demands much attention, I am bored with business! That's me.
> There is a tremendous feeling inside me, and I think inside more people than know of it, that the whole world is

323

sitting on a bomb. It is even chances if it goes off or not. The world has hitherto existed on a form of slavery—depending upon having a large number of people poor & uneducated & content, while the affairs of the world were managed by a few people comparatively rich & educated & clever. That is no longer true, & it is even chances what happens. The capitalist system has temporarily failed. If it is patched up in the next five years all may be well. If not, the world is for it. . . .

Personally I am tired of sitting on this bomb & being not wanted and envied and without security. The whole world is without security of any kind. In the next five years the bomb must either be buried or explode. No one knows which. The majority of people have lost all real interest in the issue & argue 'anything may happen, let's make the best of what we have got & know we have got'. . . .

I long for it to be settled one way or another, so that I am either to be satisfied to do my duty in that state of life, etc., and be required to do it, or else may have the chance of showing the world that I can do it in another state of life a damned sight better than they! . . .

The Socialists, Bolshevists, and Communists will not do it as well, if the bomb goes off, as we have done it. But if the world wants them to try it, they will have their chance as we have had ours. Only you & I can eventually find something *real* in life and they can't.

I don't suppose there has ever been such a time in history as this, and no one actually realizes it. The fall of the Roman Empire lasted many hundreds of years, but our civilization may collapse in a year. I'm not sure I wouldn't be glad if it did. . . .

So let's grasp what we can, be thankful for what was good, hope for the future, love, laugh & praise, and one day perhaps we shall know. . . .

On February 2nd he wrote to his mother:

It is surely a great truth that each must walk his own path in life, and build his own house, & sow his own garden.

. . . Nothing is truer than that each must find his own salvation. . . .

To make you understand too, you must remember that the sea of life is green & warm & fruitful of adventure & good to swim in, & that only now & then does one want to rest on the Rock. That is Nature & can't be helped. As a matter of fact I have got to that stage now when I am a strong swimmer—beyond the stage when little expeditions were exciting & a return to the Rock even more exciting. When I find & meet big waves now I don't want to swim back for rest & shelter any more—I just have to go on. That's all, & that's about as far as one can carry the metaphor. . . . It seems to me there is always a gap which lies between one generation & another—that while they hold fast to the same truths & the same principles, they express them differently. In other words, the big things are eternal, the little things ephemeral. The inward & spiritual grace is handed down through the ages, but the outward & visible sign changes with every generation. Only the little things & the big things in life are so inextricably bound up together that it is often hard to analyse the situation. What will happen to us all no one can tell. All we must try & do is see that we, like you, are signed of the Cross of Christ & then be content to go gaily in the dark; and meanwhile hold hard by truth. . . .

Antony was kept busy by his flying, his business at the Stores, and his Parliamentary duties, and I received few letters from him while I was abroad.

He qualified as an Air Pilot and got his wings at the end of February, and in April he bought himself a Moth aeroplane. In the letter to me announcing this, he wrote: 'I still fly like mad and like it better than anything else. I got nearly six hours in the air yesterday and enjoyed every second, feeling really tired and pleased with myself at the end.'

In the spring the Army and Navy Stores suffered the irreparable loss of their Chairman, Lord Ebury, and by his death Antony lost a personal friend to whom he was sincerely devoted. Only a week before, while Lord Ebury was lying critically ill, the death of General Everard Baring, his mother's life-long friend, had called forth the following letter:

It is awful to lose a great and loved friend. But I can't help feeling just now the vastness of existence and its continuity, so that beside the great thing somewhere which is, all our things which are so near seem really very small. Great men die and the world goes on; great projects fail, great success is achieved, old faces disappear, something which was very real and very present is for ever no more, and not a flutter in all this passes across the surface of humanity. It is the relative significance of things which upsets and appals me, and in all this the actual margin between life and death seems insignificant. . . .

The talk outside Parliament is that the end of everything is at hand. The talk inside Parliament that everything is roses in the garden also continues. I don't know about anything at all, and I don't care about anything at all. But I like flying and I like wine and I like being loved, though what with disarmament and Empire Free Trade and C— these things are becoming increasingly remote!

On May 17th he wrote again:

I arrived back from a delicious week-end in Sussex with a boy friend in the Squadron this morning, blew into the Stores full of summer spirits and summer clothes, not having seen the papers, to learn that Ebury is dead. God seems to take the best men always. I liked him such a lot and he was a real man. If I could have had a few more years working with him, I should have learnt a lot, but there must be some design in the workings of Providence, in spite of our infinite insignificance. I become more strongly a fatalist every hour of my life, and it is not good. The business will miss him even more than I shall miss him as a friend, and it has placed a great responsibility on our shoulders that survive. Just some million and a half of other people's money in our charge, and I can't look after my own hundreds!

To Lady Harcourt (Lord Ebury's daughter) he wrote:

There is nothing I can say, but I must write to you all the same. I absolutely adored your Father & feel as wretched as anyone can who isn't his son or his brother or his life-long friend. There seems sometimes a kind of plot to take from the world all the very best men of all ages, & one wonders why & tries in vain to understand. But he has left me something to think about & worship & strive after all my life. . . . All of us, in different ways, have got to have the courage & the strength of mind which he had. . . .

During the summer Antony lived in his Bond Street flat and attended to his Parliamentary duties. On June 14th he wrote me a characteristic wail about life in the House of Commons:

I would like to get out into some fresh air somewhere, and sweat with some work that is good for mind and body, and laugh a bit, and sleep under the stars. But it seems that being a successful ambitious civilised being means sitting still for sixteen hours in a smoky atmosphere, either with a lot or with a few of one's fellow human beings (according to the degree of success) and lying still in an almost equally smoky atmosphere for another 7 hours. The odd hour is spent in changing over from occupation one to occupation two. This method of life persistently carried on for about 40 years eventually produces wealth, dignity, power, position and universal respect. It is called Christian civilisation, public life, doing one's job, being ambitious, serving the State, citizenship, hard work! I doubt if I was born to it, or intended by nature, you, or God to tolerate it much longer. But meanwhile the thing is to fill in the fleeting minute by writing and telling you about it.

Tonight we shall be here till past midnight deciding whether the maternity sickness benefit of a married woman with more than 26 contributions to the Fund shall be ten or eleven shillings a week, and why. There are eight women members, four married and four single, and there are four Clydesdale members of doubtful maternal qualities. They are all speaking twice on every amendment, and they have each put down six amendments to every clause. So it is very important, and the country—not to say the civilized world— is watching with anxiety the night's deliberation.

I used to say that the world was divided into two sorts of people—those who see in business, politics and finance high romance and great deeds, and those who see in these things only the same piece of green blotting-paper every morning, varied once a week by an efficient Secretary. I am afraid that I belong by nature to the second category, but by training, environment and heredity to the first, so that even if I let Nature have its way, the force of those other influences would be too strong, and I should not be content.

But I do feel that in this last year of my young life I have been too serious, and had too much to worry about, with the result that now I can't honestly feel that anything really matters, and only wish that this much prophesied disastrous world crash would be precipitated. I wish I had been born in time for the War. It would have suited me, and brought me face to face with a physical reality which I don't feel I shall now ever encounter. If ten million years roll by I believe the world will be the same, and that only in the sweat of his brow and the work of his hands and the love of his own creation can man be happy. The thing has grown too big, too complicated and too perplexing for our simple groping minds to understand.

My only joy, and indeed my obsession at the moment, is the Air Force, where I get back to the old contentment of school, with a limited outlook, a particular job to do, and another to avoid doing, good friends, good jokes, a clean life, not too much responsibility, and a pleasant, simple, competitive atmosphere. I have got more bitten with it even than with ski-ing, and the summer weather and the dreariness of the House of Commons make it seem like good wine to the thirsty and comfort to the wounded. . . .

People say it is a wonderfully interesting time to be living in. Give me a damned boring one then. Give me security and faith, contentment and a fixed order of things—or else give me bloody war. But this kind of pin-pricking, sickening, doubtful, depressing peace without knowledge, or faith, or hope, or certainty, or duty, or truth, is getting quite unbearable.

In the midst of plenty, want; confused with duty, greed; combined with effort, insecurity and doubt. And all this in a world where the Teesta Valley is still beautiful, the sun still sets on the Taj, the shadows still lie over English lawns, the hay still smells sweet in the fields, ships still sail the seas, sheep still feed on the green hills, and men & women still love each other even unto death!

What a queer letter, and yet these are the things you are trying to deal with on a gigantic scale with your Prussian Japanese and your grimy Chinks. I wish we were in the Darjeeling hills together instead. . . .

They have made me Vice-Chairman of the Army & Navy Stores, and here again I meet the problem of replacing good but old men with new. The trouble is that England is full of unemployed in all classes, but they are none of them any good, and the men I want are not to be found anywhere.

One of the Liberals in the constituency has repudiated me for having supported the general tariff, and so I am twisting their tails a bit now with unmitigated delight. But as time goes on I feel the Tariff Reformers are going to find it exceedingly difficult to justify their reforms. I shall probably make my maiden speech on the Ottawa Conference on Thursday, which I tend to think is likely to be the turning-point in history, or alternatively the final break-up.

Everyone asks me about you and what you are finding, and how you are getting on. But the general feeling is that the thing is hopeless, and that we have to choose in the end between Japan and order and China and justice. All the Tories, of course, favour order, and, after the experiments in self-determination in Europe consequent on the Versailles Treaty, with some justification.

Antony's maiden speech, as foreshadowed in this letter, was delivered a few days later, and he wrote about it to his friend Cartland: 'Thanks for the nice letter. It was very frightening and not at all the occasion I had planned. Nor was it the speech I had prepared. But they never are. The second speech is, they say, far and away worse.'

During this summer Antony made many expeditions in his Moth to various parts of the country. He would fly down to Knebworth for the week-ends, and land on a very uneven part of the park among the trees near the house. His arrivals and departures always attracted a crowd of admiring schoolchildren, and sometimes he would fly low over the house and church, looping the loop and making wonderful turns in the air, while the villagers gazed and held their breath. We learnt to listen for the drone of his engine, and to watch for his arrival out of the sky.

In July he made a particularly adventurous flight as far as Milan to visit his sister, taking Lady Mary Erskine with him as a passenger. This flight is described in the following letters:

To his mother:

DIJON, *July* 11.

We started at 5 a.m. and crossed the Channel in the beauty of the morning, though it was rather misty and the visibility bad. We flew through France on the hottest of oppressive sultry days. The heat of the aerodromes beating up off the tarmac when we landed was unbearable.

We had a good breakfast at Le Bourget, and a bad luncheon at Dijon. Mary slept nearly all the way, and I was thrilled by the French country. Miles and miles of forests, almost like the Jainti* country, with villages on the edge.

After luncheon at Dijon we got a bad weather report from Lausanne—clouds at 3000 feet—and also a bad one from

*Northern Bengal.

Lyons and the South. As there are mountains of 4000 feet between Dijon & Lausanne I decided not to go on.

Everything had gone perfectly so far: up to time, right course, good weather, no wind, excellent pilotage, etc., but probably the best pilotage was the decision not to go on.

Now it is thundering and raining, and here we are in a funny hotel in a very provincial French town. But Mary is good to do these things with, as she takes it all just the right way.

We may be here for days as far as I can see. I have no money at all, and no one seems to like our cheques! Also we look—at least I look—like a bandit. But it's fun—adventure, life, novelty, and better than the Army & Navy.

MILAN, *July* 13.

At 6 a.m. yesterday the weather at Dijon didn't look too good and there was no news from Lausanne. On the other hand there was a good report from Lyons and the South. So I decided to choose the long way, of which I could get information, rather than risk the Alps.

We sailed down the Rhone valley in sweltering heat. We paused at Avignon, and then cut off into the hills to our left and worked our way down to the Riviera. I couldn't get through the pass I wanted to because of low clouds, and so turned back and hit the coast at Fréjus. Thence to Cannes, where we landed, had tea and filled up.

Then we went on over the sea all along the Riviera to Genoa, which was quite lovely. Blue, blue sea and sun, but with clouds all along the tops of the hills. I began to lose hope and did not know how I was going to get up the valley from Genoa. As we approached Genoa I climbed up and up over the sea to 6000 feet, and then found I could look inland right over the clouds with just the tops of the hills sticking out, and see in the distance the plains of Lombardy under a blue sky. So I climbed still higher and turned inland on a compass course, dodging the high peaks, until I saw the Po. It was fun picking up our course again in Italy, and we landed at Milan at 7.30, where Hermione & Kim met us.

As a means of travel flying is thrilling and beautiful and happy-making, but slow, unreliable on account of weather, and a bore because we have no luggage! However, I adored the voyage and was properly tired last night. We are off to Venice this evening, hot, happy and excited.

The later stages of this trip and his return journey are described in a letter to me written after he got back to London:

We stayed slap-up on the Lido, and laughed a lot, and visited Venice, and lay in the sun, and burnt the skin off ourselves, and saw a Festa, and did all the things one does do, including being driven indoors twice in the middle of dinner by the rain! We did exactly the right amount of it, and then took a flying boat to Brioni.

Brioni must be the best pleasure-place in Europe. It is an island, exactly the right size, unsophisticated and uninhabited. It has a hundred rocky bays with warm blue water and islands, and no one in sight. You walk along paths through ilex trees, and you can go for ½ hour, 1 hour or 2 hours, as you feel inclined. Everywhere it is a fairy land, and you have it to yourselves alone. Then the Hotel in which you stay has the cream of cosmopolitan society, with lovely American, Austrian and German girls, and strong bronzed men playing polo. There are all the amenities—tennis, golf, polo, etc—if you want them, but they don't obtrude, and you can easily escape. Excellent bar and a lovely place to dance under the stars, but not too good food.

I burnt my back & arms into agonising blisters the last day, and we left by air in such a storm of thunder and rain as you would not believe. It was a grand holiday.

We then went for two days to Hermione's villa on Maggiore, and then I flew home alone (Mary went on to Munich) leaving Venice (where I had had to leave my aeroplane while having a magneto mended) at 10 in the morning, flying in gorgeous weather over the Brenner to Innsbruck, and reaching Stuttgart about 8 p.m. Magnificent German aerodrome, and all conveniences, including about 30 policemen, for very little money.

The next day the weather was vile, and I had a weary time struggling against the wind and rain over the Rhine and the Ardennes with nothing but a bad French road-map and no hills marked! In bad weather air navigation is as difficult and as tiring as it is easy and simple in good. I only made about 40 miles p.h. over the ground against the wind, and it was an awful strain to read my map, as hardly anything was marked on it.

I landed at Karlsruhe—forced back there by impossible weather west of the Rhine—Saarbrucken, and Valenciennes, and popped over the Channel about 7.30, eventually reaching Hendon just as it got dark.

When I arrived at Saarbrucken (what a lovely French word!) I said something about being in France, and they said 'No, you are in Germany still. We are all Germans here'. So that was that. Then I had to pay for my beer in francs, and pass the French douane. I commented again on this. They said 'Yes, it is the French Customs Union and we use French money, but we are Germans, and in 1935 we return to the Fatherland!'

I feel ever so much better for the holiday and full of beans. . . . I am altogether happy and lucky, and can give you none of the news you would like to have.

Writing from Venice on July 14th, 1932, to Lady Gage, he said: 'I must have missed the news in the *Times* that you have got a son. O.K., good, well done, hurrah! congratulations. The Empire is tottering for want of a good man, and it won't totter any more with a new terrific Gage to learn it! . . . May all the best things in the world be his always, and life fall on his shoulders like a brave, rich and beautiful cloak.'

In a letter to his mother, written from Milan on his way home, Antony said:

The world appears to be shaking off the yoke of Democracy, and if only I were 10 years older there would be great changes in England! The hour is so ripe everywhere for a

man, and a drive, and a policy. I hope the great National
Government is the last of the *ancien régime.*

He wrote to me on August 29th:

> Politically it is high time you came home, as I have
forgotten all my Lytton Liberalism, in spite of a recent lecture from Hermione, and am just the most confirmed militarist, Fascist, autocratic tyrant that has appeared in politics
for years. They are to have another Round Table conference
on India, and are going, I understand, to make us promise
not to use bombs in the next war. It is all too fantastic and
futile for words, and what everyone wants morally, socially
and politically is for someone to come along and say 'This
is; never mind why, it just is; I say so, and will have no
argument.' Reluctantly I am forced to the conclusion that I
shall yet have to be the one to save England! It seems to me
that we have got into such a mess through trying to be fair
and rational and popular, that there is no faith, no beauty,
no prosperity, no order and no freedom left in the world. It
only needs one or two men who can't see the other side. . . .
>
> It doesn't look as if your job was going to be much more
thankful. You will find out the whole truth, or very near it,
and you will tell the world. And then it will go on the same
as it did before, and the Japs will leave the League, and
Manchuria will continue to be unhealthy. The truth seems
to be that there can only be justice and freedom where there
is strength and determination. Strength does not always
produce either justice or freedom, often it produces tyranny.
Only weakness never produces anything at all except chaos.
And the poor long-suffering peoples of the world in whose
name all these things are done are meanwhile starving in
bewildered bitterness.
>
> I have seen much on my travels this summer, and Italy is
the only country in Europe where they still believe in
liberty! In all others *ça n'existe plus,* and men are turning in
desperation to Nazis and tyrants. If we cannot be free, they
say, and we know now that we cannot, let us at least be
happy, and well-fed, and well ruled. I think the whole ten-

dency of the century is going to be a revolt against the
liberalism of 200 years! What men want is not to be poor
and free so much as to be wealthy slaves. Rule Britannia!
Britannia rule the sea! Britons never, never, never shall be
free!

I went to Salzburg in my Moth for the week-end before
last. Started after my Board on Thursday & slept the night
at Valenciennes. Arrived in Salzburg for tea on Friday, and
spent two lovely days in boiling sun by an Austrian lake.
Spent Sunday night in Munich, and was back in the office
Tuesday morning. It was grand fun. I have a passion for
getting about the world, a great love of flying, a longing to
learn German, a great admiration for efficiency, and a crazy
devotion to faith wherever I see it.

Last week-end I went to my boys' camp in Norfolk and
called at Knebs Sunday evening. . . . I am pretty full of
beans, and pretty militant, and pretty hard, and need taking
down a peg or two. . . .

Davina's baby is like all babies, and squeaks unceasingly,
but Davina is well as the dawn. Hermione has just gone
back to Italy. She is my favourite woman!

I returned from China at the beginning of October, and
in the letter which Antony wrote to welcome me at Port
Said on September 15th he said:

I was going to shoot partridges this week-end, but
am going to Paris instead. I have got a new five-year plan,
which is to do whatever amuses me, however foolish. New
for me?! Anyway I'm going to Paris.

Life I find a bit better than I did when you left. This is
because of (a) there being no House of Commons at the
moment and (b) my five-year plan!

There is published in *The Times* today a list of the 500
Peers that Asquith would have created if need were to pass
the Parliament Bill. I wish he had done it. They are all
Tories now except 300, and those are dead!

I have a passion for foreign travel which will clash
strangely with your delight in the home fields again. I loved

your letter about your flying. Will you come with me in my baby? I had a rare tossing the other day off the North Welsh coast, and was quite frightened. But it is fun to do, and gives you a sense of power, and superiority, and danger overcome. My Moth is so sweet and so slow and so casual, but very effective.

His sympathies at this time, both with Fascism and with Roman Catholicism, found expression in the following letter to his friend Mrs. Hughes in October:

. . . I have a new philosophy which started politically & has now spread to religion.

I think the whole doctrine of Liberalism which has pervaded and ruled the world since the Renaissance has been one ghastly futile blunder. Of course, like the war, it may have been necessary, and it has surely had its good points. But it is now discredited. It has shot its bolt. And so we are passing it on with an incredible cynical gesture to India & the East.

You see the whole idea of civilisation, politically, socially& religiously, has been increasingly, since the Renaissance, the idea of liberty. It has cut off Kings' heads, made revolutions, inspired poets & given flappers the vote. The will of the people must prevail. Self government is nobler than good government. The Supreme Court is the bar of public opinion. The voice of the people is as the voice of God.

When in 1816 Metternich heard the mob yelling outside the gates of the Hofburg, he turned to his friends & said— 'That, my friend, is what they call the Voice of God'!

The truth is, of course, that the people have no will & so it cannot prevail. The people don't know, & can't know. The doctrine of Liberalism has produced neither order nor liberty, but only a chaotic, faithless, unprincipled, dishonest muddle.

It is the supreme farce of history. Years ago men said that they would reach up to Heaven, & they built a great tower to that end. God looked at them & smiled and caused them all to start speaking different languages, so that in the end the Tower of Babel was a bit of a failure. That's happened

again. For the last 400 years civilised man has gradually
been discarding discipline and obedience, reason and simplicity, in this mad search after freedom, emancipation, &
self-determination. But of course man isn't big enough for
these things, either politically or morally. In politics the
crash, the multitude of tongues, the confusion, is apparent
and devastating, and the history of the next century & after
is going to be the revolution of the Right—the movement
towards order & sanity and discipline and control.

No one gives a damn now for liberty. He knows he can't
be free anyway. What he wants is work and wages, security,
and to be allowed to go about his daily business. He will
accept any government that gives him these things and be
thankful.

The movement has begun in Italy & Russia & Germany,
and is on its way in England, France & America.

That is my new political philosophy. Of course, the supreme irony of it is that as the dawn of intellectual enlighten
ment is breaking over Europe, so in the East, where there
has long been a proper understanding of these things, the
weed of liberty has begun to seed.

But the moral & religious aspect is, I think, more serious
and much the same. The revolt against the Papacy and the
founding of many new free-thinking sects from the Church
of England (and for Scotland!) downwards followed the
same lines. Leave order, leave discipline, this blind convention & intolerant tyranny, and find God in the freedom &
solitude of the individual heart. But if man can't find political wisdom by himself, heaven knows he can't find God.

That has been far too difficult for him. As a result, the
Churches are all empty, religion is no longer taught in the
schools, and Christianity is not practised at all. There is religious chaos & doubt & confusion, & the relaxation of discipline has only resulted in modifying morality to suit the sin
after the sin has been committed.

A man does wrong & then argues 'That can't have been
wrong. If there is anything wrong, then it must be the
morality which condemns what I have done as sin.' And so

Y

he scraps that bit of religious teaching. In other words, man is daily pitting his puny judgement against God's.

I have done it so often myself, & it is so grotesque really—the attempt to change Christian teaching in order to make oneself a saint instead of a sinner. You haven't done it, because you are a saint, at least compared to me you are. But I have always felt in my heart of hearts that really I was quite good, whereas I am, of course, not peculiarly perhaps, but still, of course, an ordinary human, insignificant offender against His divine majesty and the law of God.

And that's why I am attracted to the Catholic Church. I don't know much about it, but there are two things which appeal to me, if I understand them right:—

1. Catholics have mostly got what I & most of my friends have not got—faith instead of doubt, certainty instead of hopelessness, & discipline instead of laxity.

2. The Catholic Church says to me 'The whole thing is too big for you. You can't know & you don't understand, & when you think you can do both, the odds, from what evidence we have, are strongly in favour of your being wrong. The Church is blessed with the power to interpret God's will. If you bother about it, we will prove it to you, or you can prove it for yourself if you care to take the trouble (the whole Catholic argument is based on reason rather than inspiration or faith or "experience"). Therefore you take it from the Church, which knows. It won't make you good. It won't save you, but it will help you. It will give you understanding & guidance, and it will help you to live this none too easy life in the best way possible.'

Perhaps when I know more about it, I shall find that the Catholic Church is neither of these two things. But that is what I think it is. . . .

In the summer of 1932 Antony began a correspondence with Windham Baldwin, whom he had known at Eton, and to whom he had then given the name of Willow. When they met again in later years they found they had much in common, and became very intimate. They did not meet as much as each would have liked, as Antony was kept in London by his work and Willow (we only knew him by this name) was kept in the Midlands by his work in the family business at Wilden. But they shared the same friends, and the fact that they had somewhat different tastes gave them something to discuss when they met and to write about when they were separated. Some of Antony's best letters were written to Willow, who has fortunately preserved them. With his permission I reproduce some of them here in sequence from July. They fill a period when few other letters are available.

One feature in the correspondence needs a word of explanation. They imagined themselves as engaged in a crusade against a certain tendency of modern thought exemplified in the works of Noel Coward and others, from the influence of which they desired to rescue their girl friends. They called this 'The War'; they exchanged poems about it, and it was the chief topic of their correspondence during these months.

July 5th, 1932.

Dear Willow,

Though I am 'a better chap' than you, which is, of course, silly, I can't write as well as you any more. I used to write better, but I can't make my fingers work any more.

I saw your Father yesterday & he said you were quite nice, so I expect that's all right. The truth is, of course, that unless something really terrible happens to one that almost breaks the heart, and at least shakes & rattles the philosophy, everyone gets worse as they get older. Children are good, & wise, and nice, & not bothered by tiresome things. But when they grow up they are all wrong from start to finish. I was good & charitable, and happy, & nice, as a child. But I am none of these things now. Only I am worth more to anyone who likes to hire my brains. I think though that you have probably been more unhappy than me, & so you haven't grown as evil or as insolent.

I envy you in some ways, because you are detached from life, and can look down like a wise God, & give advice & have knowledge & understand. Also you are more impersonal, & less temperamental & susceptible to everything than I am. But you are more sensitive. I shouldn't like to be that. But I should like to care less about some things which are not good, & more about others which are. But your philosophy wasn't a help, was it? . . .

I think you ought to come more often to the South & this world, or rather that I should go more often to the North & to solitude. I said that I never went to bed early, but I always do. I go asleep at 10.0 always, if I can—so you will know that I appreciated our evening. . . .

You see this is the way I work! Anything to avoid doing what should be done—like school again. I only do what I like, & if I like writing to you instead of working, that's the way of it.

I wonder if I will get to Plas Newydd with you. Would it be a good plan? I think quite likely not. But still I might come & see your works one day. Will you be an important Captain of Industry one day? I suppose so. Then I shall nationalise everything by confiscation, to be funny. . . .

I will go now to a cocktail party, because that is the way to get on in politics. But why get on? Anyway I know why I drink cocktails. Because so much less dull than not! . . .

I was right glad to see you again, and wish you were in the Air Force too. It is all that is fun now.

EDWARD. *

5, HOWICK PLACE, S.W.1,†
Sept. 7th, 1932.

I think you are not very good for me. I have spent a great deal of time in recent years in trying to overcome my conviction that the things of the social world were not on

*In this correspondence all Antony's letters are so signed.

†The Army and Navy Stores.

the whole very good things, and that in my outlook on life I was probably right & they (or it) probably wrong.

I have spent that time, because being shed of that conviction would make life easier, and me more amenable & more pleasant. Also it would make people want me more, and I like being wanted. As a matter of fact I have succeeded pretty well—and then you go and talk to me like that and let me talk like that—and it's all wrong. But it's also very pleasant. What matters to me is always to have people around me, always to be wanted, & to be loved a great deal, & never to be alone or to have to think. You see, those are things you don't care about so much. But I have found that in order to achieve the end, it is necessary to see a point in point-to-points, to be able to play bridge, to adore dancing, to know which cinema star is which, & to have heard of Reinhardt, Ld Beaverbrook, Chips Channon, Olga Lynn, Noel Coward & Mrs. Corrigan, & if possible call them all by their Christian names. Now it seems Opera is thrown in, but I can't manage that.

It seems too that if you are prepared to work very hard at these things, & do them quite well, & make yourself think them important (because that is the only way of bearing them at all) then, just once in a while you get someone very beautiful & very sweet to stand with you on a high hill in the dawn, & be human & happy for five minutes, and that is very good, & very necessary to me, and worth the rest.

But I believe you manage it without! And after last night I feel inclined to try it too. . . .

5, HOWICK PLACE, S.W.
September 12, 1932.

In the office at last, with a little time to spare, and the proper setting for writing a great letter or a great epic poem! . . .

You are bad for me, I know that, but I like it just the same. I can walk on the hills in the rain, & despise the world, and come home & laugh at the X's, and be bigger than them. Or I can fly in the air, and do it. Or I can work in the office, & do it, But I can't read poetry, & feel things very much, without being sentimental, & dwelling on the hopes reared high, & the dreams brought low—Then I am unhappy & sad. It is very easy to be unhappy when you are young. It quite suits you, but I loathe it, & I can only get on, & score off the Xs, & fight the war, when I am astride the world & myself. Then I can laugh at them, & kill them with ridicule, which is good. But if I get down—it doesn't matter how intellectually superior I may feel, or how much I may know that I have got what they haven't, I get inferiority complex. Poetry & intellectual & emotional beauty have that effect on me. But physical beauty the opposite.

Now I shan't write a great epic to our war, or an epigrammatic attack on our enemy, after all. I shall just go on shooting, & working, & looking forward to the next thing, & then I shall be astride the world, & we will win the war.

I liked P.N. because I was astride the world. Because I felt I had myself & the situation in hand for the first time, & because I felt that we were the stronger, although for years & years I have known we aren't.

I wonder if I have really been fighting this war so much longer than you. The enemy is an overpowering, crushing, deadening thief, and you have to be in the full armour of virility, & spirits, and self-control, to hold him off. He has had me down so often, but I know that at P.N. we began to shake him a bit. For all your scepticism, I *know* this; and that is why I wonder if I haven't been a soldier longer than you, & if I am not better able to discriminate between a decreasing and an increasing rifle-fire. (What fun this metaphor is! and there is still 20 mins: to lunch time).

You see what we have got to do is not so much to kill the dragon as to rescue the maiden. I don't mind there being snaky dragons in the world—I loved *Cavalcade*. They give me quite a certain amount of pleasure at times.

What I do mind is anyone mistaking them for Gods, and particularly people I like. What we have got to do is rescue C—— and M—— (I think to a less extent), and all the nice *jeunesse dorée* from the fascination of this thing. We don't have to kill it. Well, in my vain way, I have been at it a long time. I have felt its fiery breath, and the awful deadening weight of its body, and the slimy cold sickly feel of its skin. It has had me down, as I say, many times, and I have shrugged my shoulders & gone, in the bitterness of my heart, to the good things—to the hills & the wise poems—& I have left the maiden still scratching the old dragon's ears. And it has made me very unhappy.

But now it's different. I have taken to scarcely noticing the beast. I have walked by armed so strong in honesty. . . . I haven't troubled to fight, and I think I begin to notice two things. The maiden just raises her eyes to see me pass, and the dragon moves as if to follow. And I don't care. That's the whole point. If I turned to look, they would be at it again. If I said 'Come on, dragon', she would hold him back. If I winked at the maiden the dragon would kiss her. But if we keep on walking past as if on our way to something interesting, in the end they'll both come too, and, in the end, the dragon will be out of his old pit, & very vulnerable.

What rot all this is, and what does it mean? It was fun to write. . . .

I have settled that these things matter: To know what you want. To have complete control over yourself, & to be always busy. I have never done either, but I am beginning.

I love your philosophy. I love your company, & I love your wisdom. But there is something about you which makes me uncertain on both the first points and enables me to have far too much time on my hands to dream & think. That's bad. But thank you for coming to stay with me, & thank you for preaching this crusade. We will have much more talk together, and, more important, some great battles. If you kill the Dragon will you let the A & N set him up & stuff him for you?

5, HOWICK PLACE, S.W.1.
October 4th, 1932.

I am sorry you won't see me any more this year, but I hope you will. I also feel that I won't see anyone any more, because it destroys equilibrium. But I know that I shall, because I really prefer losing equilibrium to being destroyed.

I like sitting here writing letters to you much better than doing dull work. And, after all, we have all our dull dreary lives to work & think & be unselfish in, but the years of youth, in which we can enjoy our loves and our little games, and our tottering equilibrium, are fast coming to an end.

As a result of our brief religious talk, Davina has produced a story about a Bishop whose Diocese was being visited by God that afternoon, which surpasses all things for cunning, witty thought. He had the greatest difficulty in keeping it from the R.C.s, and in filling his Church without divulging the secret. In the end one child ran away from the Church parade to play in the fields, and found God sitting on a log laughing!

That is one of the things you are wrong about—religion. Never mind now. I will have to put you right one day, though.

I had a good Manchurian dinner * last night, & lots more after. But subjective things are really better.

KNEBWORTH, *October 9th*, 1932.

I wouldn't have given you 'John Brown's Body' to read unless I had thought it was good, and thought too that you might like it. It isn't at all Noel Coward, you see, and it makes one feel besides the 100% Columbia super-charged Hoover Ford U.S.A.—there is probably something of virtue in the Great Republic. But of course there is, or the English would never have colonised it.

I have got to do the duty stuff by B/ham this week-end, and I shall only talk about the Manchurian Report, which needs handling properly, & will, of course, be misunderstood equally by the Tories & by the League of Nations Union. But, oh dear, I cannot feel that any, any of it matters very much. We are in the grip of great things— that fell clutch business which is altogether too big for any of our little minds. People who think that all that is wrong

*A dinner given to me by the League of Nations Union on my return from Manchuria.

with the world is profit, and/or that all you have to do is to cut wages and doles, are so equally wrong and ignorant. It is fantastic that every soap-box orator, and every petty mind that just scratches the surface of thought, should imagine that the vast machinery of the world would or could respond to their ideas. How much better it would be if, like you, 99% of the civilised world became content again to do their duty in that state of life . . . etc.

But when the Lancs cotton-merchant Tory comes and talks about monetary (pronounced moanetary) policy or the T.U. official whines about the means of production and consumption, I get the pip. But I always get the pip. I like wine & nice girls & poetry, flying, friends, thinking, being busy & feeling well. That's almost all.

5, HOWICK PLACE, S.W.1.

Oct. 13, 1932.

We will have the Civil Wars back again yet, with victory for the South, and victory for the Cavaliers, and this will be a sweeter and a simpler and a gayer life. But there is much to do, and much to change, & the insipid, crooked morality of our age must die, as the Roundheads and the Unionists should have died.

My political & philosophical & social war is a revolt from Liberty & Liberalism. I want instead of the rule of liberty— which means no freedom and no truth, no peace of mind, no order, no efficiency, no understanding—the rule of order in which these things may obtain.

The world is full not of wise, enlightened men & women, with souls & taste, and the gifts of self-determination, but of fools who don't know what to do with themselves economically, philosophically, ethically, or aesthetically. It is as if you had applied the system of Varsity organisation to a private school, & the early years of a public school. You have got the same result on a grand scale.

That is why I admire the Catholic Church. It realises what the world is, & has fitted its religion to the world— saying 'You can't be happy yourselves; you can't know; you

can't think; you're all just wet. We will make you happy, &
save you thinking, & give you that simplicity & sweetness
& gaiety which you are vaguely groping after.'

And they do it. That's the miracle—at least it's not a
miracle. It's the rational outcome of their point of view.
If they could do it to me, I would be a convert tomorrow, but
I don't think they can. I'm either a boss or a rebel. But not
so the world. And that is what we have got to do politically.
And I am going to do it in time, perhaps. Unless I marry a
lovely girl & become happy & don't care any more.

You say you have got your line of conduct from what
Mary calls our Blessed Saviour. That's good enough. You've
got it, & you're right. But no idea, no ideal, no code, no line
of conduct can exist or be perpetuated except by organization. Therefore we have organized religion, & we must support it, not because we love the Parson, or think the ten
Commandments the word of God, but just as we would support the King & the police & the Government, because they
are our institutions. The King may be rather naughty, &
the Prime Minister rather stupid, and the police a little old-
fashioned. Then we try & improve and adapt, but we are
foolish if we say Kings, Prime Ministers & policemen are all
bunkum.

And now I am being neither boss nor rebel, because—
well I can see the thing a little more clearly as a citizen than
as a soul.

That will do now. Muddled politics & religion, with a
complaint about my subjective attitude to Catholicism which
is inconsistent. But there is a theme & creed to it all, which
become increasingly mine as some things begin to harden &
crystallize in a rather soft nebulous world.

But we will pursue the subject a good deal further, & in
more detail & isolation. Also I will look up 'eclectic', & then
write about that & religious education.

I don't remember what I said about the other ordinary
war, but I don't want you to have to give your gas-mask to
——! My grouse about the war is this—I missed it. Everyone says to me, or implies, (a) 'You are lucky, it was hell—

we loathed it. We will see you never have to go through it—but we went through it & we're damned fine fellows with something you will never have', and (*b*) the flower of English youth was killed, their like will never be again. The Grenfells, the Listers, the Charterises—all the best; gone.

Give them their due—they were good. But any fool can fight a war, because he has to. There is no alternative. It is simple. It is straightforward, & when you are dead, you are great. But to live a peace is difficult, tedious, heart-breaking, complicated, twisty & uncertain. And when you are dead you are little.

The pacifists have set about me the wrong way. That's all. I admire strength, & vitality, & clarity of thought, action, & expression. And I admire death. I like black & I like white. But not grey.

> 5, HOWICK PLACE, S.W.1.
> *Oct.* 17, 1932.

I think you are clever to write a poem like that. I will forgive 'Millions have before gone', because all the rest is good rhyme & metre (which that is too, of course), but good grammar too.

Nothing is really ever as good as it was, but the whole art and joy of life consists in expecting that it is going to be better. And that, now I come to think of it, is exactly what the poem said!

I have looked up 'eclectic'. It is the one thing which religious education should not be. It is because it is *too* eclectic that we are in a mess. People should be taught one thing, taught it definitely & convincingly, & told that if they don't believe it they are fools.

It is not within our power to weigh the merits and assess the value of Mohammedanism, Buddhism, Christianity, Transubstantiation, Free-will & Predestination, Infallibility or the Nature of God, any more than it is within our power to decide for ourselves whether silver should be remonetarized, or Montagu Norman replaced at the Bank. Unfortunately we have, in the end, to come to some conclusion, &

take some action, about the last lot of things. But the first, if we were properly taught, need never worry us again.

The effect of making religion eclectic is to enable us to condone every sin we commit by believing we are probably right & God wrong. That's not so much foolish as it is futile.

Now I am going to have a bath, pick up a suitcase and go to 'Iolanthe' with M——.

I am in a rage with life, and I shouldn't be if my religious education hadn't been eclectic!

HOUSE OF COMMONS, *Nov.* 14, 1932.

Before I go off calling on people, which seems to me the proper thing to do at this hour of the day (6.0 p.m.) why not write a line?

First of all, your Father must have been very impressed by our journey to P.N. His description of fear from the air moved the House of Commons as it has not been moved since some important tariff (I forget which) was changed from $33\frac{1}{3}$ to $33\frac{2}{3}$. This sounds rude. But I didn't mean it that way—not rude to your father but rude to the H. of C. That *is* the kind of thing that moves them. But of course fear from the air is quite different from fear of the air, which is what we felt (at least I did—you weren't conscious enough) off Conway that day.

No one has understood what he meant, & we are still arguing. I say he meant that disarmament, and particularly 'local restriction', is (*a*) hopeless & (*b*) useless, and that all that matters is for you and me to like flying to P.N. better than dropping bombs on ugly people. What is more, that *is* what he meant, I am sure. But everyone else says he meant to do away with the R.A.F. and (?) the A.A.F. Perhaps that is what the *Daily Mail* said he said. Then, of course, everyone would know.

Well, that's that. I had my B/ham meeting last night in a cinema. They all came, as they thought, to see Marlene Dietrich. It was packed, & I thought I made quite a good speech.

I have been soaking in disarmament lately. It is like having to get up in the morning—bloody but inevitable.

And now for better things. I think the war has been waged not in vain. The rumour of its coming seems to have been very fearful, & I think we—but of course it's not us— have preserved one Eden to one Eve. I went to Munich fast in my aeroplane last Friday, & spent Saturday & Sunday with C——, & came back slow on Monday. . . .

You will have to come to the South again soon. It is time. I will write. I have been dreaming & vague.

5, Howick Place, S.W.1.

Nov. 22, 1932.

This is only a tiny word which I feel compelled to write, about Noel Coward.

I have had doubts about your view of him & of his influence. It is dual, I think; but I am only concerned with the public aspect—that is with the tone, effect and morality of his published & produced plays, etc.

You see I have always felt that wasn't so bad. Last night we went to his revue, and Davina said—'But he is on your side'. That was about it too. He pokes fun at the right things, & laughs at the things we must laugh at. He doesn't hate as we do—I know, but that is us & not him, and ridicule is really a better weapon than hate.

What he is like in a drawing-room, & what effect he may, as a personality, have on our Eves, is different. But his stuff is all right. He's good.

Your Mother told my Mother off for me having flown you in the storm—she seemed to think that you nearly died, which you did, & that I didn't mind, which I didn't! But all the same. . . .

I am sorry you didn't brave the wolves.* But you were, of course, obviously quite right. I must work.

House of Commons, Nov. 24, 1932.

No, of course we don't exactly see eye to eye about the war, but our eyes are quite near enough. It wouldn't do

---

*Willow had telegraphed to say he could not come to Knebworth, 'because it was winter & there were wolves about.'

if they were nearer. It wouldn't be as good or as broad or as wise a war. It would be just your and/or my prejudices. That's all right and nothing to worry about.

I agree that rat-poison isn't much good if the rats love it. I agree that Noel Coward is not, by your standards, a great artist. I think he is better than you do. I don't think he is a bad artist. Few are great artists, many are bad. He is neither.

But what is the argument on which you base your claim that he is base? Apart from your own personal opinion (which is of much more value than anything else) you say he is a bad artist because people with bad taste like his work. But people with bad taste like Shakespeare. You will say— 'If they do, then, in this respect at least, their taste is not bad'! I could say the same of Coward.

One point is this. If the rats like the poison & thrive on it, it is surprising. But if by chemical standards it remains poison, it is a miracle that the children of the Ritz like the 'Children of the Ritz' song. But it remains a song which says the right things about the children of the Ritz. That is good.

If —— likes me, and the ruder I am to him the more he likes me—I am not necessarily base. If I was trying to make him hate me, you might say I was a bad artist. But Coward isn't trying to do anything but make money, & if saying what he thinks makes him money, & if what he says is what I think ought to be said—then I am satisfied. My view is this. He is a better artist than you think. He is not great, but he is good. His view is the right one. His influence is probably bad, & his admirers are a poor lot. This is perhaps because—well, I don't know. I've suddenly got tired of the subject.

I sat down thinking I might write about it for ever, but I have suddenly got weary. It's a sign that it's not really a great subject & that I sat up too late last night. . . .

I hate the winter. I hate work. I hate emptiness, & I am full of all three.

We must meet somehow soon. But how?

Here I must interpose two letters from Antony to his sister Davina, as they introduce the subject of religion with which the correspondence with Willow closes.

Davina had written to him from Ireland about original sin, which at this time he had been discussing with Arnold Lunn, the significance of baptism, etc. Antony, whose religious views, in spite of his talks with Arnold Lunn and Mary Erskine, and his resultant sympathy with the Roman Catholic Church at the moment, were still those of a healthy schoolboy, replied on December 6th:

> Oh, what a lovely long letter, and what a good letter, and what a nice letter to answer!

Of course we don't know what Adam may be up to in the next world. He may quite likely have slipped up again, and let us in for more trouble. We can only concern ourselves with what we do know. If you were to slip up badly you might let Rosanagh* in for something which would affect her all her life. So there isn't really anything so odd about 'the sins of the fathers—unto the third & fourth generation'.

I think the relative size of the amount of water on a baby's forehead at christening, and the number of nebulae in Jeans' universe, is unimportant. What matters is that you and Rosanagh's Godparents should accept the liability of teaching her that the world is not only carnal, animal and undisciplined, but spiritual, and human, and controlled. It is a good thing that Rosanagh should learn from the beginning that the great things, and the important things, come from the soul and not from the body, from God and not from Nature. This does not mean that it is wrong or bad to like the emotions of the senses, but it does mean that these things don't even make the main currents of life. The power to appreciate these things even is of the soul and the mind.

The fact that the outward sign of accepting this truth on behalf of a baby is a spot of water only shows how little we

*Her daughter.

are, and how much we need symbols and organisations to keep us up to the mark.

The degree to which a baby is penalised by not being baptized depends of course—at least so I understand—upon the reason for its not being baptized. If it is not baptized out of defiance of the Church of God, that is bad, as it is bad not to raise your hat to a lady out of defiance. If it is just carelessness, that is also bad, because the smallness of the thing aggravates the evil of refusing it. Again, if you don't raise your hat—which is not much effort—because it is troublesome, you are futile, which is worse even than defiant. If it is a mistake—you didn't see the lady—that can be remedied.

We can't explain why we should be asked to do these little things. We can't explain why there should be a benevolent omnipotent God and also pain and evil. If we could—well, it would all be easy.

> 'The men of the East may search the scrolls,
>   And times and triumphs mark,
>   But the men signed of the Cross of Christ
>   Go gaily in the dark'.

But before we can chuck the whole thing overboard, and say 'This is nonsense, and unfair, and unreal,' we have got to disprove the truth of what happened in Palestine 1900 years ago. No one has yet been able to do that.

The more that Jeans finds out, the more remarkable it all becomes, and the more difficult to understand, which, to my mind, is a reason for clinging closer to the things we do know, and not launching ourselves without anchor or sails into what is an ever enlarging and more mysterious and more tempestuous sea.

I didn't say I was tired of hills and sun. Read it again. I said I felt increasingly that these alone were real, and good, and joy-giving, but that I didn't get them. I love life, but I don't see much now. I am weary of this blotter, and this shop, and this London, and this vile stupendous bad taste which is inescapable in all modern life. That, and the American debt, are the main problems of our time. . . .

Oh, but there is need of a great war against the modern

nonsense. 'Base' is Willow's word for it, and a good one. I shan't come to you for Xmas. I shall be at home, which is good, and I shall perhaps go to Switzerland afterwards.

In another letter to her, dated December 27th, he said:

Last year at this time I was in the depths, because all had gone as wrong as seemed possible. This year I am in the skies, because things seem better than I dared hope. . . . I scarcely dare breathe at the moment, because I have built a smallish hut on a vast plain of sand, and it may collapse and be engulfed at any moment. It appears to me immensely unimportant whether we live or die, are gay or sad, but very essential never to give up trying one's utmost quite blindly.

To Willow he wrote the next day:

KNEBWORTH, *Dec.* 28, 1932.

Will you teach me philosophy? I am wondering how you manage to live alone, & work a bit, and read books and sit by yourself. I am getting more & more like M.—must be fidgeting, must have people, sensation, occupation.

This is my Christmas holiday at home. I have been here since Friday, had a hunt, a ride, a flight or two, called on some farmers, and am so excited at going back to the office tomorrow that I can think of nothing else! It's bad, isn't it? I am also in tears because one of the farmers is very poor, his house is falling down, his clothes are in rags, & he can only have one boy to help him on the farm, & he can't pay his rent! . . .

I want a smaller, simpler, gayer life—like the Cavaliers, & all I get is wireless, & aeroplanes, & newspapers, & night-clubs, and talk in millions, & machines, & organization—like the Roundheads. And I don't know anything, & I can't concentrate on a book—which is one of the reasons I am writing this letter. . . .

I oughtn't to go to Switzerland with a £1,000 o/d,* ought I?

There is much to be thankful for yet, I suppose, though I wouldn't mind a little material bad luck to learn me!

Will there be another war soon? That would be fun.

z　　　　　　　*Overdraft.

And the correspondence closes as follows:

5, HOWICK PLACE, S.W.1.
Jan. 12th, 1933.

... Your letter to me was good & full of wisdom & help. Two things were particularly good (I) 'only Gods can stand freedom; we turn bad on it'. (Now having written it out like that, I feel I should add 'give the context of, & write a short comment on, the above')

Anyway that is true—very true, and is the reason (*a*) why I think religious education should be *less* eclectic and (*b*) why I want to be a Roman Catholic, and perhaps (*c*) why I am in politics a tyrant & an autocrat, and not a democrat, and why I believe in war & guns, and not peace and arbitration & conferences.

But:—

(2) 'I'm unsympathetic, and think everyone must help himself, and hurt himself & cure himself' and that's true too—terribly true, & that's why I don't become an R.C.

The trouble with us—the English & the educated English—is that we have had an eclectic training for generations & generations, that we have been nurtured on freedom, & that for a moment we were, as nearly as man may be, Gods. Now that's over. But anyway not the point.

But the trouble with me was the same. I have been lucky and rich & happy & prosperous, & have felt, as a boy, like a God. Then I have had no hemp, himp, homp like you, no clutch of circumstance, and I have gone bad; that's all. It would be nice to be saved by the R.C. Church and a priest. But with the other background it isn't possible, and so I shall either save myself, which will be a bore but good, or not, which will be amusing but bad.

Now I shan't write any more, but
You are mostly right.
We must certainly meet again soon.
The war's the thing.
I am happy.

EDWARD.

With those words this story may fittingly end. At the time they were written Antony's prospects were brighter than at any moment in his life. He was well established both in business and in politics. His work was congenial, and he had enough leisure to enjoy his favourite occupations. In matters which touched his heart, he was more hopeful and cheerful than ever before. We had spent what proved to be our last Christmas together at Knebworth. It was a happy time. We talked much of many things.

We talked of the Manchurian Report; I told him of my experiences in the East and of how I thought this trouble might be settled.

We talked of the League of Nations and the prospects of peace and disarmament. On this subject he was not so much militarist as martial. The difficulty to which he could find no answer was that if permanent peace were ever achieved, and armies and navies ceased to exist, there would be no outlet for the manly qualities which fighting developed, and that human physique and human character would deteriorate. In vain I pointed out to him that he himself had not been made what he was by the army or the navy, that few of the friends whom he most admired were in either service, and that life had plenty of adventure to offer without war. This never satisfied him, and the only argument with which I ever shook him was that if there were no more war there would be no more pacifists!

We talked of India, as we both knew it. His sympathies were undoubtedly with the school that regarded the White Paper policy as one of surrender, but the more he studied the subject, the more difficult he found it to support this attitude with his reason. 'I don't see much difference between you and Lloyd', he would say to me; 'you both admit that the policy has risks, and, if so, why do the d——d thing at all?' 'Because', I would reply, 'there is no policy without risks, and each man must judge for himself which risk is the greater and which the less.'

We talked of religion. He told us of the friendship he had recently formed with a Cowley Father, to whom he had given the nickname of 'Giotto',* and how when he had spoken of his Roman Catholic sympathies this friend had replied: 'Why not give your own Church a chance first, have you ever really done that?' He admitted that this advice was sound, and he intended to follow it.

We talked also of books and people, of life, of love, of the future and what it held in store—of all the many interests that we had in common. Antony was always communicative, but in these days he talked more freely with his mother than with me. The strong vein of romance in his character had never been wholly satisfied by reality. His manly tastes had found complete realization in football, boxing, ski-ing, polo and flying; but his poet's heart yearned after an ideal which ever escaped him. In his women friends—and they were many—he had found the qualities which inspired this ideal without satisfying it. Only in his last years did all the visions of his dreams become embodied in one girl, who from the age of twenty had seemed to him different from all others. She was then a child of twelve, and in the years when he was but her playmate he 'marvelled at her', and she held his heart against all others.

*'Giotto' had come to Knebworth to preach during the autumn, and after a short acquaintance had asked Antony to take him flying in his Moth. This led to a friendship which became more intimate during the early months of 1933. Antony wrote to him early in January, 'I want just to say this:—When I came to see you, before, I was unhappy. You helped me tremendously, and you helped me to help myself. Now it seems that 1933 might be the best year of my life. I don't know, but things look good, and I am perfectly certain that that visit to St. Edward's Home has more than a little to do with it. You helped me to be less bad, and I am convinced that God understood and was pleased. I have a tremendous sense of thankfulness.'

After her first ball in London, he wrote of her: 'C. was more divinely lovely than the Milky Way—so much the loveliest woman in the room that all the pretty women had to go home and hide themselves for shame.' From then onwards he lived to win her, and the last three years of his life had been entirely dominated by this great devotion. He was growing weary of being alone, and longed ardently to marry. He suffered much from the torture of uncertainty, but at the beginning of this year it seemed as if he were at last going to attain his ideal. On New Year's Day he wrote to his sister, Davina Erne, from Cranborne: 'I have a feeling that 1933 is going to be a year memorable in the life of our country, and of the world, and of our family. It is the high tide—the high tide and the turn of all that is depressing. And the year is going to mark the beginning of a new world, a new light, a great hope, and a great happiness. But it is only a feeling, and had better be left there, with heart in mouth, and a great prayer'.

He only lived for another four months. In that time he had a short but happy holiday in Switzerland; he visited Sweden, and wrote for the *Kandahar Review* an account of the ski-ing conditions in that country; he made a speech on India in the House of Commons which won him some praise, and made his friends speak of him as a man of promise. But the expectations with which the year 1933 opened were not, and never will be, fulfilled. For Antony was not born to grow old. He was the embodiment of youth, and his youth had run its course.

During these last months flying absorbed him more and more. He was living with us at Knebworth now, for just before Christmas his London flat, with his books, pictures and furniture, had been destroyed by fire. Shortly before, his overcoat and a suit-case (a coming-of-age present) containing all his personal possessions of value had been stolen

out of his motor car. Yet the loss of this property had caused
him as little concern as the loss or breaking of a toy had done
when he was a child. We saw little of him. He went to town
every morning to work at the Army & Navy Stores, and every
Sunday he went to Hendon to fly in one of the machines
of his squadron. 'It is terrible how I love this flying,' he
said to his mother one day, 'it is because it is so beautiful.'
He told her how it was producing a new science of observing
cloud formations and their effect upon the weather. Above
all, he loved to be in the air at the sunset hour, when the
whole sky was filled with colour.

On the afternoon of Sunday, April 30th, he came unexpectedly to Knebworth in his Moth with Roger Bushell, a
brother officer. It was a perfect spring day and everything
was at its loveliest. Antony and his friend played tennis, and
after tea sat talking with his mother while she was garden-
ing until nearly eight o'clock. Then the two flew back to
London together. The last I saw of him was disappearing
into the glow of the sunset above the trees.

The next day at 6 in the evening he left the Stores to take
part in a practice formation flight with his squadron at Hendon. The manoeuvres they carried out were in preparation
for a special display to be given before the Prince of Wales a
week later. As the squadron was completing a dipping movement over the aerodrome, the leader—an Air Force officer
who for that evening only had replaced the squadron's own
leader—dived so steeply, and maintained the dive so long,
that all the three leading machines actually touched the
ground. Antony was flying on the left of the leading three,
and, as in duty bound, was closely watching the leader in
front of him. His machine struck a slight rise in the ground
with great violence, overturned, and he and his passenger
were killed instantly. The subsequent enquiry established
beyond question that no blame attached to him. There had

been on his part no mistake of pilotage, no lack of skill, no error of judgement, no fault of any kind, only the rigid regard for duty which was to be expected from him. He followed, as he was bidden to do, even unto death. Thus in an instant, without warning, without anticipation, he who had always been so full of life passed into the Great Beyond, and took with him all his high hopes, aspirations and great endeavour.

Of that flower of youth which perished in the Great War he had written, 'When they were dead they were great.' His own death was as much in the service of his country as theirs had been, although no enemy hand had struck him down. In this, if in little else, he was rich. At the moment of his death he was almost without any material possessions. He was singularly free from any possessive ties. Perhaps this was because he had an unconscious knowledge that he was destined to sojourn here for so short a time. But in that short time he had tasted life to the full. He had always lived dangerously and had taken the best that life could give. In return he had also given himself heartily and generously to the service of others whenever opportunity offered.

'Mummy, do you think I shall ever be famous?' he had once asked. It was not given to him to achieve what brings fame. But if he is remembered, it will be for what he was, and not for what he did. What he was is best set forth in his own letters. That is why we who received and treasure them have wished to share some of them with others, in the hope that many may come to realize, as we do, that at the thought of him this old world seems to recapture the vigour of youth, hopes soar high, despair vanishes, hearts grow bold and limbs are strong again.

APPENDIX

THE COUNTLESS letters of sympathy and appreciation which we received helped us to realize how much affection Antony had gathered round him in his short life, and how varied were the interests which he embraced. The few that are here quoted have been chosen, not because they are the best—hundreds of others are equally valued —but because they are representative of the circles in which he moved —social, political and athletic. Only those passages have been quoted which speak of his character and his influence with those with whom he came in contact.

From Mr. Somers Somerset

I have always thought of Antony as just the nicest and most attractive fellow that I ever knew. Every time one saw him it did one good and taught one what one ought to have been; that wonderful combination of work and play that was the soul of his being and that made one envy him so much.

I don't think anyone ever had a happier life, a more perfect home, or a wider circle of friends who loved him and admired him in every possible way, so that his coming into a room was always happiness. . . . He was the splendid adventurer and has adventured 'a-tiptoe on the highest point of being' . . . his life was splendid with skill, courtesy, high-heartedness and love, and that quality of splendid courage which is above all qualities in the world. . . .

Your son was a man, and I know how proud you must be of him. . . . He was the spirit of courage, Antony was. It's awfully hard to come by, but by God it's nine-tenths of the virtues there are. . . .

From Lady Desborough

He leaves 'a white unbroken glory, a gathered radiance, a width, a shining peace, under the night'. How those words echo to every remembrance of Antony. You know how we loved him—in a different way to anyone else. I believe everybody did. One of the most vivid pictures of

360

him is leaping suddenly through the window of the little house we had in London, the summer Imogen came out. Ivo and she and I were sitting there, and we were so startled—and it was like a great rush of gladness coming in. . . .

From the Hon. Lady Grigg

. . . Antony was so rare and wonderful, he seems like the spirit of youth that would not stay with us to grow old. . . .

From Mr. Edward Murray

I, an American, found in him all that was best and finest in what is England. He was made from the stuff of which heroes are cast, and surely in all the cruelty of your grief you will never forget to be terribly proud of so splendid a son, for no one could know Antony without realizing the everything you were to him.

From Mr. Nicholas Llewelyn Davies

. . . His life was glorious, clean, unselfish and honourable. All these epithets are Antony. He was certainly the most splendid person of his age that I knew. . . . People always say that the happiest years of a man's life are the last year at his school and the years at the University. And mine were certainly no exception; and I can honestly and truly say that my biggest reason for happiness in those days was Antony. . . .

From the Countess of Sandwich

. . . Just to see him even in the distance was a joy, and to read about him was reading about such a joyous adventurer, modern and yet at heart just like an Elizabethan. . . . A great son to you both, and a great friend to you all. . . . As parents you will have the comfort that you gave to England the highest and the best. His going is a national loss— there are *very* few who had so much to give as he had. His ability was very great, but his friendliness was unique—and a hungry world, needing at this time especially those rare qualities of human kindness, will miss him throughout this generation. . . .

From Lady Phyllis Benton

. . . His courage, his irresistible charm, his great qualities of mind and character, endeared him to everyone who knew him, and made one realize a little what he must have been as a son and a brother. . . . His journey through life seemed like the flight of a star—and the light in the hearts of those who knew him will never fade. . . .

From the Hon. Mrs. Gilmour

. . . He was the most vital, the most attractive and the most genuine person I have ever known. I have heard so many wonderful tributes to him in the last few days, surely no one has ever made such a mark in people's lives, there was just no one like him. . . .

From Mr. Robert Lutyens

. . . His life was brimful—wasn't it? So much was concentrated in a little time.

He received more love and gave more delight than falls to the lot of most to be loved and to give. And if life is a trust, then did he fulfil it gaily and with great honour. . . .

From Viscountess Gage

. . . He never knew what it was to flag, and he wore a laurel crown every hour of his life. No one has ever lived more to the uttermost, to the full strength of courage and fitness and vitality. He is a joy to remember and a shout of encouragement. . . .

From Mr. A. B. Ramsay

When Antony was at Eton, we seemed to be one family watching him and devoted to him, and he inspired me so forcibly by his vitality and promise that I think I caught something of what you felt and hoped and prayed for in your son, and understood the pride of his parents. I remember when he was Captain of my House, how often I wondered about his future and about the great things for which he seemed to be born, and how grateful I was for his unfailing enthusiasm and loyalty. Great things has he done, for he has set a fine pattern to young men who are born in such a position as his, and also he has won for his class high estimation among the rising generation of England, and at this time no better service can be done for our country. Everywhere I have heard him spoken of with honour and with admiration, and have felt the kindling of fine ideals from his high spirit and noble purpose.

In his political life his seriousness was always recognized, for he looked beyond the present convenience or utility and was clearly guided by the best principles, and so he stood out among the younger states-men....

From Lady Ruth Balfour

... He was so wonderfully full of vitality, he counted life cheap that was not lived to the last ounce. I remember talking to him last year about flying. He said 'People often say now that a young man leads a soft life sitting at the wheel of a car or behind the joystick of an aero-plane—but to be a good airman you must keep absolutely fit and in perfect condition.' Obviously, I felt, his boxing and his ski-ing were a means to that end.

He talked to me of his other interests, of his commercial ambitions, of politics and the world's troubles, but behind it all I felt that it was through flying that he hoped to quicken his mind and temper his limbs to fine steel, and that so quickened and tempered he might give of his best to help others.

I felt that to him it was a dedication of all his soaring, joyous nature. He was fired with enthusiasm. He could not have kept from it, and one would not have wished him to.

The world will always owe most to those pioneers who, like him, go forth and dare everything without counting the cost. Such natures are an inspiration while they live and an example in their death....

From Baroness De Brienen

... He was such a remarkable young man, beloved by all who knew him—gay and yet serious—ready to play, but also to work—helping those who wanted help by his good works, his courage, his example. I have never met anyone who had such a great personal charm.... I have never met any young man who could be compared to him—he was one that once met is never forgotten....

From Lady Jekyll

... How wonderful your boy was in his courage and skill and fine endeavour and lovable character. I wish I had known him better—but all the beautiful time is yours for always and it is Life that takes away and changes and spoils so often, not Death, which is the warden and not the thief of our treasures....

From Mr. Duff Cooper

. . . I had grown so very fond of Antony during the last eighteen months, and I was proud that he should like to start his political career by working with me—that career which I had no doubt must have led him to the very highest places.

On every question that I discussed with him I always found that he had formed his own independent view, very definite and very sensible, and that he could express it perfectly.

Most amazing of all his qualities was, I thought, his unspoilt modesty, in spite of all his physical and mental gifts, which might have been enough to turn the head of anyone less sweet and simple.

I have been very touched this morning by the number of people here in the War Office who have come to express their sympathy, and have asked me to convey it to you—from the Permanent Under-Secretary down to the office-keepers. He had made himself so much loved by all. . . .

From the Rt. Hon. Stanley Baldwin

. . . Antony was the salt of the earth, and you have had such love and companionship as fall to few. . . . Many of us thank God for his friendship, a possession to be cherished with life itself. . . .

From Sir Edward Grigg

. . . Of all the young men of his age that I have met, he seemed to me the soundest and the best. He felt things with an instinct that always struck me as wonderfully straight and right, and with all his ability, his gift of sympathy, his gaiety and his charm, he looked like having the world at his feet. . . .

From Lord Francis Scott

. . . I only knew Knebworth slightly, remembering him as a delightful boy at Eton and having met him on a few occasions since he grew up, but I had always followed his career, as he seemed to me to embrace all that was best in the youth of our race. As one gets older, one thinks who are the young men coming on who will take the lead in the future, and who will uphold the finest traditions of our country, and it always seemed to me that Knebworth stood out among his contemporaries as being endowed with the great qualities that count—courage, charm, ability and sound sense, which of course go to make up leadership. . .

From the Chairman of the London Unemployment Association

... You have lost your boy and we have lost a leader. He fought our battles in our early days. His enthusiasm cheered us and his shining idealism inspired us. He was beloved by us in East London, as he was admired in the greater world . . . you and England have lost a noble son. . . .

From the Chairman of the Shoreditch Business Men's Association

... Lord Knebworth presided at our last Meeting, and his death will be deplored by thousands of people of every class in this Borough, where despite his short connection with it, he had made and retained a host of friends and admirers. . . .

From the Chairman of the Baldock Conservative Association

... In every way we were so proud to have him as our representative in Parliament, and he was such a splendid specimen of English manhood, a great sportsman as well as a great gentleman, and his place in our esteem and affection can never be replaced.

From Mr. Hugh Seebohm

... The memory I cherish most is of his fearless honesty. His courage and high purpose led him not into heresy (as he suggested to me after his last speech in Hitchin) but into leaving no stone unturned which might possibly serve to pave the way to better things. His courage and the clearness of his vision made something of which the world is in sore need, fettered as it is by outworn prejudices and torn by the savage attempts to replace them by others.

I think you will like to know that 'following Knebworth's lead' is a not infrequent expression at our meetings. . . .

From Mr. George H. Woodman

... In 'Knebby' the common people of England have lost a great friend; a gentleman in every sense of the word. I, as many others, only knew your son from his frequent appearances in the Ring for charity. . . . So I am writing to tell you that we, his boxing associates, without any of the pomp and ostentation which he so disliked in life, deeply, sincerely, mourn a gallant gentleman, whose only motto in life appeared to be 'Play the game'. . . .

From Mr. D. Martin (Police Station, Hammersmith)

. . . It was as a sportsman and amateur boxer that I knew Lord Knebworth.

When I was Secretary of the 'K' division Police Boxing Club, he was a frequent visitor at our tournaments, and on two occasions he came and boxed for us. His contest at Ilford with P.C. Barnes, who was then Police Champion, will be long remembered by those who were privileged to see it. By his gallant display and sporting spirit Lord Knebworth endeared himself to the large company present, who gave him the finest ovation ever given to a boxer in that part of London. All his sporting friends will mourn the loss of his young life, and I am sure, like myself, they will feel glad to have known so fine a sportsman and gentleman as Lord Knebworth. . . .

From Sir Frederick Gascoigne (in a speech at the Annual Meeting of the Army and Navy Stores)

He showed the same characteristics of courage, energy and strength of purpose in his voluntary training for the defence of his country, in which cause he lost his life, as he did in the other spheres of business and politics, in which, in spite of his slender years, he had already begun to make his mark.

He had been a Director of the Society for four years, Vice-Chairman for twelve months, and had already developed such a keen insight and interest in the business that, combined with his youth and his natural abilities, it had been hoped that these attributes would have been available for the Society for many years to come.

From Herr Werner Salvisberg (a famous professional Swiss ski-er)

. . . It was a great pity that it was just our friend Knebworth who had to start first for the eternal ski-grounds, just as he was best in a position to overcome these sad times with his supreme humour.

Whenever we of the Swiss University team think of the races against the University team of Great Britain, we remember not only his bold *Schussfahrten*, but even more his perfect sporting behaving and his youthful agreeable voice.

We love to remember the races of which he took part, and not less the *Stimmung* he caused wherever he appeared. We think with pleasure of the beer parties and similar less sportive occasions, when he was always our very best companion. In one word, we shall never forget him. . . .

From Mr. Arnold Lunn (in the British Ski Year Book)

. . . He was a grand talker, he had a first-class brain, and he was remarkably well-informed. I remember his acute and completely pessimistic forecast at a time when politicians were trying to believe that the depression, which had just begun, would soon pass. He possessed in full measure and overflowing the gracious gift of humour. He was the best possible company. One can say all this, and yet fail to recapture the secret of his infectious gaiety. . . .

It is tragic that men like Irvine, Waghorn and Knebworth should die young, but it would be far more tragic if our race ceased to produce men who are prepared to prove, if need be by dying, that there are worse things than death. The mountains, the air and the sea, are great avenues of adventure, not in spite of, but because of the toll of young lives which they exact. *Sicut cursores vitaï lampada tradunt.* The torch of life, a life more abundant than mere existence, is passed on by those who die to prove that danger and hardship are an integral part of the life which is best worth living. . . .

From Mr. Frank Henley (Commandant, Metropolitan Special Constabulary Reserve, No. 2 Group Business Houses Division)

. . . Lord Knebworth was a Commander of this Division, and has taken a great interest in the Special Constabulary. A fortnight ago he inspected the Drill Squad, and only this morning I received a letter from him of congratulations for the success attained by the Squad on Sunday.

To us, Lord Knebworth was an ideal Englishman, sportsman and gentleman. His life will be an inspiration to all. . . .

From Air-Commodore W. F. MacNeece Foster (Headquarters, No. 1 Air Defence Group, R.A.F.)

. . . Of all the remarkable young men, who have joined the Auxiliary Air Force in recent years, nobody could fail to put him in the very forefront. It has always seemed to me when we met that the Auxiliary Air Force attracted him most strongly in two ways. There was first the most sane and healthy patriotism, divorced from military aggressiveness—and then there was the joy of adventure, the love of the air and the satisfaction of a very perfect technique in flying. His Commanding Officer had often spoken of him to me as 'the perfect Auxiliary officer', and as such he will always remain in the memories of those who knew him. . . .*

From Mr. Arthur Bryant (in the Ashridge Journal, June 1933)

. . . Man's life at its best is either a record of achievement or an inspiration. Wren, dying full of years, sitting upright in his chair, left behind him a glorious legacy of work accomplished—St. Paul's dome, riverside Greenwich, Hampton Court, Chelsea and the belfries and spires of a hundred churches; Julian Grenfell falling in battle in early youth, a trumpet call in men's hearts to remind them how valiant, how beautiful, how generous man at his best could be. So it was with Antony Knebworth. Had he lived he might have given to England in a new age gifts of leadership and imagination which she sorely needs, and a selfless service, which none who knew him could doubt for a moment. The gods, who slay those whom they love young, willed it otherwise.

That quaint eager dark face—of a heroic boy poised for fighting—remains as I write clearly photographed in my memory. I see him in a rocky wood of mountain ash leaping as an arrow to save my dog which had blundered in pursuit of a rabbit almost across the edge of a cliff; leading without orders and with the most delightful calm long columns of men and women with banners through the dense East London crowd to their appointed place, when the arrangements for marshalling them had broken down; coming into my room where I was lying sick to say good-bye before catching an early train from North Wales to London, when he was going straight to the office, in the most ragged and torn pair of grey flannel trousers upon which I have ever set eyes. The secret of personality is a thing hard to define, but unmistakable where it exists. Antony Knebworth's was apparent in every word that he spoke and every act he did.

*When giving me permission to quote from this letter, Air-Commodore MacNeece Foster informed me that, had he lived Antony would shortly have been chosen to command the Squadron.